SUCCEEDING AT SUCCESSION

Succeeding at Succession

Founder and Leadership Succession in
Christian Organizations and Movements

PETER BUNTON

WIPF & STOCK · Eugene, Oregon

Wipf & Stock
An Imprint of Wipf and Stock Publishers
199 W. 8th Ave., Suite 3
Eugene, OR 97401

www.wipfandstock.com

PAPERBACK ISBN: 978-1-6667-6682-0
HARDCOVER ISBN: 978-1-6667-6683-7
EBOOK ISBN: 978-1-6667-6684-4

06/07/23

To my wife, Ruth Ann,
with gratitude for your love and support in all things,
including the writing of this book.

To my children, Brooke and Wesley, of whom I am proud.

Contents

Part III: Cases of Succession

Part IV: Aspects of Succession

Part V: Succession Gestalt

Part VI: Succession and Organizational Self-Reflection: Successor Identification, Power, and Ceremony

Part VII: Fears, Failings, and Findings

Acknowledgments

My sincere and abiding gratitude is expressed to those who have helped with the writing of this book. My thanks in particular are extended to the following:

- Dr. Justin Thacker, for his invaluable and constructive criticisms of my research and writing

- those who have at times given input, specifically Dr. Anne Dyer, Dr. Walter Riggans, and Dr. George Bailey

- Rev. Larry Kreider, international director of DOVE International, and Rev. Ron Myer, Director of DOVE USA, for their encouragement and granting of times to facilitate my research and writing

- Nancy Leatherman and Hillary Vargas, who have provided guidance concerning style and textual corrections

- Randall Leaman for his encouragement to see this work to completion

- those who consented to be interviewed to provide data for this research

Abbreviations

GKI   Generative Knowledge Interviewing
LMX   Leader-Member Exchange Theory
LSSC   Leadership Succession and Strategic Change
TAR   Theological Action Research

Introduction

Time means succession, and succession, change.

—NABOKOV, *PALE FIRE*

FOR AN ORGANIZATION TO achieve longevity, new leaders must be in place to provide strategic and operational guidance and decision-making so that the organization may flourish and transform into its future. For new organizations to endure beyond their founders, a way must be made for founders to relinquish, and for others to assume, organizational leadership. These statements are, of course, true of any organization, be it a commercial enterprise, nonprofit organization, educational institution, club, church, or social movement. The first time such a transition in leadership occurs is, of course, founders' succession; subsequent changes in primary leadership are referred to as "leadership succession" or "organizational succession." The crucial nature of leadership succession in the business world was grasped by Jack Welch, chief executive officer (CEO) of the corporate giant General Electric, who nine years before his anticipated retirement commented, "From now on, . . . [choosing my successor] is the most important decision I'll make. It occupies a considerable amount of thought almost every day."[1] Even in the four Gospels in the Bible, we see Jesus spending considerable time teaching and modeling ministry, preparing others to succeed him in his proclamation of God's kingdom. Indeed, his goal was that his disciples would do greater works than even he himself did: "Very truly I tell you, whoever believes in me will do the works I have been doing, and they will do even greater things

1. Slater, *New GE*, 8.

than these, because I am going to the Father" (John 14:12). That's pretty good leadership succession! From the writings of those in organizational development, we see that succession may be social, structural, and organizational. With the Bible's frequent turning to the topic, moreover, whether it be the leadership succession of Moses to Joshua (Deut 31) or the continuance of prophetic ministry from Elijah to Elisha (2 Kgs 2:1–18), we find that succession may also be spiritual, indeed a topic requiring theological reflection. With the growing number of social scientific studies on the matter, however, it may indeed be the case that organizational scholars have treated it more seriously than have systematic or practical theologians.

ORGANIZATIONAL DEVELOPMENTAL UNDERSTANDINGS OF SUCCESSION

The crucial and potentially problematic nature of succession began to draw the attention of organizational scholars in the 1960s, with Grusky famously leading the way.[2] This has led to a growing field of succession studies and research literature, which has become increasingly specialized as scholars examine facets of succession including successor origins,[3] power,[4] organizational performance,[5] strategic change,[6] leadership style change,[7] and succession frequency.[8] In this book, we will review such literature to seek to gain an understanding of the organizational and business world's conceptualizations of succession.

STUDY OF SUCCESSION WITHIN CHRISTIAN ORGANIZATIONS

In turning to Christian movements and organizations, we find this field of study sparse. Where there has been reflection on leadership succession, we find that the literature may be placed broadly into three categories. The first category is that of practitioner literature, aimed at describing succession

2. Grusky, "Corporate Size," 261–69; Grusky, "Effects of Succession," 83–111.

3. Cannella and Lubatkin, "Succession," 763–93.

4. Block and Rosenberg, "Toward an Understanding of Founder's Syndrome," 353–68.

5. Carroll, "Dynamics of Publisher Succession," 93–113.

6. Hutzschenreuter et al., "How New Leaders Affect Strategic Change," 729–55.

7. Tashakori, *Managerial Succession*.

8. Kesner and Sebora, "Executive Succession," 327–72.

processes, often within a church, particularly a large or megachurch, or offering practical advice to those in such organizations facing succession, particularly pastoral succession within a church congregation or parish.[9] The second category contains a limited number of theological reflections, a category which itself falls further into two subcategories, namely those in disciplines of biblical theology (for example Tushima),[10] exploring biblical models and attempting to provide biblical warrant for certain guidelines or principles of succession (such as Fountain),[11] or the subcategory of writings in practical theology, such as Pugh's work on contemporary successions within new church movements.[12] The third category of literature is empirical study of leadership succession, particularly founder succession within newer Christian networks or organizations. Within this category, however, I found only three attempts at such empirical study of succession. Owens studied the founder's succession within the Church of God in Christ (COGIC).[13] Peterson studied succession at Liberty University, an evangelical Christian institution in Virginia.[14] Wheeler undertook a study of several American megachurches, usually examining succession from the founding pastor.[15]

In this book, I will review some of the literature from the business world to show how organizational scholars might assist us in understanding the many facets of succession, as well as consider some of the theological literature on the topic. We will spend time seeking to learn from the three larger empirical studies mentioned above (Owens, Peterson, and Wheeler). Yet, ultimately, they may prove of little help due to some deficient research methodologies and an almost complete lack of theological analysis of the succession within churches and Christian institutions. This book will explore such a lack further, showing that the religious beliefs and theologies of founders must to be taken into account when seeking to understand succession praxis.

---

9. See the bibliography for titles on pastoral succession, such as Cionca, *Discerning the Time* (on succession timing); Antal, *Considering a New Call* (on the emotional processing of the departing pastor); Mead, *A Change of Pastors* (on transition phases); and Weese and Crabtree, *The Elephant in the Boardroom* (on the relationship between congregational size and succession.)

10. Tushima, "Leadership Succession Patterns."

11. Fountain, "Investigation," 187–204.

12. Pugh, "Succession Plans," 117–30.

13. Owens, *Never Forget!*

14. Peterson, "Case Study."

15. Wheeler, "Leadership Succession Process."

HOW DID THIS BOOK COME ABOUT?

A few years ago, I was drawn to the topic of succession within new Christian church movements and mission agencies. This was in part, or perhaps largely, due to my own personal situation. I spent many years serving in a large, international Christian mission agency, the founders of which were then aging. I have more recently served in an international network of churches, the first church of which was planted in 1980. With the founder-director still in post, in the last years founder succession has become a relevant and needed topic on our agenda. My initial reading and investigation of the topic led me to realize how many networks of churches exist that had been initiated in the 1970s and 1980s, many of which had recently undergone founder succession or were going to need to face that issue soon. Indeed Kay, in his now classic work on apostolic networks in Britain, writes, "The next major challenge facing almost all the networks is to find the right person to fill the shoes of their founding apostle."[16] As if following Kay's cue, many of the networks he studied did so in the years following. Wider investigation led me to realize that there was little study of such contemporary successions, particularly founder succession, and indeed that the few attempts that had been made actually obfuscated the topic, particularly through deficient methodologies. While empirical study of succession in Christian movements had begun, it had in fact started on a wrong footing. This led to my conducting research for a PhD to be awarded by the University of Manchester, United Kingdom. During this research, I examined several case studies of such succession, especially succession in the organization International Aid Services (based in Sweden), in the movement of churches Newfrontiers (begun in the United Kingdom), and in the church network Grace Network (founded in the US). In this book, I will draw from these case studies and other examples, largely from successions within the last decade or so, rather than further into history. Furthermore, analysis and comments are reserved largely for evangelical movements, but with some reference to newer movements within other types of churches. Within Roman Catholicism, for example, the term founder is usually reserved for those founding a new religious order. Several key Roman Catholic texts specifically honor those with the founding charism for a religious order (see chapter 6). There is, however, no study examining what happens when the founder moves on, namely the question of founder succession. In examining this matter within Catholicism, we find that succession is usually of a post-mortem nature! "For better

16. Kay, *Apostolic Networks*, 350.

or worse, the founders of religious institutes tend to stay in the role until death."[17] This may explain the lack of study of such founder's successions.

RESEARCHER POSITION

Turning to my own place as one studying this topic, I wish to acknowledge the potential limitations deriving from my position. This work may be viewed as both emic and etic. It is emic in that I am an evangelical Christian engaged in full-time Christian ministry, a position held in common with many of those studied in this work. I suggest that such a position proved advantageous as participants were inclined to trust the researcher. I was aware, however, that I could be sympathetic to their position and needed to develop critical *epochē*, that is "the bracketing out or suspending of a researcher's pervious ideas, thoughts or beliefs about the truth, value or meaning of the religion [culture, event, or community] under study."[18] On the other hand, I simultaneously was in an etic position, for I was not part of the organizations studied. This allowed a greater measure of *epochē* and a more critical perspective.

As a male, I am aware that I was largely studying men in Christian leadership (despite my efforts to identify women who might have been included in such a study). My purposive and snowball sampling did not lead to identifying women meeting the criteria of either being a founder or successor to the founder of a larger scale international Christian agency. Given this, I sought to activate gender considerations in my research interviews by posing relevant questions concerning the role of women. Yet, as many of my findings are taken from an exclusively male sample, I am aware of limitations in application to other populations.

I am aware, furthermore, that as a white male, I can offer limited perspective on, or of, those of other races or of the work of post-colonial approaches to scholarship. Indeed, this book cannot be a decolonizing work. Such works are needed when studying succession within contemporary evangelicalism, but delineation led to such matters, important as they are, being outside the narrow scope of this book, particularly as, given the concepts and language of decolonizing methodologies, I am at the center of colonization, not the margins.[19]

17. Correspondence from Rev. Dr. Thomas P. Gaunt, SJ, PhD, Director of Center for Applied Research in the Apostolate, Georgetown University, Dec 13, 2017 (cited with permission).

18. Cox, *Introduction to the Phenomenology of Religion*, 49.

19. See Woodley and Sanders, *Decolonizing Evangelicalism*, 52–56, for an understanding of the possibilities of "anti-colonial" work from those at the center of

PROSPECTIVE READERSHIP

For whom is this book? It is written partly with organizational scholars and theologians in mind, but mainly for Christian leaders, pastors, leaders of nonprofit agencies or businesses, and for founding entrepreneurs who wish to ensure longevity for the churches, missions, and organizations that they lead. Part I aims to explore further the nature of leadership succession and founder succession, beginning to parse the multiple facets and dynamics in conceptualizing, planning, processing, and enacting succession. It raises issues of theory and theology. Part II reflects on how we might study succession, paying attention to theological studies and providing a critical evaluation of existent study on succession within Christian movements. It also explains in outline how I sought to study this topic and why I have undertaken this in the way I have. Part III explains how analyzing cases of succession provides data fruitful for a deeper understanding of succession and introduces three examples of such cases to inform much of the subsequent reflection upon succession.

Part IV examines nine aspects of contemporary successions among Christian organizations and movements, including leadership styles, gender considerations, power, theology, and succession ceremonies. Part V introduces the notion of a "succession Gestalt" and seeks to show how this may be produced, whereas Part VI examines the crucial necessity of theological self-reflection or reflexivity in organizational succession. This part examines such reflexivity regarding the matters of successor identification methods, power to make decisions, and succession ceremony. Part VII draws some conclusions as well as suggests potential lessons or guidelines for those navigating leadership succession.

Having engaged with the content of this book, it is hoped that the reader will become aware of the richness of the topic of leadership succession including among Christian organizations and movements. Furthermore, it is hoped that readers become better informed to engage with the issues at a theoretical, theological, and practical level. Perhaps this work might just help Christian organizations survive for the benefit of the generations following!

---

post-colonial society, and the work of decolonization undertaken by those on the margins.

PART I

Thinking about Succession

Chapter One

What Is Succession?

An Introduction to the Issues Involved

SUCCESSION, ACCORDING TO WEBSTER'S *Dictionary*, is "a coming into the place of another," or "the act of . . . coming after another in order or to an office."[1] Succession implies both temporality and position. It is almost invariably used of leadership office, whether monarch, president, CEO, or pastor. It is regarded as important because leaders, whether in government, business, or the church, so often set the direction of those entities they lead, including in terms of objectives, strategies, and methods to reach them and the pace of achieving them. Given leadership's ubiquity and thus succession's universality, it might seem a straightforward concept. Just about everybody will have an understanding of what succession is, as they have indubitably lived under an instance of leadership succession in some form.

This universality, however, may betray the reality that succession is rarely a simple process. Someone has already laid down the methods through constitutional framing, and often great deliberation has taken place as to whom to appoint. Founder succession, however, may not have the benefit of prior constitutional framing. In the organizational world, scholars in the 1960s began to realize the heretofore unseen complexities of the topic. Since then, a world of succession studies within organizational development has grown, often leading to great specialization. Chapter 2 will seek to provide an, inevitably rather cursory, overview of some of the developments in

1. "Succession," in *Webster's Dictionary*, 1819.

3

understanding organizational succession, to help us see at least some of the issues and dynamics involved.

Following this, chapter 3 will concentrate more specifically on the phenomenon of founder succession, as there is much research to indicate that such a succession may raise unique issues not experienced in subsequent leadership changes within an organization. This will lead to some comment in chapter 4 on organizational succession within an international context, as a greater number of organizations in business and in Christian ministries in today's world find themselves in such a context. Taking place within an international setting, succession may produce its own set of dynamics and questions.

Finally, chapters 5 and 6 respectively consider the topic of succession and founder succession within churches and Christian organizations to reflect upon some of the particular issues and nuances within such organizations that may be different from the world of business. This itself raises issues of theology, indeed whether there is even one theology of succession that is normative for Christian groups, or whether, even here, there are multiple apposite models of theology to guide succession (chapter 7). Chapter 8 summarizes what can be learned from research thus far. We find that to date there has been little inclusion of theological analysis in the study of succession in Christian movements and organizations. There is much to learn.

Chapter Two

Aspects of Succession
Learning from Organizational Studies

IN THE LAST FEW decades, an increasing number of facets of succession have been examined in multiple ways. This chapter adumbrates a number of key themes that have emerged and anticipates that such themes will help us understand successions further.

ORIGINS

Perhaps the great founding debate in succession studies became that of successor origins; that is, the "internal/external question": Should one appoint from within or from outside the organization? This question grew in importance as people sought guidance in how to find the most appropriate leader to enhance organizational success. The debate hinged upon the different characteristics of internal or external successors, how they are received, and their styles and comparative performances. Interest in successor origins began with Grusky[1] and developed during the 1970s (thirteen studies) and 1980s (eighteen articles).[2] Previously in the Western world, there had been a widely held assumption that one's career was within one company; company loyalty led to promotion. If external appointments increased performance,

---

1. Grusky, "Corporate Size," 261–69; Grusky, "Effects of Succession," 83–111.

2. For a review of such literature, see Kesner and Sebora, "Executive Succession," 327–72.

5

this challenged the one career/one company philosophy. In addition, at this time, leadership theory was still focused on the leader rather than other factors such as culture, contingences, or leader-follower relationship (such as leader-member exchange theory [LMX]).[3]

Two schools of thought on the matter of origins developed. Cannella and Lubatkin found that low performing firms have greater rates of outside succession,[4] whereas Wiersema studied 146 companies in the US, finding that an external successor brought greater strategic change.[5] This research implies that external succession is helpful, certainly if an organization needed greater change. There was, however, growing evidence supporting the advantages of internal succession. Of significant influence in this field, with scores of printings in multiple languages, is Collins and Porras.[6] This is a study of eighteen "visionary" (American, but often multinational) companies that have endured over generations, comparing each to another company in the same market, with the aim of identifying those characteristics leading to success. Collins and Porras found that succession is facilitated if the company has an "enduring purpose that goes beyond the original founding concept"[7] and that visionary companies appoint CEOs from within the company. Indeed, their frequency of internal appointments was six times greater than the comparison companies.[8]

Ocasio[9] found that as founder CEOs' tenure increased, it became more likely that outsider succession would occur, but offered no empirical reasons for this, suggesting that as others had experienced only the founder as leader, they were unable to see likely candidates within the organization. Shen and Cannella[10] studied over 300 firms; they showed that outsider succession was positively associated with negative performance post-succession. My concern with this (and with much of the research), however, is that it extrapolates findings from investor and stock market reactions rather than other longer-term performance measures, thus limiting the reliability. Allgood and Farrell[11] found that insider appointments were better when the predecessor voluntarily departed, but that external appointments were a

---

3. See Northouse, *Leadership*, 161–184, for an introduction to LMX.

4. Cannella and Lubatkin, "Succession," 763–93.

5. Wiersema, "Strategic Consequences," 73–94.

6. Collins and Porras, *Built to Last*.

7. Collins and Porras, *Built to Last*, xix.

8. Collins and Porras, *Built to Last*, 10.

9. Ocasio, "Institutionalized Action," 384–416.

10. Shen and Cannella, "Revisiting the Performance Consequences," 717.

11. Allgood and Farrell, "Match between CEO and Firm," 317–41.

better match when the predecessor was forced to leave. The limitation with many studies is that they examine one variable as it correlates to origins, rarely taking into account a number of variables such as broader social and environmental factors which impinge upon an organization.

It will be seen later that this debate from the business world has great relevance to Christian organizations, which tend to attach considerable significance to successor origins. In chapter 15, it will be seen that there is unanimous preference for internal succession within new Christian organizations, but that the reasons for this are different to those found in the above studies.

FREQUENCY OF SUCCESSION

Frequency became a subject of interest as it was seen that frequency and performance (both as antecedent and consequence) were related. Performance is a key driver for not only business but also most organizations, including Christian ministries. In the 1970s, nine studies examined frequency; in the 1980s, there were nineteen studies.[12] Higher frequency of succession was detrimental to firm performance[13] while numerous studies began to show that performance was an antecedent of succession, with lower performance correlating with higher succession rates.[14] Of course, correlation does not mean causation, and, again, a number of studies would have been better served if multiple environmental variables had been examined, as Cannella and Lubatkin sought to do as they studied correlations between performance and origins (above).[15]

It would appear that there are no studies of frequency of leadership succession in Christian organizations, nor whether performance (however measured) is an antecedent to such succession. Mentzer does attempt such an application with regard to congregational performance post pastoral succession.[16] He measures the level of donations and congregational attendance (see chapter 5), which shows that application of such theories is possible to Christian groups.

---

12. Kesner and Sebora, "Executive Succession," 327–72.

13. Eitzen and Yetman, "Managerial Change," 110–16; McEachern, *Managerial Control and Performance.*

14. Morck et al., "Management Ownership," 293–315; Huson et al., "Internal Monitoring Mechanisms," 2265–97; and others.

15. Cannella and Lubatkin, "Succession," 763–93.

16. Mentzer, "Leader's Succession-Performance Relationship," 191–204.

CONSEQUENCES

Grusky also found that performance was likely to be adversely affected by the disruption of succession (the "vicious cycle" theory of succession). Guest questioned this, positing the "common sense" theory that an organization will strive to choose a good candidate who will improve performance.[17] Gamson and Scotch examined this further by studying the dismissal of sports teams' managers.[18] They found that the predecessor and successor had little influence over performance, thus developing a third theory, that firing a leader was ritual scapegoating ("scapegoating" theory). These theories heavily influenced subsequent understanding of leadership succession appointments.

Consequences of succession were examined when Kelly examined successors' leadership actions during their first months of tenure, finding that the majority initiated organizational infrastructure realignments before seeking to change company strategy.[19] McTeer et al. conducted a major study of professional sports teams across the main four sports in the US.[20] The findings were that, in most sports, performance in the next full season following leadership change had not significantly improved over the season in which the change occurred or the full season prior. Not only did this seem to support scapegoating theory, but also it pointed again to the holy grail of leadership theory: "Does leadership matter?"

The study of succession consequences might prove fruitful for Christian ministries. Which of the three theories (if any) applies? Do Christian organizations engage in scapegoating when performance is declining? As will be shown (chapter 20), succession within the network Newfrontiers was highly disruptive, involving the cessation of employment for a number of long-term staff and indeed the cessation of Newfrontiers as a single movement. This might suggest an interpretation of "vicious cycle" theory; the subsequent stability of the new apostolic spheres and concomitant church growth after two years of transitions may, however, suggest that, although disruptive, the succession was not part of a repetitive cycle. Indeed, I argue that the three cases I study in depth, and on which I report later, certainly espoused a "common sense" theory. In so doing, with Grace Network and International Aid Services, there was little disruption. Yet, as projection of blame onto others seems to be an attested human trait, something that Jesus spoke against (Matt 7:3–5; Luke 6:41–42), it is likely that some Christian

---

17. Guest, "Managerial Succession," 47–54.

18. Gamson and Scotch, "Scapegoating," 69–72.

19. Kelly, "Management Transitions," 37–45.

20. McTeer et al., "Manager/Coach Mid-Season Replacement," 58–68.

organizations might engage in scapegoating as a way of dealing with organizational difficulty. This may well explain the appalling behaviors exhibited in the founder succession process within the Church of God in Christ (shown later in my review of Owens).[21]

PROCESSES

The first study of the actual processes of succession was undertaken when Vancil[22] found organizations employed one of two methods for successor selection, namely "horse race" (giving potential successors roles and tasks and observing which one displayed the most needed leadership capabilities) and "relay" (agreeing upon a successor, who then spent a period of time in training by working alongside the predecessor). These models were later refined by Friedman and Olk[23] who developed the following typology for succession methods: crown heir (similar to "relay"), naming the successor (usually chosen by incumbent), and allowing the successor a period of role socialization before assuming responsibilities; horse race (incumbent firmly in control); "coup d'état" (usually out of concern, the board takes control of decisions in spite of the incumbent); comprehensive search, inquiring widely within and without the organization for suitable candidates (which usually involves many actors). The problem with this is a confusion between appointment methodology (whom to appoint) and socialization, the latter concept pertaining to preparation for a role and learning of the required knowledge and values.[24] For example, an appointment might be made through "horse race" method, but then socialization might still occur following the relay method. Vancil's work, moreover, is less reliable due to his self-selecting sample, namely a group of CEOs who believed they had led successful transitions. This provides limitations to findings and transferability. However, while examples of research from the 1980s and 1990s, Vancil as well as Friedman and Olk have shaped ongoing understandings of processes as well as provided the terminology for their description.

Dyck et al. undertook a longitudinal study of a failed succession in a family-owned firm.[25] The main research question was to find causes for unsuccessful succession ("success" was not clearly defined in this research, but the successor resigning within six months of appointment was deemed

21. Owens, *Never Forget!*
22. Vancil, *Passing the Baton.*
23. Friedman and Olk, "Four Ways to Choose a CEO," 141–64.
24. See the next section for further treatment of the concept of socialization.
25. Dyck et al., "Passing the Baton," 143–62.

"failure"). Dyck et al. developed the "relay" metaphor further than Vancil by examining the implied metaphor within "relay," namely that of "passing the baton." They examined four factors within baton passing: sequence, timing, baton-passing technique, and communication. They saw, for example, when studying "technique" that "title, power, control, and responsibility often do not transfer simultaneously"[26] and that *this is problematic*. The research reached a number of conclusions: The greater the similarity between the skill sets and managerial styles of incumbent and successor, the more likely it is that the succession will be successful, but less likely that superior organizational performance will result; and the greater the level of agreement between incumbent and successor on the mode of succession, the more likely it is that the succession will be successful. The researchers, however, fail to see the relevance of organizational life-cycle theory, for the next cycle might indeed require leadership skills different from the founder, which may explain the finding of similarity leading to lower performance. In chapter 15, I will show that Christian organizations also may not understand this; they prefer internal successors, tutored and mentored by, and thus often like, the founder.

Research into succession processes is crucial for Christian ministries. Both Wheeler[27] and Peterson[28] show how Christian ministries employ the relay succession method. There is room for an examination of why Christian groups choose this (pragmatism or theological rationale), its consequences, and for comparison between ministries that adopt other methodologies. This alerts us to the potential importance of processes and methods as enactments of underlying theologies, something that occupies a good deal of this book.

SOCIALIZATION

Socialization is the adaption of an individual or group to the needs and expectations of others, often to the broader culture of the society we inhabit. In organizational terms, it refers to the processes of adapting to a new company or role, learning it values, or indeed simply being trained for a new position.

Any new incumbent, even an internal appointment, needs socialization. Attention has been drawn to the transmission of tacit knowledge as part of that process of succession. Kikoski and Kikoski found that high

26. Dyck et al., "Passing the Baton," 149.

27. Wheeler, "Leadership Succession Process."

28. Peterson, "Case Study." Both Wheeler and Peterson are reviewed fully in chapter 10.

functioning organizations are influenced by the tacit knowledge of their leaders;[29] this raises questions of which knowledge is to be transmitted during leadership succession and how the transmission is to be affected. Peet[30] conducted a study to test the efficacy of Generative Knowledge Interviewing (GKI) as a method of tacit knowledge transmission, by introducing "generative listening" to discern the tacit "core capacities" embedded in the patterns of the stories. This test was successful: Staff grew in understanding their roles and core capabilities, as well as in taking less time to make decisions. The GKI process helped them understand why the outgoing leader's results were achieved and assisted performance replication. Peet claims that the method thus produced organizational generativity, but there are few empirical findings to substantiate this.

STRATEGIC CHANGE

Sakano and Lewin[31] studied eighty-one Japanese firms that had experienced CEO succession (1988–89) and revisited these cases (1991–92) to assess the successions' impact on change. They found CEO succession did not affect organizational restructuring. They attributed findings to Japanese firms' taking a long-term view and thus a preference for evolutionary rather than revolutionary change. This begins to show a relationship between culture, leadership perceptions, and performance (a topic to be addressed more fully in chapter 4).

The literature on leadership succession and strategic change (LSSC) exemplifies some of the growing specialization within succession studies. Hutzschenreuter et al. identify sixty-eight articles on LSSC.[32] A good deal of the literature examines whether the impetus for strategic change comes from within or is external to the leader. Much of the literature draws on developments from cognitive psychology, studying the cognitive differences between predecessor and successor, and states that the impetus is internal. Other studies, however, maintain that strategic change comes through external drivers such as the mandate to implement change. I suggest that rather than isolating one driver for change, it would seem a reasonable hypothesis that there are many drivers. Indeed, Zúñiga-Vicente et al. found the realignment of power relationships to be the external driver but they came to recognize that environmental factors such as business regulation

29. Kikoski and Kikoski, *Inquiring Organization*.
30. Peet, "Leadership Transitions," 45–60.
31. Sakano and Lewin, "Impact of CEO Succession," 654–71.
32. Hutzschenreuter et al., "How New Leaders Affect Strategic Change," 729–55.

could drive change as well as internal reactions of leaders to those environmental factors, thus offering a more nuanced understanding.[33]

There have been few studies applying leader life-cycle theory to LSSC due to an assumption that long-tenure leaders are less likely to initiate strategic change. Zúñiga-Vicente et al. found, however, that long-tenure leaders could perform extremely well in the area of change. This is supported elsewhere:

> Long tenure may reflect leaders' ability and willingness to continuously initiate appropriate strategic change. As a result, new leaders following long-tenured predecessors may find their firm better aligned to the environment than new leaders following short termed predecessors, reducing the need for post-succession strategic change.[34]

However, it should be noted that "there is virtually no research that addresses the influence that an incoming leader's cultural identity may have on the LSSC-relationship."[35] This shows the gaps in understanding correlations between cultural identity and strategic change. Successors in international ministries will need to be mindful of how change is perceived and handled by different nationalities.

PSYCHOANALYTICAL REFLECTION ON SUCCESSION

As the subject of succession studies has become more specialized, it has simultaneously become more diverse. Eisold[36] attempts a psychoanalytical reflection of the dynamics of succession, noting that, since Freud, succession has been seen in the light of the Oedipus drama of father-son conflict and power usurpation, namely that successors are destined to live in guilt about overcoming their predecessors and not to go beyond their achievements. Eisold suggests that we have been interpreting succession with an inadequate metaphor (Oedipal)[37] and ignored the more helpful one of Orestes,[38] where there is a communal and political element to the succession development, as seen in the establishment of the first court of law and jury to judge the deeds of Orestes and to discern who is to succeed. Thus,

---

33. Zúñiga-Vicente et al., "Facilitating and Inhibiting Factors," 235–65.

34. Hutzschenreuter et al., "How New Leaders Affect Strategic Change," 741.

35. Hutzschenreuter et al., "How New Leaders Affect Strategic Change," 745.

36. Eisold, "Succeeding at Succession," 619–32.

37. Sophocles, Oedipus the King.

38. Aeschylus, Eumenides.

succession and justice are determined not by the predecessor and successor but by a more dispassionate organ from the community. Eisold applies this to modern institutional succession, suggesting that we consider three matters: the creation of a mechanism to permit others to make impartial judgments on behalf of the community; the recognition of the emotions of those involved in succession, which necessitates the above mechanism so that irrational emotions do not dominate the succession process; and that we take into account the broader social and economic milieu in which the organization undergoing succession locates itself. Eisold suggests one practical application of the establishment of a search committee for an institution's successor that represents the interests of different stakeholders.

While a thoughtful reflection from literary models, Eisold's work is not an empirical study of successor appointment mechanisms. It is helpful, but its conclusions require testing. Applying this approach to the subject studied by Dyck et al., namely a father-son transition (see above), may have proven helpful to understand the powerful relational dynamics of the business succession and why it ultimately failed.[39] As there are few studies applying psychoanalysis to succession, it might be fruitful to investigate the extent to which Christian ministries employ or require some kind of dispassionate organ to assist succession. The methodologies and participants in ministry succession could be examined to ascertain which transitions are the least disruptive and produce the best performance. In chapter 18, I apply Eisold's recommendations to an understanding of paternal-filial succession within a Christian organization and posit that his principles were of assistance in defense of charges of nepotism.

LESSONS AND DEFICITS

This very brief overview of just a few of the findings of succession research begins to show us the subject's complexities, but also that solid lessons may nonetheless be learned about the importance of taking matters such as origins or organizational change into account. Despite numerous succession studies, however, there are still considerable deficits in research. First, there is a lack of attention to the issue of gender and its relationship with the multifaceted issues of succession. The four academic reviews of the literature in the last decades make no mention of gender issues.[40] Second, succession

---

39. Dyck et al., "Passing the Baton," 143–62.

40. Gordon and Rosen, "Critical Factors in Leadership Succession," 227–54; Kesner and Sebora, "Executive Succession," 327–72; Giambatista et al., "Nothing Succeeds Like Succession," 963–91; Hutzschenreuter et al., "How New Leaders Affect Strategic

studies have not thus far taken into account the perspective differences of social generations as leadership is transferred. Weil shows perspectival differences among generations in Germany,[41] while Cherrington in her study of generations in China shows that social generational change is not merely a Western phenomenon.[42] How should international Christian organizations take into account generational transfer, especially when some cultures have rigid understandings of age deference?[43] Third, there has been scant research on succession within international organizations. Fourth, the myriad of studies are not conducted within the context of Christian ministries. A rigorous application of theory and methodology and examination of aspects such as internal/external succession, antecedents, consequences, post-succession performance, process, and socialization might assist ministries in their preparation for succession.

Change," 729–55.

41. Weil, "Cohorts, Regimes, and the Legitimation of Democracy," 308–24.

42. Cherrington, "Generational Issues," 302–20.

43. Hofstede, *Culture's Consequences: Comparing Values.*

Chapter Three ————————————————

Founder Succession in Organizational Studies

"The great entrepreneur must, in fact, be compared in life with the male *Apis Mellifera*. He accomplishes his act of conception at the price of his own extinction."

—J. K. GALBRAITH

THE PREVIOUS CHAPTER INTRODUCED a number of concepts which may have to be taken into account during succession. In this chapter, we turn to a specific type of succession, namely succession following the founding entrepreneur of a business or founding visionary who began a nonprofit organization. It became clear that founder transition was different from other forms of succession when Carroll found that organizational failure rates were higher after founder succession than after non-founder succession.[1] This also raises questions for Christian ministries. A number of issues have come to light requiring consideration and which might help shape how we proceed when facing succession today.

---

1. Carroll, "Dynamics of Publisher Succession," 93–113.

15

ENTREPRENEURIAL LEADERSHIP STYLE TO PROFESSIONAL LEADERSHIP STYLE

Tashakori undertook a detailed study of cases where external leaders replaced owner-founders of businesses.[2] Her key finding is that founder succession is usually from an entrepreneurial style of leadership to a professional style. Entrepreneurial management may serve well in the early stages of enterprises, but growth and complexity mean it can become an impediment in later stages. None of the founders in her study was able to make the transition to a professional role. She found that succession is made complex (even hindered) by founders' reluctance to relinquish control, due to emotional/psychological factors such as perception of self-importance, unknown future roles, their need to achieve, fear of their own mortality, or financial concerns for the future. Transition often occurs when the organization grows too complex for the founder to manage or when there is a need to turn to outside investors, who will then usually require board representation and concomitant power. Transitions were successful when successors had "substantial"[3] realized power and that predecessors had little continuing power.

While there is much in Tashakori to inform an understanding of founder succession, she portrays styles as exclusive categories. I argue that styles are not oppositional. Indeed, according to situational leadership theory, I suggest they are fluid, and indeed should be. As the nomenclature implies, situational leadership theory posits that different situations demand different types of leadership. Indeed, "to be an effective leader requires that a person adapt his or her style to the demands of different situations."[4] This involves an analysis of the skill levels and motivation of the employees or followers, and indeed how those change over time. The leader then changes the degree of direction or supportiveness in this changing context. Leadership style is thus adapted to the competence and commitment of the subordinates.[5] Tashakori's binary understanding makes no room for such nuances. Indeed the clear demarcation of leadership styles actually dissipates in one of the cases I describe later, that of the international mission and aid agency International Aid Services (see chapter 16).

---

2. Tashakori, *Managerial Succession*.
3. Tashakori, *Managerial Succession*, 82.
4. Northouse, *Leadership*, 99.
5. Northouse, *Leadership*, 99–100.

SUCCESSION AND FOUNDER-EMBEDDED ORGANIZATIONAL CULTURE

Schein shows the significance of the founder in the establishment of organizational culture and the subsequent problems this may pose for the successor.[6] The founder will establish the culture by setting the tone for and ways of dealing with external adaption (primary task, core mission and strategies) and internal integration (conceptual categories, boundaries for inclusion/exclusion, allocation of power, and allocation of rewards). The founder embeds cultural elements in many ways, but Schein found the three most potent media are deliberate role modeling, teaching, and coaching by the founder; those matters which leaders measure and control; and leadership reaction to critical incidents and crises. Founder-owners and professional managers tend to differ in four key areas: motivational and emotional orientation, analytical orientation, interpersonal orientation, and structural/positional perspectives. Entrepreneurs subconsciously embed non-economic assumption into the culture, which a professional manager will want to rationalize. This can create conflict as such rationalization attempts challenge perceived organizational culture.

While not an exact parallel, Schein's work in part points to the seminal writing of Weber and his theory of the routinization of charisma. According to Weber,

> The term "charisma" will be applied to a certain quality of an individual personality by virtue of which he is set apart from ordinary men and treated as endowed with supernatural, super-human, or at least specifically exceptional powers or qualities. These are such as are not accessible to the ordinary person, but are regarded as of divine origin or as exemplary, and on the basis of them the individual concerned is treated as a leader.[7]

In Weber's understanding, routinization is the establishment of rules, constitution, eligibility tests, and economic structures of a new (religious) group or community. Thus, according to this theory, a pioneering leader with charismatic authority is often succeeded by others who formalize and bureaucratize. While sidestepping the many debates on Weber,[8] I suggest that it is not inevitable that the second-generation leadership routinize and diminish charismatic authority, or, put in Schein's terms, that they

---

6. Schein, "Role of the Founder," 13–28.

7. Weber, *Theory of Social and Economic Organization*, 358–59.

8. One search yielded over eighty-seven thousand pieces of literature on Weber. See http://www.worldcat.org.

rationalize leadership (although this may indeed be common). In the case of Newfrontiers, a large international network of churches originating in the United Kingdom, efforts were made to maintain charismatic authority by dissolving established bureaucracies upon founder succession and releasing fifteen new leaders to gather a number of existing churches and with them establish entirely new church networks (further details in chapter 20). This conforms with Ukah, who, in his study of the Redeemed Christian Church of God (RCCG) in Nigeria, shows that not only is routinization *not* inevitable but that the successor can enhance the charismatic nature of leadership and church, providing a "double founding" and "recharismatization."[9]

CONTINGENCY PROBABILITY OF FOUNDER SUCCESSION

Rubenson and Gupta increased understanding of founder succession by offering a contingency model.[10] They seek to predict when founder succession will help the organization by evaluating the founder's continuing utility and power to allow or prevent change. They suggest that succession is unlikely in the following three scenarios: no great change in organizational needs; change in needs with an adaptable founder; change in needs with a lack of adaptability in the founder but where the founder is able to impede succession. Where there is a change in needs, lack of adaptability, and where the founder is able to impede succession, it is impeded. While accepting these conclusions from Rubenson and Gupta's sample, they seem to posit a Machiavellian view of humanity and not take into account matters such as generativity. It is possible to surmise that founders of Christian organizations, although having the ability to impede succession, might actually desire it for the good of their organizations and for purposes of generativity. Indeed, I suggest this was the approach in a number of cases, which I explore in further detail later. Whether such contingency probabilities as mentioned here can be identified in Christian ministries is a topic needing research. The underlying matter, however, suggests the importance of power distribution in succession.

9. Ukah, *New Paradigm*, 83.
10. Rubenson and Gupta, "Initial Succession," 21–35.

FOUNDER'S SUCCESSION AND
ORGANIZATIONAL ZEAL

Haveman and Khaire[11] examined contingency factors, particularly the extent of the ideological zeal of a founder, the managerial role played by the founder, and organizational affiliations, expecting these to moderate the relationship between founder succession and performance. For this research, they studied the magazine industry in the United States.

Their major contribution to the study of founder succession is the introduction of the concept of "organizational zeal" among founders. Founders who were not intensely ideological created "instrumentally-rational" organizations to achieve value-neutral ends, while those with high degrees of organizational zeal produced value-rational organizations which reflected firm principles rather than efficiency or profitability.[12] The authors found support for the following hypotheses: The succession of founders in line positions will have greater impact on organizational failure than the succession of founders in staff positions; the difference between the impact of line and staff founder succession will be greater for strong-ideology rather than weak-ideology organizations; the difference between the impact of the exit of a founder who plays multiple roles and the exit of a founder who plays a single role will be greater in strong-ideology organizations than in weak-ideology organizations. The major conclusion of this research is that "intense ideological orientation increased the detrimental impact of founder succession on organizations' survival chances."[13] While helpful, the method of measuring zeal (content analysis examining frequency of certain words deemed to signify "zeal") is limited. It ignores the context and that words may also signify latent content in discourse. Such nuances are not taken into account in such quantitative content analysis.

There are no studies relating organizational zeal to Christian organizations. The above study would suggest that such organizations, presumably established with strong organizational zeal and a compelling mission, might find founder transition problematic. Yet, it would seem likely that founders of Christian movements and organizations are motivated by generativity; that is, the desire to give themselves to those who will come after them so that they leave a legacy of faith and good works that will survive after they have relinquished leadership or passed on. Indeed, we would expect that

---

11. Haveman and Khaire, "Survival Beyond Succession?," 1–43.

12. Haveman and Khaire, "Survival Beyond Succession?," 4, following Weber, *Theory of Social and Economic Organization*.

13. Haveman and Khaire, "Survival Beyond Succession?," 27.

such Christian leaders are, therefore, especially diligent in ensuring succession conducive to organizational longevity.

RATES AND ANTECEDENTS OF FOUNDER SUCCESSION

Wasserman conducted the first large-scale exploration of founder-CEO succession, by studying 202 internet companies.[14] His study showed that the rate of founder-CEO change increases after the company finished development of the initial product; the rate of founder-CEO change will increase after each round of outside financing; the more money raised by a company in its latest round of financing, the higher the rate of founder-CEO succession; in insider-controlled firms, the rate of founder-CEO succession will be lower than in outsider-controlled firms. In essence, Wasserman points to a paradox of success—the founder's achieving critical milestones (product completion and rounds of financial investment due to growth) cause a significant rise in the probability of founder replacement.

This study, of course, may not be generalizable to other industries, as the internet industry changes rapidly, and may, in fact, need greater amounts of shorter-term investment. Also, those companies studied were those that had raised new rounds of investments, biasing the study toward the more successful entrepreneurs. While providing helpful understanding of the antecedents to succession in new enterprises, it is probable that the findings here are less applicable to Christian organizations, where success is harder to quantify or commodify compared to matters such as capital investment. Founders of ministries rarely need to step down due to increased tranches of capital investment from others.

CULTURAL AND RELIGIOUS CONTEXT OF FOUNDER SUCCESSION

From a study in Nigeria, Ukaegbu examined founder successions and enterprise durability, a concept defined as follows: "The prospects for a firm to exist for long after the death of its founder without a significant decline in human and material input as well as organizational output."[15] Ukaegbu's work shows how local contextual realities moderate founder succession. In 1991, Ukaegbu studied twenty functioning businesses and five that ceased with the founder's death, finding in these latter cases that issues of

14. Wasserman, "Founder-CEO Succession," 149–72.
15. Ukaegbu, "Entrepreneurial Succession," 28.

inheritance and family conflict were the primary causes of business cessation. In 2001 the five businesses remained non-functional, while a further four founders had died, three of whose businesses were now also defunct. The crucial moderator seemed to be familial conflict, which was more common in polygynous families. Not only do polygynous families have a greater number of members, increasing the probability of conflict, but also the wealthier a man becomes, the more likely (among Muslims in modern Nigeria) he is to take more wives.

For the purposes of this book on Christian organizations, Ukaegbu introduces the crucial nature of local religious and cultural context in mediating and moderating founder succession. This is something which we should note, especially with regard to international Christian agencies.

POWER AND POWER DISTRIBUTION

Block and Rosenberg attempted to discern whether founders of nonprofit organizations exercise greater levels of power than non-founder CEOs.[16] Their evidence showed in multiple ways that a greater percentage of founder leaders exercise greater influence and power than non-founders, including in matters such as reduced board meeting frequency and higher frequency of founders establishing board agendas and approving minutes before distribution. Founder succession, therefore, is likely to be from one who has higher levels of organizational power. A further area for research might be to link this to the findings of Haveman and Khaire and examine the relationships between zeal and power distribution.[17]

Perry and Yao studied power distribution subsequent to external succession.[18] Wasserman[19] had already shown that external CEO succession was more common when replacing the founder; in selecting only external succession, Perry and Yao found that 73 percent of their study was founder succession. This study sought to understand the relationships between predecessors' and successors' four dimensions of power as identified by Finkelstein:[20] structural power, ownership power (connections to the owner and/or founders), expert power, and prestige power. They found strong support that a predecessor founder's status will be positively related to

16. Block and Rosenberg, "Toward an Understanding of Founder's Syndrome," 353–68.

17. Haveman and Khaire, "Survival Beyond Succession?," 1–43.

18. Perry and Yao, "To Get the Best New CEO," 505–25.

19. Wasserman, "Founder-CEO Succession," 149–72.

20. Finkelstein, "Power in the Top Management Teams," 505–38.

post-succession structural power. This is due to a number of factors, such as founders having stronger attachments,[21] as well as boards wanting to retain access to their knowledge.[22] There were mixed findings concerning the predecessor's structural power being negatively related to the successor's expert power. Indeed, if the predecessor was expected to remain involved, it was found less likely that the organization would attract a successor with prior CEO experience. In short, the study found that if predecessor founders remained more involved after succession, the predecessor's power negatively related to a successor's expert power but less so to prestige power. With regard to subsequent performance, it was found that keeping a former CEO with some power showed higher return on assets, but it is less likely to attract an experienced or prestigious successor, thus providing a conundrum for those making leadership appointments.

There is greater generalizability of this study due to the examination of both a larger number and a wider diversity of organizations. There are, however, limitations. The research was based on announcements and plans, not actual distribution of power as it developed in the post-succession period. It also did not seek to compare cases where predecessors were not involved and how this related to power, growth, and other factors. The study, furthermore, did not examine any causal relationship between predecessor and successor power. Applying this methodology and studying power distribution within founder-led international Christian ministries could, however, be fruitful for a deeper understanding of the succession dynamics. Indeed, in chapter 27 we will seek to determine exactly where power lay in some of the decision-making around succession within the Christian organizations studied. The determination of power is vital to understand how succession is navigated.

FOUNDER TRANSITION AND ORGANIZATIONAL IDENTITY THREAT

Other work alerts us to a further matter which may be a dynamic and of significance in founder succession, namely that of "organizational identity threat." For Balser and Carmin, "Organizational identity is the set of features that members understand to be central, distinctive, and enduring within their organization,"[23] while the identity threat is "when organizational members interpret events or situations as challenges to or violations

---

21. Wasserman, "Stewards, Agents, and the Founder Discount," 930–76.

22. Clutterbuck, "Handing Over the Reins," 78–85.

23. Balser and Carmin, "Leadership Succession," 186.

of or danger to that which they believe are central and distinctive features. Such threats can be external, for example a reduced donorship, or internal, such as prioritising one value over another."[24]

After the departure of the charismatic founder of Friends of the Earth, a nonprofit organization advocating for environmental sustainability and the many issues of justice surrounding it, new leadership challenged the decentralized nature of the charity and increased oversight and accountability between the regional offices. Many felt there was a loss of founding values and goals, resulting in internal conflict. In studying this, Balser and Carmin showed how founder succession may "bring to the surface latent differences in understandings of identity and be interpreted as internal identity threats if individuals believe modifications will devalue features they regard as central and distinctive to their organizations."[25]

While this is a study of one organization and may not be generalizable, it does highlight the potential difficulty in founder succession, particularly in a nonprofit organization where people devote themselves to a founding vocation (organizational zeal) rather than profit motive. It fails, however, to examine correlations between identity threat and other succession characteristics, such as origins; that is, whether external appointments caused greater identity threat than internal. This may be a helpful concept to bear in mind for Christian organizations which, one presumes, are also started with a deal of zeal and commitment to spiritual goals rather than financial profits. Those planning succession may wish to minimize identity threats as leadership changes hands in order to retain membership and people committed to the organization for the longer term.

FOUNDER'S SYNDROME

Given the potentially problematic nature of founder's transition, a term has gained circulation, namely that of "founder's syndrome." McLaughlin defines this as "the imbalance of power in a nonprofit organization in favor of the founding executive that occurs because of the unique advantages of assembling the board and staff of the organization."[26] This may make it difficult for founders to relinquish positions of power. McLaughlin, despite the title *Moving Beyond Founder's Syndrome to Nonprofit Success*, writes less about succession strategies and more about an attempt to understand founders, their passion and their often idiosyncratic management, which

24. Adapted from Balser and Carmin, "Leadership Succession," 187.

25. Balser and Carmin, "Leadership Succession," 198.

26. McLaughlin, *Moving Beyond Founder's Syndrome*, x.

can lead to enmeshment of identity between the founder and the organization as well as compelling vision but little strategy, leading to loss of original focus. Adams suggests a number of explanations for this dynamic within charities, including the likely ongoing influence of the founder even post-succession; that many founders have not been good managers, thus leaving structural problems for their successors; an overdeveloped sense of loyalty between the founder and staff/volunteers; and fundraising dependence on the founder's relationships.[27]

Much of the literature, such as the two examples cited above, emphasizes the person and style of the founder in the creation of founder syndrome. I suggest this shows that such literature stems from a latent and unacknowledged leadership theory of leadership as trait or style, such as found in Kirkpatrick and Locke's study, which articulates the six traits that distinguish leaders from others: drive, motivation, integrity, confidence, cognitive ability, and task knowledge;[28] or in Stevens,[29] which details the entrepreneurial behavior of nonprofit organizations' founders, finding fourteen entrepreneurial behavior patterns.[30] I suggest, moreover, that trait-based theory may be inadequate as others participate in the syndrome's creation by elevating the founder and his/her achievements, which thus produces insecurity among followers when succession occurs. Studies applying leadership theory to founders' succession, such as leader-member exchange theory (LMX) might thus provide a more nuanced understanding of succession. For example, this theory conceptualizes leadership not so much as emphasizing a leader's traits, skills, or style, nor the follower context, such as in situational leadership. Rather, LMX focuses on leadership as "a process centred on the interaction between leaders and followers."[31] Perhaps such psychodynamics partly explain a fascination for founders within the church, yet little interest to date on what happens post-founder, a matter taken up more fully in later chapters.

27. Adams, *Founder Transitions*.

28. Kirkpatrick and Locke, "Leadership" 48–60.

29. Stevens, "In Their Own Words."

30. For a fuller understanding of trait approaches to leadership, see Northouse, *Leadership*, and Jung and Sosik, *Who Are the Spellbinders?*

31. Northouse, *Leadership*, 161.

Chapter Four

Succession in International Organizations

Leadership and Culture

MANY ASPECTS OF MODERN life, whether it be business, education, the arts, or Christian ministry, are increasingly international in scope and ways of operating. As we read the book of Acts of the Apostles in the New Testament, we see that the Christian church from its outset was international and multicultural, as witnessed by the peoples gathered at the day of Pentecost (Acts 2) and indeed throughout the entirety of the book. Today there are both large international Christian agencies, such as Youth With A Mission, Operation Mobilization, or Samaritan's Purse, as well as many networks of churches with congregations in multiple nations.

Given the above, it would seem pertinent to ask whether succession within multinational organizations takes on specific characteristics due to the international and multicultural nature of the organization being led. In which ways, if any, might succession in international organizations differ from succession in a local or monocultural context? Unfortunately, there appear to be no empirical studies of founder succession in such international agencies, nor indeed within international organizations in any other field. There is some research into the competencies needed to lead large international organizations, and considerable work studying the relationship between leadership and cultures. This chapter will briefly refer to these issues; studies of such issues, however, omit treatment of succession.

INTERNATIONAL LEADERSHIP COMPETENCES

Adler and Bartholomew pioneered the way in attempting to articulate the competences needed in a transnational organization, where traditional hierarchies tend not to exist and transnational leaders need a "career home" rather than a geographic home.[1] While a study of fifty international organizations, they were all headquartered in the US and Canada, thus, ironically, producing findings that still lack true international perspective. Trompenaars and Wooliams turned to matters of intercultural competences in leadership, finding "intercultural competence in reconciling dilemmas is the most discriminating feature that differentiates successful from less successful leaders and thereby the performance of their [international] organizations."[2]

There has been no application of the findings on transcultural competences to the field of international ministries. There is scope to explore the extent to which the required competences are the same as or different from the business world. In the field of Christian ministry, one would expect the need for competences to include fundraising and donor management in different cultures, as well as motivation of staff and volunteers who bring to their work cultural expectations of leadership.

LEADERSHIP AND CULTURE

With the numeric growth of transnational companies, the issue of the relationship between culture and leadership has become pressing. One influential study is that of Trompenaars and Hampden-Turner, who researched thirty thousand participants in thirty companies in over fifty countries to identify the best leadership for transnational organizations.[3] The authors' main thesis is that every culture must handle three dilemmas: relationships

---

1. Adler and Bartholomew, "Managing Globally Competent People," 61.

I use the terms "international" and "transnational" interchangeably, in common with much of the literature. Trompenaars and Hampden-Turner, however, make a qualitative distinction, defining the "transnational" organization as "the genuinely international organization . . . in which each national culture contributes its own particular insights and strengths to the solution of worldwide issues and the company is able to draw on whatever it is that nations do best" (*Riding the Waves of Culture*, 12).

2. Trompenaars and Wooliams, "Getting the Measure of Intercultural Leadership," 164. Trompenaars (Dutch) is one of the most influential writers in the business world (see Thinkers50 and THT Consulting in the bibliography).

3. Trompenaars and Hampden-Turner, *Riding the Waves of Culture*. This has sold several hundred thousand copies in multiple languages (http://www.amazon.com/Riding-Waves-Culture-Understanding-Diversity/dp/0071773088).

with people, such as individualism versus communitarianism or specific versus diffuse; attitudes to time; and attitudes toward the environment. Trompenaars and Hampden-Turner conclude that there is no single best way of organizing or managing an international business because organizations must adapt "not simply to the environment but also to the views of participating employees."[4] Thus, organizations actively select, interpret, choose, and create their environments. Trompenaars and Hampden-Turner, therefore, decry a universal absolute approach to leadership, contrary to the position of House et al. (see below).[5] Trompenaars and Hampden-Turner do not, however, treat issues of succession. How their notions of "specific" versus "diffuse" and temporal understandings impact succession are, therefore, matters open to research.

Hofstede examined culture and work by studying one hundred thousand respondents in over fifty countries.[6] His main contribution has been to show five major dimensions where cultures differ: power distance, uncertainty avoidance, individualism-collectivism, masculinity-femininity, and long-term-short-term orientation. He has been particularly influential in highlighting the notion of "power distance." This concept is defined by Hofstede as follows:

> The power distance between a boss B and a subordinate S in a hierarchy is the difference between the extent to which B can determine the behavior of S and the extent to which S can determine the behavior of B.[7]

Cultures that are more egalitarian tend to be "low power distance" cultures, where followers (employees, congregants) are more likely to initiate discussion, even criticize leadership. In "high power distance" cultures, followers are more deferential, less likely to criticize leaders, wishing to know the leaders' opinions and desires so these may be unquestionably followed.

Hofstede's framework is helpful to leaders of international Christian ministries who need to understand, facilitate, and motivate workers and volunteers from many cultural backgrounds. Indeed, power distance might intersect with theology in that some might infuse cultural understandings of high power distance with the notion of divine calling and be even less likely to initiate or criticize. His research, however, does not address issues

4. Trompenaars and Hampden-Turner, *Riding the Waves of Culture*, 14.

5. House et al., *Culture, Leadership, and Organizations*.

6. Hofstede, *Culture's Consequences: International Differences*; Hofstede, *Culture's Consequences: Comparing Values*.

7. Hofstede, *Culture's Consequences: Comparing Values*, 83.

of succession. It would surely be fruitful to address how power distance relates to selecting leaders and, indeed, who is to participate in the process.

The Global Leadership and Organizational Behaviour Effectiveness (GLOBE) Project[8] presents a strong body of findings on culture and leadership, particularly the relationship between culture and leadership effectiveness, as it is based on a study of seventeen thousand managers from 950 organizations in sixty-two countries. Building on Hofstede's five dimensions of culture, they offer a more nuanced model for the study of the relationship between culture and leadership by examining nine cultural dimensions and six global dimensions of leadership. The extent of their research has for the first time led to an attempt at a "universal" understanding of leadership, as they posit leadership attributes which are universally desirable, universally undesirable, and culturally contingent. Universally desirable attributes consist of the following:

- trustworthy

- dynamic

- decisive

- intelligent

- dependable

- plans ahead

- excellence oriented

- team builder

- encouraging

- confidence builder

- informed

- honest

- effective bargainer

- motive arouser

- win-win problem solver

- positive

- foresight

- just

- communicative

8. House et al., *Culture, Leadership, and Organizations.*

- motivational

- coordinator

- administratively skilled

Attributes universally seen as negative are as follows:

- nonexplicit

- dictatorial

- loner

- ruthless

- asocial

- egocentric

- irritable

- noncooperative

This project's major contribution to understanding the relationship between culture and leadership was their finding that cultural values do not directly predict leadership behavior but they do drive the cultural expectations that in turn drive leadership behavior. This is a significant finding, one which may be difficult to challenge given the vastness of their study, which makes their conclusions more generalizable than those of others. While suggesting universal attributes, the study is actually of multiple contextual expectations of leadership. This still leaves the gap of how to lead when there is no one dominant set of contextual expectations, but, as in the case of an international ministry, there are multiple contextual expectations from a diverse group of followers. Despite their claims, the study fails, therefore, to offer a truly transnational or transcultural understanding of leadership helpful to those leading transnational organizations. Notwithstanding this, their framework of attributes may be our best understanding of international leadership yet.

Northouse criticizes the GLOBE project for the conceptualization of leadership as how it is viewed rather than conceptualizations such as what leaders do and also that the universal positive attributes ignore context.[9] Such comments suggest, however, that Northouse's critique comes from the perspective of leadership as action or behavior.

The GLOBE project continued its extensive research by studying one thousand CEOs and five thousand managers in twenty-four countries in

---

9. Northouse, *Leadership*, 405–6.

order to examine CEO leadership behavior and effectiveness.[10] They offer empirical evidence to support the congruency hypothesis of leadership, a hypothesis that leader effectiveness is predicated upon the extent to which leaders enact the type of leadership actually expected to be outstanding within that society.[11] This work also indicates those leadership styles which produce more effective results and greater follower participation. They indicate that there is a strong link between charismatic/transformational leadership and performance—in fact, it is universally effective.

With such findings, House et al. answer Northouse's criticism and offer a general theory of strategic leadership which transcends national boundaries. Such a general theory of strategic leadership has both "mission critical leadership competencies" and "important leadership competencies."[12] Mission critical leadership competencies are activities leaders must perform to high levels to produce extraordinary results. Such qualities are as follows:

- visionary
- performance oriented
- decisive
- inspirational
- administratively competent
- integrity
- diplomatic

Important leadership competencies are activities which do not need to be performed at such a high level as the first set. They are as follows:

- self-sacrificial
- collaborative
- participative
- team integrator
- bureaucratic[13]

This offering could be a crucial assistance to those seeking to lead international Christian operations. It also, however, raises the question of whether

10. House et al., *Strategic Leadership across Cultures.*

11. See House et al., *Strategic Leadership across Cultures.*

12. House et al., *Strategic Leadership across Cultures*, 360.

13. The term "bureaucratic" in this context means leading according to guidelines and norms and fairly administering rewards.

the competencies suggested apply equally to ministries as to businesses. There is room here for significant comparative research. Again, these studies do not, however, address succession; there is no work on the relationship between culture and succession, culture and founder, or succession within international organizations.

Chapter Five

Succession in Christian Organizations and Movements

THUS FAR, THIS BOOK has sought to explore some of the many issues concerning leadership succession within businesses and to a lesser extent nonprofit organizations. It has also introduced some of the specific dynamics that can shape succession when it is the transition from the founding entrepreneur or leader, and furthermore introduced the notion that many organizations today are international, posing the question of whether the multicultural nature of the organization also should be taken into account when planning for and executing succession. In this chapter, we turn our attention specifically to Christian ministries and church movements to reflect on understandings to date of leadership succession. The following chapter focuses on the subcategory of succession, namely founder succession. This paves the way for a subsequent chapter where we reflect on those seeking to draw forth a theology of succession for such organizations or movements.

CHRISTIAN LEADERSHIP SUCCESSION

In seeking to examine Christian literature on succession, it is perhaps surprising how little on succession is available in the general literature on Christian leadership. Many influential classics of Christian leadership do not address it. This is the case with classic works such as Sanders's *Spiritual Leadership*, with currently over one million copies sold.[1] Practitioner authors such as De Pree[2] and Maxwell[3] are both prolific and well read. More than one million copies of both Maxwell's *Developing the Leader within You* and *The Twenty-One Irrefutable Laws of Leadership* have been sold.[4] These works also do not address any specific issues with regard to succession. It is, furthermore, instructive that Banks and Ledbetter in their review of Christian leadership literature do not address the succession issue at all, despite referencing some three hundred publications.[5] Avoidance of the issue might be explained by the publications' desire to impart skills or methods for those Christian leaders faced with the immediate quotidian practicalities of leadership rather than helping them plan for the future.

PASTORAL SUCCESSION

Notwithstanding the above, there have been many publications providing guidance for clergy and congregations undergoing pastoral succession. Such advice is usually along the lines of establishing a search committee and how that should engage in candidate search. While much that is written in this category may indeed provide helpful advice for a congregation seeking to find a new minister, there is usually little in such works that draws on conclusions from empirical data rather than advice from former experience. As the purpose of this book is to address leadership succession within larger Christian organizations or church movements, I will largely sidestep the details of how to secure a new pastor for a congregation. Those interested in congregational leadership succession and wishing to refer to published works in this field may consult the bibliography.

PRACTITIONER ADVICE

There are, however, several works by practitioners which seek to give general guidance to Christian organizations in dealing with succession. They

1. Sanders, *Spiritual Leadership*. Statistics taken from https://www.amazon.com/Spiritual-Leadership-Principles-Excellence-Believer/dp/0802482279.

2. De Pree, *Leadership Is an Art; Leadership Jazz;* and *Leading without Power*.

3. Maxwell, *Developing the Leader within You; Developing the Leaders around You; Twenty-One Irrefutable Laws of Leadership;* and others.

4. Information from back cover of Maxwell, *Developing the Leader within You* (2005 ed.).

5. Banks and Ledbetter, *Reviewing Leadership*.

are not empirical but seek to give practical advice from experience. One such example is McKenna,[6] who from his experience in leading a Christian ministry suggests that succession is a cycle comprising twelve components: remembering our story, reading our culture, understanding our life cycle, accepting our role, timing our leave, completing our task, announcing our decision, celebrating our successor, making our exit, managing our emotions, letting history be our judge, and leaving our legacy. Such points may be helpful for one considering succession and provide some general yet reasonable advice.

EMPIRICAL RESEARCH ON CONGREGATIONAL LEADERSHIP SUCCESSION

There is little empirical research on congregational leadership succession, although six credible exceptions have been found.[7] The benefits of greater engagement with empirical research on congregational succession may be seen, for example, in the work of Mentzer, who examined whether leadership transition in a church affects performance, concluding that turnover is positively associated with organizational performance if it is operationalized in terms of attendance but not of funds raised.[8] This study shows that the subject of studies in the business world (performance) and the methodologies (quantitative studies) may also be employed when studying Christian organizations.

A further helpful example of learning from empirical research on succession is found in Dollhopf and Scheitle.[9] They analyzed 1,321 congregations in the US to examine whether leadership transitions in congregations are associated with membership decline or congregational conflict, as well as whether characteristics of the leader or congregations moderate any associations. Some of their key findings are that churches in areas measuring lower on socioeconomic scales were more likely to experience post-succession conflict within the congregation than those in more affluent communities. They also found that post-succession conflict was more frequent where a female pastor was appointed but acknowledge that any correlation

---

6. McKenna, *Leader's Legacy*.

7. Mentzer, "Leader's Succession-Performance Relationship," 191–204; Avery, *Revitalizing Congregations*; Lummis, "What Do Lay People Want in Pastors?"; Anthony and Boersma, *Moving On, Moving Forward*; Antal, *Considering a New Call*; and Dollhopf and Scheitle, "Decline and Conflict," 675–97.

8. Mentzer, "Leader's Succession-Performance Relationship," 191–204.

9. Dollhopf and Scheitle, "Decline and Conflict," 675–97.

between succession and gender within churches is complicated by other variables. Given research showing little difference in approaches to ministry between male and female clergy,[10] and bearing in mind that Dollhopf and Scheitle also found higher incidents of conflict in congregations in poorer neighborhoods, and that McDuff and Mueller show that women are more likely to be appointed to congregations in poorer areas,[11] it is possible that location and social-economic milieu are more likely causal factors in post-succession conflict than leadership gender.

These studies provide a hint that issues researched in business succession (internal/external appointments, performance, expectations, antecedents) are relevant to churches as well as businesses and that empirical research is possible and may be fruitful in Christian organizations. In the following chapter, attention is drawn more specifically to founder succession within Christian ministries.

10. Simon and Nadell, "In the Same Voice," 63–70.
11. McDuff and Mueller, "Gender Differences," 465–91.

Chapter Six

Founder Succession in Christian Ministries

IN TURNING TO EXAMINE literature on founder succession within ministries, it should be noted that there have, of course, been numerous examples of founders within the Roman Catholic and Protestant traditions. This frequency, together with the reverence for such founders in both ecclesial traditions, makes it surprising how the matter of what comes after the spiritual founder is not well examined in either Catholicism or evangelicalism. For example, Hanks provides sixty examples of evangelical founders.[1] This is a work written to show the influence of (evangelical) Christians in creating a moral fabric for society. It contains short biographies of the founders and a brief history of the organizations initiated. It is a work of encyclopedic entries which helps show the extent of evangelical initiatives. It does not, however, address the issue of leadership transference and succession from these pioneering figures. As with the Roman Catholic literature, it has undertones of hagiography. Schattschneider[2] might have been helpful as a study of Zinzendorf (1700–1760), in effect the founding leader of the renewed Unitas Fratrum (or Moravian Church)[3] and his successor, Span-

1. Hanks, *60 Great Founders*.

2. Schattschneider, "'Souls for the Lamb.'"

3. The Unitas Fratrum began in the fifteenth century. I am regarding Zinzendorf as the founder of the *renewed* church as, under Zinzendorf's leadership, it experienced

genberg (1704–92); this study, however, is a work of comparative missiology rather than a study of leadership succession processes.

As previously mentioned, there also appears to be a lack of attention to founder succession within Catholicism, where the term "founder" is only used with regard to founders of religious orders. There was some interest in the subject of founders during the Vatican II period, an approximate twenty-five year period (1964–89),[4] in which literature appeared in three forms: references in official Vatican statements (forty-five references in *Lumen Gentium,* eleven in *Evangelica Testificatio,* and eleven in *Mutuae Relationes*); articles from the 1975 conference "The Spirit of the Founders and Our Religious Renewal";[5] and several scholarly books, of which two are the most comprehensive.[6] On the whole it would seem that while inspired by founders, Catholicism has shown little interest in studying succession, perhaps due to its post-mortem nature.

Notwithstanding the above comments, there are, however, four recent and relevant pieces of literature concerning founder succession within Protestant ministries.[7] Two contribute little to understanding the subject; two are helpful. In this chapter, some of the findings are explained so that we can learn from them. In chapter 10, we will return to some of these works when we consider how we might study leadership succession, considering their methodologies and methods further.

FOUNDER SUCCESSION IN THE CHURCH OF GOD IN CHRIST (COGIC)

Owens studied succession from the founder of COGIC, Charles Mason (1866–1961), to the (soon disputed) leader, Ozro T. Jones (1891–1972).[8] The title of his work, *Never Forget!—The Dark Years of COGIC History,* points to the purpose of this study, that Christians would learn from a tragic example of navigating founder succession. Jones was elected by a presiding

---

a rebirth as a residential religious community and became a pioneering missionary movement within evangelicalism.

4. There appears to be no literature before or since.

5. I have used the 1977 English translation of the French conference papers published as "Spirit of the Founders and Our Religious Renewal." See Canadian Religious Conference, *Spirit of the Founders.*

6. Lozano, *Foundresses, Founders*; and Romano, *Charism of the Founders* (originally published in Italian in 1989).

7. Kondrath, "Transitioning from Charismatic Founder," 83–115, also includes one example of a Roman Catholic ministry.

8. Owens, *Never Forget!*

body of bishops and functioned as denominational leader for two years. Some claimed that he had not been appointed according to the denominational constitution. There were rival boards and rancorous meetings, at times to which the police were called to maintain peace. Finally, the courts imposed the need to determine a legal constitution, which, when enacted, elected a leader other than Jones.

This work is historical, citing numerous articles, minutes, sermons, and conference proceedings. It is constructed, however, in a way that is confusing, neither adequately giving an account of events nor accounting for events. There is a confusing attempt to evaluate the outcomes according to organizational theory with comments stating that routinization of charisma was taking place under Mason's leadership yet others stating that it began later. In particular, Owens[9] relies on organizational understandings drawn from Morgan and his notions of "bureaucratic authority"[10] and "traditional authority."[11] Owens' central explanation seems to be that the post-succession conflict was due to protagonists using the language of and appealing to bureaucratic authority,[12] while some assumed the organization was led by traditional authority. It was, furthermore, made complex by Jones initially appearing to lead with bureaucratic authority but later employing charismatic, even autocratic, authority.[13] While Owens' methods are discussed more fully in chapter 10, from this study, it is clear that a succession mechanism should be agreed before it is needed.[14] It is also a salutary lesson that disastrous founder transition may occur, even in Christian organizations.

FOUNDER SUCCESSION AT LIBERTY UNIVERSITY, VIRGINIA

Peterson examined founder succession at Liberty University, an evangelical institution in Virginia, US.[15] Succession occurred in 2007 following the death of the founder, Jerry Falwell Sr.; the successor was his son, Jerry Falwell

---

9. Owens, *Never Forget!*, 81.

10. "This type of legitimate authority exists when the foundation of power is the correct application of formal procedures and rules" (Morgan, *Images*, 172).

11. "This type of legitimate authority exists when power is vested in people who embody and symbolize the traditional values of customs and practices of the past" (Morgan, *Images*, 172).

12. Owens, *Never Forget!*, 186.

13. Owens, *Never Forget!*, 190.

14. Owens, *Never Forget!*, 188.

15. Peterson, "Case Study."

Jr. It was decided, largely by Falwell (senior), in 2003, that his son would be the successor. Thus, this was a case of "crown heir" succession according to Friedman and Olk's typologies of successor selection (see chapter 2).

There is little to learn from this study, as it largely gives us data about how people reacted to the news of the succession, with comments from participants such as that the succession was a work of God. The conclusion that the identification of a successor and subsequent mentoring can contribute to smooth transition, while true, is simplistic; it is, moreover, naïve, as shown in failed founder succession in other ministries where successor identification and mentoring also took place, such as in the case of the Crystal Cathedral.[16] The work also fails to explore the father-son dynamics raised by Eisold.[17] Due to the lack of reflexivity on the nature of the emic positioning of the researcher, I argue, furthermore, that the work helps us little as it is not merely reflective of, but even constitutive of, the official organizational discourse of the institution being studied, a matter to be explored further in chapter 10.

FOUNDER SUCCESSION IN AMERICAN MEGACHURCHES

Wheeler is considerably more helpful in furthering an understanding of founder succession within Christian ministries.[18] His is a study of succession in three megachurches in the US. It is not described as a study of founders but of megachurch pastoral succession; two of the transitions were from the founders who had long tenure; the third from the pastor of forty-one years, who had followed a founder of three-year tenure. According to Carlson and Donohoe, succession following such a long tenure usually has the same dynamics as founder succession.[19] All three cases were deemed "successful" because financial income and attendance remained stable, ministries continued well, and there was no obvious division.

This qualitative study employed sound methodology, using fifteen semi-structured "life world" interviews[20] of the same (or functionally equivalent) actors in each of the three cases, all of which were examples of relay succession. There are a number of findings, which may help others in

16. Lavietes, "Rev. Robert Schuller."
17. Eisold, "Succeeding at Succession," 619–32.
18. Wheeler, "Leadership Succession Process."
19. Carlson and Donohoe, *Executive Director's Guide*.
20. Kvale, *InterViews*, 29–30.

understanding successions and how to prepare for them. The key conclusions are as follows:

- Transitions are "complex multi-layered change processes,"[21] often associated with structural, cultural, and relational change.

- There is a positive relationship between organizational performance and relay succession. This supports similar findings from Zhang and Rajagopalan.[22]

- The role played by the founder/predecessor leader is crucial in facilitating succession. It is facilitated if the founder initiates the discussion, thereby enabling others to participate in honest ways. Others involved and affected by the succession find it helpful, as does the founder, if he/she has a plan for post-succession life. It is beneficial, furthermore, if the founder supports the successor in public.

- Preservation of core ideology is a stabilizing factor during time of transition. This confirms the findings of Collins and Porras.[23]

- Succession affects multiple categories of people, not just the predecessor and successor.

Of course, as with much detailed qualitative study, the results may not be generalizable, but may nonetheless be transferrable to other cases.

FOUNDER TRANSITION AND ORGANIZATIONAL CHANGE

Kondrath studied founder transition in three Christian ministries, one an outreach to the homeless, one a network of prayer groups, the third a small international network of churches.[24] This is not a study of the processes of transitions, nor matters such as antecedents, characteristics of the successors, performance, and socialization. As a pastoral theologian, Kondrath focuses on the relational dynamics of founder succession. His main argument is that leadership transition from the founder is not merely about a change of persons but also of both structure and leadership style. An organizational shift is needed. It is unhelpful to focus on the person of the leader; vision should not be transferred from the founder to another individual

---

21. Wheeler, "Leadership Succession Process," 311.
22. Zhang and Rajagopalan, "When the Known Devil," 483–500.
23. Collins and Porras, *Built to Last*.
24. Kondrath, "Transitioning from Charismatic Founder," 83–115.

but should become the responsibility of a designated group who ensures its continuation. There must be transfer of trust from a founder to trust in the community, its goals and structure.

For Kondrath, dissemination of information and communication is the key. Charismatic leaders who feel their mission is divinely inspired may fail to see the need for helping others to understand the raison d'être of the ministry. Beginning better communication can itself be a change of organizational culture. Communication at this stage must not be merely cognitive but affective. Followers will have many emotional responses to change, such as sadness, grief, fear, or insecurity. Members also need to be in greater communication with each other as they become less centered on the leader. In particular, members may need to process their position and relationship with regard to the founder, what this meant to them, and what new relational possibilities there might be after the transition. Kondrath, furthermore, observed that differences might emerge. They may have existed before, but loyalty to the founder inhibited the discussion of divergent values. The disequilibrium and surfacing of differences may then be blamed on the new leader.

Kondrath's central suggestion is that founder succession is not merely a person-to-person transference but will inevitably raise many other issues of relationship, structure, vision, and values. This is a helpful contribution to understand the corporate dynamics of founder transition.

LESSONS FROM FOUNDER'S STUDIES IN CHRISTIAN ORGANIZATIONS AND MOVEMENTS

From the above four studies a number of lessons may be drawn. Such lessons include the following:

- the importance of a clear plan of succession (Owens)
- the necessity of a clear understanding of the nature of the organization and its basis of authority (charismatic, tradition or bureaucratic) (Owens)
- that founder succession is not merely about the replacement of one person but requires an organizational paradigm shift (Kondrath)
- the benefit of outside consultants and/or a board to help navigate succession (Kondrath), thus supporting Eisold
- the need for socialization of successors (Wheeler)
- the influential role of the predecessor post-succession (Wheeler)

These studies also point to areas of further potential research, including comparative studies of ministries which employ the methodology of relay succession and those adopting other methodologies, the kinds of successor socialization needed, the processes of succession within Christian agencies, and comparative studies on those which employ consultants and those which do not (Kondrath). I will return to some of these works again in chapter 10 to learn how best to reflect on how succession has been and is to be studied.

Chapter Seven ───────────────

Theology of Succession

THE SURPRISING OBSERVATION IN the four studies mentioned examining founder succession within Christian organizations is the lack of theological data and analysis. Owens examines the conference and committee meetings, decisions, and polemical arguments against such decisions, and seeks analysis from understanding of authority from the field of organizational development.[1] Peterson explains the process of the appointment of the successor (largely a decision and announcement of the founder) and how the staff at Liberty University reacted to it rather than any theological interpretation of leadership at the institution.[2] Even Wheeler[3] seems to concentrate on succession plans and the perspectives and feelings of key protagonists in the succession. Yet, these were all Christian organizations and leaders with either overt or implicit theological positions on the nature of leadership and the raison d'être of the organization in question. It would seem reasonable to ask whether the understandings of the theology of leadership among the key protagonists in each case affected how they viewed the succession and to include this in the analysis. This has thus far only happened in a very limited way. Indeed, in what has been written in this book so far, much has been drawn from the organizational field, as there is scant literature

1. Owens, *Never Forget!*
2. Peterson, "Case Study."
3. Wheeler, "Leadership Succession Process."

on succession within practical theology or missiology from which to draw. Some, however, have begun to address the theological nature of leadership and succession. In this chapter, I seek to review two attempts at theological reflection on succession to assist my later framing of a theological and not merely organizational analysis.

Kay Fountain has theologized succession by inquiring into several Old Testament cases from which she hopes to produce "guidelines" for today.[4] Fountain concludes with "principles" of succession as follows:[5] God chooses leaders; existing leaders make God's choice public; the successor must be given opportunities to prove himself/herself and thus gain credibility in the eyes of the people; mentoring by the predecessor is to be provided, particularly so that the successor might grow in servanthood; at the appropriate time, a public ceremony of power transference should take place.

Without so knowing, Fountain espouses "crown heir" appointment followed by its implementation through "relay" succession.[6] A critical reflection on Fountain's proposed theology, however, reveals its problematic nature. First, in terms of her methodology, it is not possible to generate the kind of nomological conclusions drawn by her; three (biblical) cases cannot provide substantive and multi-contextual guidelines, particularly when one of the cases (Elijah to Elisha) must surely be categorized as an "extreme" case.[7] Second, her "principles" raise questions of hermeneutics. Do the Old Testament offices of prophet and king continue today, and if so, what aspects of them and their succession models are transferable to contemporary international Christian organizations? Is it possible, in the post-Pentecost era, to view the Old Testament description of several successions as normative for the church, as Fountain seems to suggest? The participants in the case studies explicated later (chapter 14) did not seek to draw normative guidelines from the Old Testament at all.

My third critique of Fountain is that theology alone is insufficient for providing a normative approach to succession. We have already seen, there are many factors in successions; these can often only be examined when taking into account matters such as human relationships, power, zeal, and so forth. While such matters may be the subject of theological reflection, they may

4. Fountain, "Investigation," 189.

5. Fountain, "Investigation," 202.

6. Vancil, *Passing the Baton*; Friedman and Olk, "Four Ways to Choose a CEO," 141–64.

7. The term "extreme" is common in the literature on case study methodology (see for example, Yin, *Case Study Research*). There can, of course, be good reason to study an extreme case, as it may be of interest in its own right or may point to matters not usually observable in typical cases.

also be understood from different theoretical positions. While definitions of the concept of "leadership theory" may be hard to find (although there are many definitions of specific theories), I posit that it is simply a way of "conceptualizing" leadership,[8] or that a theory is an "approach to leadership,"[9] a way of perceiving it, which emphasizes matters other than the numinous or authoritative religious scriptures (matters such as behaviors, traits, or situational factors).[10] In her work, Fountain ignores theoretical understandings of leadership, which can nonetheless inform theology. An example of how theory might inform theology on this matter is seen with Fountain's framing of the Elisha succession as a "continuation" of Elijah. This was appropriate in this specific case, but I argue that contingency theory helpfully shows that often a successor should not be a "continuation." Contingency theory of leadership posits that "effective leadership is contingent on matching a leader's style to the right setting."[11] Thus, the second-generation leader might need a different style and traits to meet the different contingencies of his/her times; thus, contextuality impinges on normativity. Given the variety of ways that church leadership is understood around the world, there are many contextual factors which might shape succession today, something ignored by Fountain. This is not to say, however, that contextuality and normativity are necessarily in opposition to each other. A study of biblical leaders may reveal both normative principle and contingent variables in interplay in the shaping of leadership thought and action.

Fourth, Fountain's work stems from a priori assumptions that God speaks and shows who the leader is. There is no problematizing of this assumption to examine how that might happen today, when (usually!) chariots of fire do not appear in organizational board meetings when succession appointments are deliberated.

Theologizing succession from scriptures was taken up by Pugh, seeking to find a "biblical basis for Pentecostal and charismatic leadership transition today."[12] His investigation into the succession theologies of Britain's

8. Northouse, *Leadership*, 4.

9. Northouse, *Leadership*, 2.

10. See Northouse, *Leadership*, for descriptions of different approaches to, or conceptualizations of, leadership. For a standard definition of leadership, see Burns, *Leadership*, 18: "Leadership over human beings is exercised when persons with certain motives and purposes mobilize, in competition or conflict with others, institutional, political, psychological, and other resources so as to arouse, engage, and satisfy the motives of followers."

11. Northouse, *Leadership*, 123. There are, of course, greater complexities to this theory than such a definition might suggest. For an introduction to the nuances of contingency theory, see Northouse, *Leadership*, 123–36.

12. Pugh, "Succession Plans," 117.

new apostolic networks found divergent positions. Some held there should be no human involvement at all; it was entirely left to God to make the matters obvious, a position that still raises the question of how God intervenes and makes the appointment obvious. Several networks did not privilege any particular scripture as normative, thus suggesting they did not espouse a normative theology of succession. Pugh provides a nuanced interpretation of several Old Testament successions and thereby seems to posit a theology of succession largely resting on two constructs; leadership in the church is, or should be, charismatic and plural. All the new apostolic networks in the UK are categorized as having charismatic leadership, according to Weberian theory.[13] Thus, in succession, a crucial matter becomes "maintaining the charisma."[14] For charisma to continue, Pugh stresses the need to avoid a transition to other types of authority (traditional or hereditary) that tend toward bureaucratization. This connects to the second pillar of succession theology, namely that it should lead to plural leadership, for such leadership itself mitigates bureaucratization. Pugh posits that Jesus disseminated charisma to a group and believes that Kondrath's recommendation for modern founder succession also adopts this approach with Kondrath's stress that a board or group become the repositories of organizational vision, not an individual.[15] For Pugh, Jesus did not appoint one successor; the Spirit was deposited primarily in a community.[16]

Pugh has gone further than most in examining succession from a theological position as he attempts to articulate a normative basis for leadership succession today. It is interesting that it is Newfrontiers, one of my case studies, that Pugh holds to be one of the better examples of his succession theology: "It is the kind of transition that can take place in a strong and growing organization possessed of a core community who are faithful custodians of the founding vision. Plurality is at its heart and the Spirit drives the process prophetically."[17] His normative approach to the dissemination of charisma is underlined, for Newfrontiers' succession is "the ideal type and the goal . . . [which] should be to try to move in the direction of a plural rather than a singular investment where succession is concerned."[18]

Pugh's work brings together a biblical understanding as well as empirical comment from new church networks today. While helpful, a number

---

13. Pugh, "Succession Plans," 120.

14. Pugh, "Succession Plans," 120.

15. Kondrath, "Transitioning from Charismatic Founder," 83–115.

16. Pugh, "Succession Plans," 128.

17. Pugh, "Succession Plans," 128.

18. Pugh, "Succession Plans," 129.

of critical comments are to be made. In Pugh's theology, bureaucratization works contrary to maintenance of charisma, and thus Christian succession. I posit, however, that some amount of bureaucratization may be necessary as part of the succession process. In organizational literature, this is clear both with Tashakori[19] and Schein.[20] Both show that charismatic founders may lead with idiosyncratic styles, producing irrational policies and decisions. This was seen in that, after the highly charismatic leadership of Zinzendorf, the Unitas Fratrum needed Spangenberg to systematize theology and structures. Indeed, an understanding of organizational life-cycle theory[21] may help in this regard, as well as realizing that in addition to charisma, a contingency approach may be necessary for organizational survival. Indeed, the "dissemination" of charisma attempted by Newfrontiers almost required a greater level of routinization on some issues as Newfrontiers Together formed (chapter 14).

I argue, furthermore, that Newfrontiers was not the example of diffusion and dissemination lauded by Pugh. It was rather a reduplication or multiplication of leadership around individual apostles, rather than dissemination to a group. Each of the fifteen apostles were to have exactly the kind of power and authority exercised by Virgo within their "sphere."[22] This was not a move to group leadership but a division of one organization into fifteen separate ones, each having the same power structures as the former.

Pugh's suggestion of "an ideal type" of succession returns us to the matter of normativity. Given the diversity of leadership in international Christian organizations and the thorough research of the GLOBE project showing how cultures and leadership behaviors correlate,[23] what may be needed, rather than normativity, are many contextual theologies of succession. Moreover, as with Fountain, we need to ask whether a purely theological imperative is adequate, but rather whether an interdisciplinary model of succession in which theory and theology are mutually in dialogue would be more helpful. There have been no substantive attempts at such a study.

To recapitulate, the question of succession theology has rarely been studied; it is highly problematic, raising matters of hermeneutics, methodology, and the fundamental matter of whether there is normative theology of

19. Tashakori, *Managerial Succession.*

20. Schein, "Role of the Founder," 13–28.

21. Adizes, *Corporate Lifecycles.*

22. In Newfrontiers, "sphere" is the word employed for the (metaphorical) area of an apostle's ministry. The term is taken from 2 Cor 10:13: "[We] will confine our boasting to the sphere of service God himself has assigned to us." See, for example, Devenish's explanation in *Succession or Multiplication?*, 34.

23. House et al., *Culture, Leadership, and Organizations.*

succession, or, whether such theologies can at best only be contingent and contextual. It is not this book's aim to answer definitively whether there is a normative theology, nor to seek to construct one, should one even be possible. Fountain and Pugh have provided helpful initiation into the matter of succession theology; it would require a different book to develop this matter. This work will examine, however, the construction of the succession enactments of several organizations and the theologies which shaped them and seek to highlight a number of issues to be considered in leadership succession.

Chapter Eight

Conclusions

What Do We Already Know about Succession?

FROM THE ORGANIZATIONAL WORLD, we see that organizational success and longevity are positively correlated with internal succession.[1] At times of forced departure, however, external appointments may be needed.[2] Organizations usually employ one of four methodologies of succession,[3] with "relay" succession being common in Christian ministries.[4] For relay succession to be successful, however, title, power, control, and responsibility must transfer simultaneously.[5] Due to the personal dynamics of incumbent/ successor relations, a dispassionate group must be involved in the appointment and transitional processes.[6]

There are further complicating and potentially detrimental dynamics when succession follows the organization's founder.[7] Founders profoundly influence the organization by the embedding culture;[8] they have greater

---

1. Collins and Porras, *Built to Last*; Ocasio, "Institutionalized Action," 384–416; Shen and Cannella, "Revisiting the Performance Consequences," 717.

2. Allgood and Farrell, "Match between CEO and Firm," 317–41.

3. Friedman and Olk, "Four Ways to Choose a CEO," 141–64.

4. Wheeler, "Leadership Succession Process," and Peterson, "Case Study."

5. Dyck et al., "Passing the Baton," 143–62.

6. Eisold, "Succeeding at Succession," 619–32.

7. Carroll, "Dynamics of Publisher Succession," 93–113.

8. Schein, "Role of the Founder," 13–28.

49

levels of power than non-founding leaders.[9] Succession almost ineluctably leads to a change of style from entrepreneurial to professional leadership,[10] which may lead to perceptions of organizational identity threat.[11]

There has been little attempt to apply the theories of organizational development to Christian organizations, yet there are signs that such application can be fruitful.[12] There have also been few attempts to study Christian founder succession, but those studies do point to the importance of all actors' agreeing the nature of authority within the movement[13] and indeed of the clear release of authority.[14] Intentional relay succession may provide smooth transitions,[15] but founder successions are complex as they bring structural, relational and cultural change.[16] Both Wheeler[17] and Collins and Porras[18] point to the key role during transitions of core ideology preservation in supporting organizational stability.

In review of the studies undertaken thus far into founder succession in Christian organizations, we do find a few attempts to examine and learn from this topic. Yet, as I explain in chapter 10, such attempts have started on a wrong footing. There are vast gaps in the literature on Christian succession and international succession and little theological reflection thereon. This book will continue now to contribute to these matters in terms of providing a salient methodological approach to the study of such matters. It will proffer fresh case studies to describe successions. By bringing organizational and theological considerations to bear on reflections on founder succession, this book will highlight some of the key themes and indeed potential problems in leadership or founder succession in Christian organizations and movements.

9. Block and Rosenberg, "Toward an Understanding of Founder's Syndrome," 353–68.

10. Tashakori, *Managerial Succession*.

11. Balser and Carmin, "Leadership Succession," 185–201.

12. Mentzer, "Leader's Succession-Performance Relationship," 191–204; Dollhopf and Scheitle, "Decline and Conflict," 675–97.

13. Owens, *Never Forget!*

14. Early, "Second Generation Leadership," 1–8, 55.

15. Peterson, "Case Study."

16. Wheeler, "Leadership Succession Process"; Kondrath, "Transitioning from Charismatic Founder," 83–115.

17. Wheeler, "Leadership Succession Process."

18. Collins and Porras, *Built to Last*.

PART II

Studying Succession

Chapter Nine ————————————————

Introduction to Studying Succession

BEFORE CONCENTRATING ON THE main thrust of this book, namely how Christian organizations have navigated succession and the main themes in such successions, it is pertinent to pause to consider how exactly succession can be examined and studied. This is crucial because there are different paths available to be taken and indeed that researchers have taken; each path will lead to different data collection. Of course, this takes us into the realm of research methodologies and methods. Methodology is the overall framework for studying a topic, including the worldview and epistemology behind such frameworks. Methods are the specific tools employed to produce or gather data and the specific ways in which such data can be analyzed. For the general reader, probably even leaders in ministries and organizations, this may hold less interest than the practical findings and potential applications of studying succession. Given this, much of the methodological approach and analysis of data gathering is summarized in this chapter. Those particularly interested in such matters may refer to my work, available in digital format.[1] What follows is further comment on three studies of founder succession mentioned in Part I. Subsequently, an approach to study succession is suggested. This approach is then tested in a pilot study (briefly reported here). The content of this part

---

1. Bunton, "Founder Succession," 86–123. The digital version is available at https://www.research.manchester.ac.uk/portal/files/164141071/FULL_TEXT.PDF.

should help the reader understand how the conclusions in the later parts of the book were reached.

Chapter Ten —————————————————

Designing Research into Founders' Succession

Learning from Others

UNIVERSITY, DENOMINATION, MEGACHURCH— AN INTRODUCTION TO THREE CONTRIBUTIONS

AS PREVIOUSLY MENTIONED, PETERSON's work is a study of leadership succession from the founder of Liberty University in Virginia, US.[1] Liberty University is an evangelical university founded by Jerry Falwell Sr. in 1971 with the mission to "train Christ-centered men and women with the values, knowledge, and skills essential to impact their world."[2] Peterson reports that with thirteen thousand residential students and approximately ninety thousand registered for online educational provision, it is "the largest private, non-profit, higher education institution in the United States."[3] Upon the founder's death in 2007, Falwell's son Jerry Falwell Jr. was appointed as chancellor and successor. Peterson's aims are to investigate the succession processes and provide guidance to help "ensure successful and smooth transitions among colleges and universities."[4] He concluded that the founder engaged in the specific succession design of "relay succession" by using the

1. Peterson, "Case Study."
2. Liberty University, "Statement of Mission & Purpose."
3. Peterson, "Case Study," 54.
4. Peterson, "Case Study," 17.

"crown heir" strategy, and that the transition was successful with universal agreement due to both the planning and skills of the successor.[5]

Owens's book *Never Forget!*[6] is a study of succession from Charles Harrison Mason (1866–1961), the founder of The Church of God in Christ (COGIC), a largely black Pentecostal movement in the US, to his immediate post-death successor, Ozro T. Jones (1891–1972), and of the disputes which arose challenging this succession. It seeks to chronicle and comment on the transition period 1961 to 1968, with a view to evaluating the leadership styles in operation. Conclusions include the following: that a succession mechanism must be decided before its enactment is required; if appeals are made to bureaucratic legitimacy, those who win the argument are those best at "maneuvering" within bureaucracies;[7] seeking to resolve matters through legal channels increases the likelihood that those better at handling bureaucratic procedures will have their view upheld; the leadership style enacted was a "bureaucratic, collective leadership style" that under Jones changed to an autocratic leadership style.[8] Owens believes that this research supports the theory that charisma is routinized in succession from founders with charismatic authority (following Weber, but also Glassman and Swatos, and Marger),[9] and that his study is "conclusive" in confirming the "inherent instability of charismatic organizations in the area of leadership succession."[10]

Wheeler, in "Leadership Succession Process," researches leadership succession within Protestant megachurches in the US, most being founder succession.[11] The research aims to provide a "rich description of three megachurch succession processes,"[12] to understand this succession in relation to theory as well as provide assistance to other megachurches facing leadership succession.[13] Wheeler identifies the consistent theme of "relay succession"[14]

---

5. Peterson, "Case Study," 117.

6. Owens, "Dark Years (1961–1968)" is a PhD dissertation, while Owens, *Never Forget!* is a published book, largely based on this dissertation. As I have not been able to find the dissertation in digital form, comment is made on the published version due its accessibility to other researchers.

7. Owens, *Never Forget!*, 188.

8. Owens, *Never Forget!*, 190.

9. Glassman and Swatos, *Charisma, History, and Social Structure*; Marger, *Elites and Masses*.

10. Owens, *Never Forget!*, 201.

11. Wheeler, "Leadership Succession Process."

12. Wheeler, "Leadership Succession Process," 5.

13. Wheeler, "Leadership Succession Process."

14. Friedman and Olk, "Four Ways to Choose a CEO," 141–64.

and posits a five-phase process of succession.[15] I summarize those phases as follows:

1. Realization by the predecessor and others in leadership of the need for deliberation on succession. This discussion on succession was activated by matters such as age considerations of the predecessor leaders, the current leader's desire to leave the pressures of directing a large ministry, or an invitation to pursue a leadership role in another organization.

2. Phase of identification or recruitment of the successor.

3. Public announcement of the successor and concomitant mentoring by other senior leaders. This phase served as a proving time for the successor to demonstrate public and private capabilities as a leader as well as a season of transference of various roles and functions from the predecessor to the successor.

4. Exit of the leader, including a ceremony with symbolic enactments.

5. Post-succession adjustments to new realties.

As previously stated, it is not my intention to write a full methodological analysis of previous research; for that, the reader is referred to Bunton.[16] However, any student of succession should realize that methods affect the findings that are presented and the conclusions drawn. I argue that what has been presented to us thus far as observations of and lessons for succession in Christian movements is not always reliable; indeed, it may well obfuscate our understanding of the topic. In this chapter, I will attempt to show the critical importance in the study of succession of both the concept and practice of "reflexivity" and of research design.

THE RESEARCHER—ISSUES OF REFLEXIVITY

Reflexivity is a metaphor from grammar indicating a relationship of identity between subject and object, thus meaning the inclusion of the actor (scholar, author, and observer) in the account of the act and/or its outcomes. In this sense reflexivity shows that all knowledge [including that of scholars] is "subjective."[17]

15. Wheeler, "Leadership Succession Process," 340–41.

16. Bunton, "Founder Succession."

17. Hufford, "Scholarly Voice," 57.

Elsewhere, I have sought to provide a fuller treatment of reflexivity as it purports to the study of religion, showing its relevance and importance in practical theology.[18] In practice, reflexivity often means acknowledging and taking into account one's personal demographic characteristics, such as gender and race, worldview, methodological framework, one's position with regard to the subjects of study, and a priori assumptions. In this section, I aim to comment on how these aspects of reflexivity affected data collection and analysis and question the findings of much of the research to date on succession in Christian organizations.

Reflexivity in Studying Liberty University

Peterson's research was conducted while an employee of and as a doctoral candidate at the university. Research committee advisors were drawn from the university's faculty. These factors call for due reflexivity in several areas. These are inadequately addressed in this research, which leads to some significant weaknesses in both the data collection and interpretation.

Firstly, there is a general lack of personal reflexivity with regard to the researcher's demographic characteristics and their potential role in the data collection and analysis. We do not know Peterson's race, but we do know his gender (male). We have no knowledge of the race of the research participants nor how race might affect the perspectives and data. There is a lack of acknowledgment of how gender might influence the researcher's knowledge production. This is of particular pertinence with regard to Peterson's adoption of the interview and focus group methods. There appears to be no awareness in the construction of questions of neither the interviewers' position of power and how this might affect responses, nor the potential for patriarchal assumptions of privilege in the guiding of an interview by an interviewer, nor that knowledge production may result from the type of relationship established between the interviewer and interviewee. The data analysis does not assess the responses on a gender basis, which would have provided a deeper understanding of perspective on the leadership succession at Liberty University.

This, of course, is part of a further issue, namely the lack of methodological reflexivity. At times Peterson appears to attempt a positivist methodology, yet, at other times, his framework appears constructivist. The former is seen with comments such as "the researcher detached himself from experiences in order to garner a better understanding of what actually

---

18. Bunton, "Reflexivity in Practical Theology," 81–96.

transpired."[19] If detachment is the aim, there is, however, little indication of *epochē*.[20] Yet at the same time (even on the same page), Peterson seems to adopt a non-objectivist position, placing himself firmly inside the research topic, thus presumably attempting a *verstehen* approach; that is, of identifying and empathizing with the participants.[21] Peterson decides that affinity with the interviewees (his colleagues) and employment within the institution are strengths, gaining him access to "key players" who trusted him.[22] This methodological confusion makes the data less reliable, as we do not know the details of how it was obtained and on which assumptions it was analyzed.

Of greater concern is the lack of acknowledgment of the disadvantages of his being embedded in the research subject. He is aware of potential bias in three areas:[23] The researcher's discomfort could pose a threat to the value of data obtained and analyzed; the potential lack of preparations for the field research; and bias might affect his conduct of the interviews.[24] Lack of due reflexivity, however, is evident in that he does not elaborate on any potential "discomfort," does not elucidate potential lack of preparation, and does not acknowledge potential bias in interviewing nor any strategy to mitigate this. Indeed, Peterson takes these potential disadvantages out of context and misapplies them to his situation, as Poggenpoel and Myburgh's comments are of highly sensitive interviews concerning termination of pregnancy among adolescents. While sensitivity to interviewees is needed in all cases, Peterson is misapplying the observations to his far less sensitive situation. Indeed, his references to Poggenpoel and Myburgh are not only irrelevant; they obscure the real problem, namely that the institution being studied is his employer (and the employer of his research advisors). This work reveals a strong institutional discourse that Liberty University is a thriving establishment blessed by God. Peterson's lack of reflexivity as an employee severely undermines his research, which itself becomes not only reflective of that discourse, but also constitutive thereof.

The consequences of lack of reflexivity in the researcher's complicated position may be seen in the areas of documentary analysis, appropriate coding and category identification, and omission of highly pertinent discourse analysis. Not only were crucial documents not analyzed (minutes of the

---

19. Peterson, "Case Study," 52.

20. Defined more fully in my introduction.

21. See Roof, "Research Design," 68–80, for more on research design, including *verstehen*.

22. Peterson, "Case Study," 52.

23. Citing Poggenpoel and Myburgh, "Researcher as Research Instrument," 418–21.

24. Peterson, "Case Study," 51.

board of trustees, correspondence between the founder and his successor) but also there was no accounting for the social production of those that were analyzed. This is particularly the case with regard to Peterson's analysis of articles from the university's own journal, *Liberty Journal*. Peterson fails to acknowledge that the purpose of *Liberty Journal* is the official dissemination of information about the institution and the promotion of the institution to the wider public.[25] While such aims are legitimate, these should be accounted for in any documentary analysis; indeed, such documentary content is part of the official institutional discourse.

A second consequence of the lack of reflexivity was the omission of key coding and the overlooking of categories vital to understanding the succession processes; or, if such codes were part of the data categorization, analysis did not take place or was not reported, thereby omitting an opportunity for gaining a fuller understanding of the leadership succession. One such unreported category rich in analytical possibilities is that of "God" (or "theology"):

> They pulled behind Jerry [Jr.] because God had done it just exactly right. He brought Jerry, Jr. on the scene just in time. He exposed him to all of us. He gave him enough power and authority to be able to, for us to accept him (Comment of an administrator).[26]

A further overlooked category here was that of leader-follower theory, such as LMX.[27] This omission may be seen in the following data:

> He was more than a man, He [*sic*] was a movement (Member of Board of Trustees).[28]

> The man was always bigger than life (A vice-president).[29]

> You know, Doc (J. F. Sr.) was invincible. He was convinced he wasn't going to die. He had told all of us he wasn't going to die. So who were we to object to that . . . (Laughter) (An administrator).[30]

25. Volumes available at https://www.liberty.edu/journal/.

26. Peterson, "Case Study," 109.

27. Previously defined in chapter 3 as "a process centered on the interaction between leaders and followers" (Northouse, *Leadership*, 161).

28. Peterson, "Case Study," 79.

29. Peterson, "Case Study," 79.

30. Peterson, "Case Study," 80.

Coding for "leader/follower" might have led to further categories, such as the ascription of charisma. The omission of such categories means that the researcher was ill attuned to the hagiographical tone of the responses and thereby missed a significant opportunity to report on organizational myth-making and discourse constitution. The respondents' answers are examined for "manifest content" but not "latent content;" that is, "interpretations about the content in texts that imply something about the nature of the communicators or effects on communicators."[31] There seems to be a lack of awareness that subjects might recreate and change the social world in their (re)telling of it; that there may be a prevailing institutional discourse which the respondents reflect and constitute; and that indeed there may be discursive limits at Liberty University.

It is noteworthy that Yin's work on case study research, a work from which Peterson draws heavily, provides a specific caveat about interviewing in a "closed" educational institution where respondents are likely to provide the same or similar responses:

> Such consistent responses are likely to occur when interview-ing members of a "closed" institution, such as the residents of a drug treatment program or the teachers in a closely knit school. The apparent conspiracy arises because those being interviewed all aware of the "socially desirable" responses and appear to be providing corroboratory evidence when in fact they are merely repeating their institution's mantra.[32]

If such specific advice had been heeded, a fuller analysis of the responses might have produced interesting and rich data. This leads to my third point, that a discourse analysis method may have helped with data interpretation, but this approach would not be possible without due reflexivity. Rather wor-rying is the following comment:

> As a researcher, who was close to the case being examined, po-tentially, the data collected might have appeared to contradict the mission of the organization or did not reflect well on the school. In this type of situation, counsel was sought of the com-mittee chair and the other members of the committee to see if the alternative explanations for the data could be derived.[33]

It would seem that this research is not only reflective of the institutional dis-course but is also, moreover, constitutive thereof, maybe even intentionally

31. Nelson and Woods, "Content Analysis," 120.

32. Yin, *Case Study Research*, 125.

33. Peterson, "Case Study," 73.

so. Lack of reflexivity has in fact undermined the research in its entirety, meaning that there is little we can draw from this work to further an understanding of succession.

Reflexivity in Studying COGIC

This work is devoid of reflexive comment, except for the statement that the researcher is an elder in the Church of God in Christ.[34] Owens believes this information is providing "full disclosure."[35] This lack of reflexivity is problematic in several ways. We do not know how his interview data were gathered and analyzed. By not providing details of his interview sample, we do not know the gender of the participants. From the names of participants, we assume that most were men. It is likely that the lack of reflexivity means that there is lack of taking into account any gender bias in the data gathering and analysis.

Issues of race are central to this research, but unacknowledged. COGIC is primarily a black church. The Pew Forum's *Religious Landscape Study* 2014 states that 84 percent of members identify as "black."[36] While historical statistics on the racial demographics of COGIC have been difficult to find, the founder and successor were black; reports contemporaneous with the succession events being researched confirm the racial constituency of the church.[37] There is, however, no comment on the race of the subjects nor of the researcher. Investigation shows that Owens is white.[38] There is no reflexivity concerning how a white American interviews and studies black Americans and how any assumptions concerning race affect his interviewing or analysis. This is a significant omission.

Thirdly, while Owens informs us of his leadership position within COGIC, he provides no reflection on how this might affect the research. If interviewees are less likely to reveal opinions to an elder in their denomination, this might affect collection. An elder might be predisposed to believe official church accounts, thus affecting analysis. He might not wish to present matters which reflect poorly on the church or its leaders. The lack of acknowledgment of such things or suggested mitigation strategies means the reader might not have full confidence in the data.

---

34. Owens, *Never Forget!*, 23.

35. Owens, *Never Forget!*, 23.

36. Pew Research Center, "Members."

37. Means, "Negro Bishops," 23, cited in Owens, *Never Forget!*, 139.

38. https://www.linkedin.com/in/drrobertowens.

There is, furthermore, a lack of methodological reflexivity with regard to a possible unacknowledged positivism, to the historical method and to data collection methods (interviews). There are some hints that the study at least aims to be based on a positivist methodology by the desire to "prove" (not test) a hypothesis[39] and the conclusion that the study proves "conclusive" in confirming the "inherent instability of charismatic organizations in the area of leadership succession."[40]

This work is essentially historical research, the events in question having taken place some thirty-five years prior to research. The historiographical method is, therefore, of central importance, but there is no comment concerning historiographical approaches. There is lack of recognition that religious history is often "emic history" drawing on "emic narratives,"[41] and how such emic narratives are constructed and should be interpreted by the historian. Perhaps the following is the closest to an overt, stated historiographical methodology:

> Neither does the author of this work wish in any way to cast aspersions upon the characters, morals, or spirituality of any person mentioned within the context of either the case study or the evaluations contained here-in. No judgments are expressed or implied as to the motives, objectives, or reasons associated with any of the events discussed in this work.[42]

This could mean that the author is at least in part attempting neutrality and objectivity, a kind of naturalist history, or Rankean "*wie es eigentlich gewesen war*,"[43] that is "how it actually had been" (my translation). The desire for no judgment, however, speaks to the role of the historian. While not wishing to ascribe moral judgment, surely it is the role of the historian to evaluate, suggest responsibilities for actions, or to suggest interpretations for the decisions and speech reported. Indeed, Owens *does* make many interpretive judgments, certainly with regard to evaluations of leadership style, concluding that Jones was autocratic. An unclear historiographical method has led to a subconscious "nomological" approach, seeking to find "regularities" from which generalization may be made.[44] This relates to some of the confusion with regard to a single case leading to transferable conclusions.

---

39. Owens, *Never Forget!*, 15.

40. Owens, *Never Forget!*, 201.

41. Rüpke, "History," 285.

42. Owens, *Never Forget!*, 23.

43. Moses and Knutsen, *Ways of Knowing*, 121.

44. Rüpke, "History," 287.

The data gathered through a specific collection method such as the interview is also impaired by inadequate reflexivity. We do not know which approach to interviewing was taken nor the interviewer's position and stance. There is no acknowledgment of issues which affect data reliability such as reactivity and social desirability. We do know that the interviewees were not asked the same questions,[45] which we assume means the interviewer had an (unacknowledged) a priori understanding of what he wished to ask each specific participant; this, however, is not explained.

The effect of the lack of due reflexivity in Owens means that there is a lack of methodological clarity and that we question the reliability of the data collection. Moreover, we cannot judge any bias in the interpretations due to lack of knowledge, and we do not know how his position as leader and his race affect the conclusions.

Reflexivity in Studying American Megachurches

Wheeler in his research shows a greater degree of reflexivity than Peterson or Owens, certainly with regard to potential effects of his professional position, his experience and methodology. His research, however, is limited in its effectiveness due to lack of reflexivity concerning both race and gender, which affect the reliability and transferability of his findings.

Wheeler states that he is a pastor of a large congregation and that this could prove problematic as he might seek to interpret according to his own experience in similar contexts to those being studied. Such reflexivity allows for an acknowledgment of potential problems but also promotes mitigation strategies in his design; he is conscious of his need to root interpretations in the data rather than prejudgments.[46] He does not, however, write that this could have been helped by others scrutinizing his findings for possible prejudgments.

He acknowledges, furthermore, that he underwent a transition similar to those being studied; toward the end of his research, he transferred church leadership, in effect becoming a "predecessor" leader of a large church. While he speaks of the "powerful feelings of loss,"[47] there is no exploration of how such an experience might affect the research. What was his relationship with the church board during the transition? If negative, did this bias his interpretation of board members' perspectives in the research? Does his personal transition mean that he is more likely to empathize with the

45. Owens, *Never Forget!*, 22.

46. Wheeler, "Leadership Succession Process," 79.

47. Wheeler, "Leadership Succession Process," 84.

predecessors in the study and less likely to provide fair interpretation of the successors? Deeper reflexivity should have taken place at this point, and a counter-balancing strategy could have been developed (for example, asking the successor leaders to comment on whether his interpretation seems unduly biased toward the predecessor perspective).

Wheeler fails, furthermore, to reflect on his race and gender, which limits the usefulness of the data and interpretation that he provides. This lack of reflexivity particularly pertains to his two samples—the churches and the specific participants within those succession events. There is neither comment on his racial characteristic nor comment on the racial demographics of the three megachurches in which in-depth interviews were conducted.[48] Not only are there different approaches to worship and spirituality in American black, Hispanic, and Caucasian churches, but there are also very different understandings of leadership.[49] Given this, the dynamics of succession can be different for, "in the African American church, the identity of the congregation is heavily linked to that of the pastor."[50] The leadership of the black community, whether against slavery or the modern civil rights movement, has always been the religious leaders; therefore, remembrance of and comparison to a former leader is more acute in black congregations. Dollhopf and Scheitle show that Protestant churches of many types show a negative association between leadership transition and membership change, but black Protestant churches in the US show a positive association.[51]

Wheeler cannot be criticized for not studying the relationship of race to succession. Due acknowledgment of this important issue and provision of demographic information would, however, help to locate this study and to see potential limitations to its conclusions. Lack of personal reflexivity on racial factors is, therefore, problematic.

Having identified the church sample, further sampling then took place with regard to the individuals who were interviewed. A serious omission is the lack of comment on the participants' gender. A reading of the text reveals that they were all male. We are not told, however, that this work represents the *male* perspective on leadership succession. The single gender nature of this research limits how the data may be interpreted and the kinds of conclusions drawn. The research takes no account of any female actors in the transitions; this is not acknowledged. Richer data could have been

---

48. An internet search revealed that Wheeler is white: https://www.facebook.com/meredith.wheeler.71.

49. Paris, *Black Religious Leaders*.

50. Watkins, *Leading Your African American Church*, 6.

51. Dollhopf and Scheitle, "Decline and Conflict," 675–97.

collected had female staff members or predecessors' and successors' spouses been interviewed. We do not know, furthermore, whether this omission was solely a lack of gender reflexivity on the part of the researcher or whether only men occupied the leadership or board positions. If the latter, this should be acknowledged in the data and findings. If only men are in leadership positions, analysis could take place within the framework of "theology in four voices," a quadripartite theological model of the following: normative theology (scriptures, creeds, etc.); formal theology (theology of theologians and dialogue with other disciplines); espoused theology (a group's articulation of its beliefs); and operant theology (the theology embedded within the actual practices of a group).[52] Assessing which of these voices shaped the single gender leadership appointments could provide a more nuanced understanding of the successions.[53]

Omission of gender reflexivity is even more significant given research which shows that congregations who have had leadership changes in previous two years are more likely than others to experience serious conflict, even more so if the leader is a woman.[54] Thus, leadership gender may well be crucial to understanding succession consequences and thus to generating theory.[55]

In summary, in all three studies there was insufficient methodological reflexivity and awareness of the potential effects of the researcher's gender, race and personal locus in the study. These matters limit the reliability of findings, and in the case of Peterson, transform the research to be constitutive of the official discourse of the organization being studied.

RESEARCH DESIGN IN THE STUDY OF FOUNDER SUCCESSION IN CHRISTIAN MINISTRIES

The second aspect of methodology to be examined is that of research design, examining the research aim and methods, evaluating their appropriateness and use, and considering whether alternative methods might have

---

52. Cameron et al., *Talking about God in Practice*, 53–56.

53. These theological "voices" are taken up in Part VI.

54. Dollhopf and Scheitle, "Decline and Conflict," 675–97.

55. Although, as previously mentioned in chapter 5, the relationship between succession, gender, and conflict is complicated by other variables, as Dollhopf and Scheitle, "Decline and Conflict," 675–97, acknowledge. See also Simon and Nadell, "In the Same Voice," 63–70, and McDuff and Mueller, "Gender Differences," 465–91.

been conducive to aim attainment. As mentioned before, further analysis is provided in my previous work.[56]

Research Design in Studying Liberty University

Aims

Peterson aims to "explore"[57] leadership succession at Liberty University, to provide an understanding of this succession "process,"[58] to provide information on the actions taken prior to and during the transition,[59] and to produce insight and guidelines for other universities about to undergo founder or leader succession.[60] To achieve his purposes Peterson adopts the case study design. Following Yin's typologies of case design—single-case (holistic), single-case (embedded), multiple-case (holistic), and multiple-case (embedded)—Peterson is aware that he has chosen a "single-case" design.[61] While not acknowledged, Peterson has in fact attempted a single-case (holistic) design.

Justification

Peterson provides three (contradictory) justifications for adopting the case study approach to this subject. First, he states that all case studies provide insights for application in other settings.[62] Secondly, he writes that the qualitative case study approach is useful where there is "lack of theory or an existing theory fails to adequately explain a phenomenon."[63] His third justification is that case study, particularly a single case study, is appropriate when examining extreme or unique cases.[64] The researcher makes repeated references to the "unique" nature of the leadership succession studied: "A

---

56. Bunton, "Founder Succession."

57. Peterson, "Case Study," 3.

58. Peterson, "Case Study," 16.

59. Peterson, "Case Study," 15.

60. Peterson, "Case Study," 17.

61. Peterson, "Case Study," 49.

62. Peterson, "Case Study," 18.

63. Merriam, *Qualitative Research*, 15, cited in Peterson, "Case Study," 19.

64. Peterson, "Case Study," 50. This is taken from Yin's *Case Study Research*, which enumerates five justifications for single-case research: critical case (for testing well-formulated theory); extreme or unique case; representative or typical; revelatory (phenomenon not readily accessible); and longitudinal.

unique aspect to the leadership transition at Liberty University was the relationship between the founder and the second-generation leader. They are father and son";[65] "There was a unique transition";[66] "The case was s [*sic*] a bounded system with three unique aspects."[67] This third justification (uniqueness) is, of course, in tension with the first (applicability), as will be discussed later.

Case Study

It is with regard to the use of case study that Peterson's intended aims and his methods do not align. Four main points will be made concerning his adoption of the case study. Peterson misunderstands the nature of many case studies when he asserts that all case studies may be "applied to other like situations and settings."[68] The literature is overwhelming that some cases are highly individual and may not be applied, such as a "deviant" case,[69] or one interesting in its own right.[70]

Not only is there misunderstanding and contradictions of case study theory, but also of the specific case he is studying. As was shown, this is regarded as a unique study. In one sense, of course, any case is unique; transition from the founder, furthermore, does only occur once in the life of an organization. There is much about the case, however, that is not unique: There are multiple studies of leadership successions (see chapter 2); founder succession is, moreover, not unique (see chapter 2); father-son founder succession has occurred elsewhere,[71] as has father-son founder succession within Christian ministries.[72] Abramson provides a helpful framework for understanding appropriate reasons for unique studies, notably that they help elucidate the upper and lower boundaries of experience and they facilitate prediction by documenting "infrequent, non-obvious, or counterintuitive occurrences that may be missed by standard statistical (or empirical) approaches."[73] While a unique case study may, therefore, be valid, this study is not, however, the unique case believed by the researcher.

---

65. Peterson, "Case Study," 92–93.

66. Peterson, "Case Study," 101.

67. Peterson, "Case Study," 101.

68. Peterson, "Case Study," 18.

69. Lijphart, "Comparable-Case Strategy in Comparative Research," 691.

70. Punch, *Introduction to Social Research*, 122.

71. Dyck et al., "Passing the Baton," 143–62.

72. Lavietes, "Rev. Robert Schuller."

73. Abramson, *Case for Case Studies*, 190.

Indeed, given this, Yin's third type of single-case study, "representative or typical," may have been a more appropriate justification for this study. Indeed, the researcher himself refers to other institutions facing the same issue of leadership succession.[74]

Peterson's confusion raises two problems. First, that a research design aiming at transferability should not study a unique case, and secondly that, if this is indeed not a unique case, then there is data which might be transferable precisely because it is not unique, in fact somewhat typical. The stated goal of transferability may have been achievable had the researcher understood the nature of the case he was studying.

Methods

INTERVIEWS

Interviewing, while a valid method, is problematic in this study. There is no articulation of the philosophical approach to interviewing taken in this research, nor acknowledgment of the interview type (see Roulston for an overview of six conceptualizations of interviewing).[75] The interview conception, furthermore, affects the issue of reactivity. The researcher seems unaware that he may have influenced the data and does not account for potential social desirability influencing the responses. While the researcher did provide for confidentiality to respondents, many of the interviewees were being interviewed about their employers by the researcher who was also an employee of the institution. There is no acknowledgment or attempt to account for concern for employment or advancement if responses were not in accord with the institutional discourse. Moreover, the content of the structured questions shows that the questions do not adequately procure data to answer the overall research questions. The first research questions concern methods of planning and processes, but actual interview questions probe issues of succession criteria and candidates, rather than methods and processes. The interviews proceed to address reactions, responses, and the changing roles of the interviewees. The questions are more appropriate for a study of succession consequences and reactions rather than method and processes.

---

74. Peterson, "Case Study," 18, 19, 21, 22, 27, 28, 29, and elsewhere.
75. Roulston, *Reflective Interviewing*.

Alternative Approaches

Are there other methods or approaches which could have helped better to achieve the overall aims? In addition to better handling the case study rationale and data collection, I suggest that four further things could have helped this research achieve its goals: the employment of a single case (embedded) design; broader coding, based both on the literature and the actual data; a discourse analytical method; and greater reflexivity. The matter of coding from the data, discourse analysis, and general comments on reflexivity have already been treated in this chapter. Here, comment will be restricted to case design and coding based on the literature.

I suggest that a single case (*embedded*) design might have proven more fruitful for richer data collection. The existing research, without recognition, already embedded subunits in the study (for example, members of the board of trustees, alumni, faculty members); these were treated as subunits in the interviews and focus groups. The data from such subunits could have been exploited to provide a richer description by providing a comparative analysis of the responses of each subunit. Structuring the design accordingly would not have required further data collection and could have led to a more nuanced understanding of the succession.

The second matter which would have improved the quality of the data and made richer analysis possible is a different approach to coding. Had Peterson undertaken a broader survey of theoretical literature on leadership succession, even founder succession, a number of categories might have been available to him, such as "insider/outsider" succession,[76] entrepreneurial/professional management styles,[77] authority types,[78] LSSC,[79] power distributions,[80] and organizational zeal.[81] Such an approach would have placed the study more firmly within the corpus of existing literature and have enabled greater nuance in the analysis and conclusions.

76. Cannella and Lubatkin, "Succession," 763–93; Ocasio, "Institutionalized Action," 384–416.

77. Tashakori, *Managerial Succession.*

78. Weber, *Theory of Social and Economic Organization.*

79. Hutzschenreuter et al., "How New Leaders Affect Strategic Change," 729–55.

80. Block and Rosenberg, "Toward an Understanding of Founder's Syndrome," 353–68.

81. Haveman and Khaire, "Survival Beyond Succession?," 1–43.

Research Design in Studying COGIC

"The purpose of this work is to describe, interpret, and evaluate the leadership styles and organizational types present in the Church of God in Christ with respect to the period of time this work terms 'the Dark Years' (1961–1968)."[82] Owens aims to "provide guidance to organizations so that they may avoid the disruption, dislocation, and turmoil" which COGIC faced upon founder succession.[83] Owens writes, furthermore, that he wished to "prove" (not test) a hypothesis that insight into theories of practices of organizational leadership will be gained. His specific questions were to find "lessons which can be learned from COGIC's Dark Years," to establish what prevented an orderly transfer of power, to determine which type of leadership style was operating in COGIC and to learn how COGIC refined and institutionalized the succession process. To answer these questions, Owens utilizes the case study approach with the methods of interviewing and documentary analysis.

Aims

There are a number of problems with the stated aims of this research. First, the matter of "proving" a hypothesis is problematic in the following three ways. The hypothesis is poorly defined. Indeed, a general hope that insight into types of organizational leadership will be gained is not a hypothesis at all; it is not something specific that can be tested and found to be supported by empirical data. There is, furthermore, no mention of any literature or previous research which might lead to hypothesis formation. Moreover, there appears to be confusion as to whether the "hypothesis" is being tested through a quantitative study of some kind or multiple case study or single case. Despite Owen's comment that this research is "built upon the multiple-case study model,"[84] this approach is in fact a single case study.

The second problem with the research aims is that of providing guidance. This speaks to the matter of generalizability or transferability. A single case study is not adequate grounds for such goals; it can merely hint at some potential guidelines from one case, acknowledging that further research would be necessary. It is a mistake to infer conclusions from this historical case study to other cases. According to Owens, "The first and foremost lesson that can be learned" is the following: "If an organizational leader desires to see a seamless transfer of power after he passes from the scene he

82. Owens, *Never Forget!*, 15.
83. Owens, *Never Forget!*, 15.
84. Owens, *Never Forget!*, 21.

needs to have the mechanisms in place prior to that passing."[85] While this is true in this historical case, and indeed would seem common sense, from one study it cannot be concluded from empirical data that this is necessary for all Christian ministries. His second lesson, that those "most adept at bureaucratic maneuver" will triumph once appeals are made to "bureaucratic forms" may also not always be the case.[86] The literature on succession would need to be reviewed or other cases studied in order to make such a generalization.

Transferability is also suggested by Owens' belief that his study is "conclusive" in confirming the "inherent instability of charismatic organizations in the area of leadership succession."[87] Given the references in this research to other works on charismatic authority and routinization, this statement has some credibility. However, this conclusion is weakened by a lack of due examination both of alternative explanations (that is, interpretation according to other theories, such as LMX)[88] and of disconfirming research. Indeed, I suggest that routinization of charisma is not inevitable. Andelson shows that charismatic leadership may continue beyond the founder where there was a theology which allowed for multiple people to be charismatic;[89] Melton shows that in the modern world, new religious movements often focus far less on founding charisma and power concentration;[90] and Ukah suggests that not only is routinization *not* inevitable, but that the successor can enhance the charismatic nature of leadership and church, providing a "double founding" and "recharismatization."[91]

Case Study

As previously noted, the matter of transferability is made complicated by the author's confusion concerning case study typologies. Owens believes that his research is "built upon the multiple-case study model" and that this model, therefore, allows for generalizations: "The author does contend that case studies (built upon the multiple-case study model) may contain specific information concerning events, characteristics, and experiences

---

85. Owens, *Never Forget!*, 188.
86. Owens, *Never Forget!*, 188.
87. Owens, *Never Forget!*, 201.
88. See, for example, Northouse, *Leadership*, for other applicable leadership theories.
89. Andelson, "Postcharismatic Authority," 29–45.
90. Melton, "When Prophets Die," 1–12.
91. Ukah, *New Paradigm*, 83.

useful in moving from specific to general knowledge."[92] It seems that he confuses his use of multiple sources to mean this is a multiple-case study. There is, therefore, a belief that an approach has been taken which allows for generalization, even citing Yin that case studies may generalize from specific data to theoretical proposition.[93] However, Yin makes the analogy to scientific experiments, that one does not generalize from one experiment but from multiple experiments that have replicated findings. A single-case study may lead to theoretical propositions, but only tentative ones, as part of wider research.[94] A misunderstanding of case type by Owens has led to conclusions not supported by the data from a single-case.

If this is a single-case study (in fact a single-case [holistic] design), this means, furthermore, that an opportunity has been missed to appreciate the strengths of its type and to produce solid data and conclusions in keeping with the type. This may been seen by categorizing the case according to Yin's five types of single-case design, namely critical case, testing well-formulated theory, extreme or unique case, representative or typical, and revelatory or longitudinal. With different purposes and questions, Owens could have presented this case as either a "critical" case or an "extreme" case. If he had viewed this as "critical," the theory of routinization of charisma could have been tested more thoroughly, giving due credence to alternatives. If examined as an "extreme" case, it could have been celebrated for something interesting in its own right,[95] still contributing to the "horizontal accumulation of knowledge."[96]

Methods

INTERVIEW SAMPLE

Interviews constitute a "major part of the original, primary sources."[97] They are problematic in a number of ways. For interviews to provide data to be analyzed to answer a research question, appropriate and adequate sampling must take place. Interviewees were indeed chosen because they

92. Owens, *Never Forget!*, 21.

93. Owens, *Never Forget!*, 21.

94. Yin, *Case Study Research*, 15.

95. Punch, *Introduction to Social Research*, 122.

96. Eisner, *Enlightened Eye*, 210–11. I suggest the category "extreme." Whatever disagreement, misunderstanding, or conflict an organization might undergo during transition, it is indeed rare, especially for a church, that matters are so acrimonious that police are called to church meetings.

97. Owens, *Never Forget!*, 20.

were "contemporaneous participants and/or observers" and "have relevant knowledge of the events."[98] We do not know how many were interviewed, their demographic characteristics, or whether they were offered anonymity. The report, therefore, does not provide much of the information needed to be able to assess the trustworthiness of the data collected from the interviews and thus how it could be interpreted. It is, furthermore, unacknowledged that, as the interviews were taking place over thirty years after the events examined, it was only surviving participants who could be interviewed. The most concerning aspect of the interview method of data collection with this sample is that people were interviewed about events over thirty years prior, from which we assume that a number, or even most, of those interviewed were very old indeed. Owens believes that this time has allowed "for the heated emotions and passionate spirits of the Dark Years to have cooled, and yet the memories and observations are still sharp."[99] No reason is given for asserting that memories are still sharp. It is likely that memory is very unreliable and that the data collected will not be trustworthy. If it could be shown that the documentary evidence corroborates interview accounts, for example, this also would have provided greater trustworthiness in the data. There is, however, no systematic attempt to establish trustworthiness in this way. In this case, it is doubtful whether the interview method produced reliable data.

Historical Documents

Space does not allow an expatiation on the many documentary categories. What is of significance, however, is the lack of critical analysis of these documents. This may be seen in Owen's view that the denominational accounts by the Recording Secretary should be considered objective. I posit that such accounts are laden with judgment: "The battle for authority was on. It had begun with the say as to whether or not there would be an offering taken during the fast. The Executive Board had won, and the offering was taken."[100] To describe the suggestion of an offering as a battle for authority is clear imputation of motive on the part of the recorder. Believing that the official record was objective may have led to a misguided analysis of the institutional discourse.

98. Owens, *Never Forget!*, 20.
99. Owens, *Never Forget!*, 12.
100. Cornelius, *Pioneer*, 82, cited in Owens, *Never Forget!*, 122.

Alternative Approaches

In my more thorough critique of Owens' work, I suggested a number of approaches that may have been more helpful, including an understanding of the extreme case that was being studied and its inability to lead to generalizability. In particular, this work is an example of studying succession that hardly takes into account the theologies discernible through speech and actions. In fact, it was a deliberate strategy of the researcher to eschew comment on theology: "*The author* of this work *in no way* attempts to address the spiritual aspects of the Church of God in Christ. This *is not* an examination of the spirituality, biblical correctness, or appropriateness of any of the actions described."[101] More comprehensive coding for such matters would have given data rich in analytical possibilities, which also would have provided alternative perspectives, even supported the conclusion better. For example, one of the main premises of the work is that Mason led by charismatic authority. There is ample evidence in the data to show in greater depth how charisma functioned, particularly how it was ascribed. There is a hagiographical tone to writings concerning Mason, the founder. Elder Brown, for example, believed Mason's "judgment is unquestionable";[102] that he had "divine qualities";[103] that "he is anointed over and above his fellows."[104] Such references provide data which show the process of charisma ascription, yet these are not fully analyzed to gain a better understanding of charismatic authority within newer religious groups.

Owens's work, therefore, is a study of which the aims require different methods.

Research Design for American Megachurches

Aims

Wheeler also shows some confusion between aims and design. For example, a significant aim is to provide a "unique theoretical contribution to succession research."[105] Yet, for example, there is no attempt to apply the grounded theory approach needed for theory generation. There is no subsequent

101. Owens, *Never Forget!*, 200 (emphasis in original).

102. Mason, *History and Life Work of Elder C. H. Mason*, 85, cited in Owens, *Never Forget!*, 40.

103. Owens, *Never Forget!*, 41.

104. Owens, *Never Forget!*, 41.

105. Wheeler, "Leadership Succession Process," 8.

interviewing as the researcher refines the codes and categories to provide higher-level theoretical categories. Wheeler does not use the data in this way nor the mode of interviewing and analysis required. The researcher's stated aims would require different approaches, such as grounded theory.

Methods

SAMPLE

Previously, I stated an omission of sample characteristics (race, gender). The findings may also be limited in that there is no investigation of why the churches of the study were favorable to participation, nor why others were unfavorable. The data collected, therefore, may only be from megachurches generating a certain discourse that is a self-belief in a narrative of success.

INTERVIEWS

"The in-depth interview was the key method in the case studies."[106] This, Wheeler believes, is significant because the greater part of succession research had been archival field study.[107] Taking Kvale's threefold typology of interviews (structured, semi-structured, and transformational),[108] he adopts the model of "semi-structured life world interviews."[109]

Wheeler shows considerable awareness of matters which might affect data collection through interviews, such as the potential for social desirability to affect answers; he attempts to mitigate this by providing confidentiality and assuring interviewees that answers are neither correct nor incorrect. He understands his interview methodology and methods. This increases confidence in the data collected and reported. He does not, however, articulate an interview philosophy. Certainly, the interviews are constructivist and appear to be in line with Kvale and Brinkmann's metaphor of the traveller collecting stories rather than the more positivist miner's extraction metaphor.[110]

---

106. Wheeler, "Leadership Succession Process," 60.

107. Giambatista et al., "Nothing Succeeds Like Succession," 984, cited in Wheeler, "Leadership Succession Process," 61.

108. Kvale, InterViews, 5–6.

109. Wheeler, "Leadership Succession Process," 61.

110. Kvale and Brinkmann, Interviews, 48–49; Davidsson Bremborg, "Interviewing," 311.

The interview guide lists forty-two questions.[111] These include nine specifically seeking data concerning process; four on the participants' personal gifts and contributions; four on the profile of the successor; three on recruitment; one on successor socialization; two on congregation preparations; four on post succession roles; one on successor preparations; two reflecting on the concept of "success"; and seven reflecting on lessons learned (and thus related to transferability). They are appropriate questions to provide data for analysis in helping the researcher attend to his study's aims of a rich description of processes and personal experiences as well as inter-case comparison (if the same questions were used in each case). It has already been suggested that the methods do not facilitate theory generation. There are no questions framed with some a priori assumption of theory, certainly after the first round of data collection. There is no account of grounded theory phases, and no secondary (or tertiary) interviews took place which would be necessary in a grounded theory approach. The interviewing goals and question content of this research are not well suited to theory generation.

Analysis

It is difficult to assess whether the analysis was conducive to achieve the research aims. There is no stated approach to analysis, despite Wheeler's awareness of analytical theories, citing Yin's four modes of case study analysis,[112] as well as Kvale's five approaches to qualitative analysis.[113] Although citing such analytical approaches, Wheeler does not state which of these (if any) he employs, which makes an evaluation of his analysis more difficult. This is an omission. We are simply told that analysis "paid attention to concepts, stories and themes" of the interview and archival data.[114]

Alternative Approaches

Wheeler accomplished his research goal of providing a rich description of the processes of succession, with an intimate account of the inner life and emotions of those closely affected. Such accounts are, therefore, useful data

111. The following categories and quantification are mine, not Wheeler's.

112. Wheeler, "Leadership Succession Process," 75. Wheeler cites the 1994, 2nd ed. of Yin, *Case Study Research*. Throughout this book, I cite the 2009, 4th ed.

113. Wheeler, "Leadership Succession Process," 75.

114. Wheeler, "Leadership Succession Process," 75.

for our understanding of founders' succession in Christian organizations. Wheeler's work does fill a gap in the literature which had previously been based on archival research. Insight into succession processes is provided and a composite, five-phase processual model is suggested (previously cited earlier in this chapter).[115] It is a lack, however, that important categories were not included in the analysis, despite these themes reported in the data. For example, despite multiple references in the interview data to "God," "Christ," and "gifts," there is no analysis of the underlying theological understanding of leadership succession. Such coding would have given much richer understandings of the process and experiences. Not taking theology into account when seeking to understand and describe megachurch succession would seem a grave omission, as it is theology that affects so much of the thinking and ministry of those being interviewed. Similarly, other forms of analysis, such as semiotic analysis of the many symbolic references in the data, would have greatly assisted a description of the succession processes. For example, the employment of physical symbols such as a baton used during a leadership transference ceremony,[116] a sword used to "knight," and a golden sprinkler head presented[117] could have "matched the form of the discourse to its social function."[118] A deeper understanding of the succession process might have been gained by a semiotic "pragmatic" analysis of the signs and their function in the transference of leadership. Are the knighting and passing of batons indexical icons constructed through performance and enhancing communication through what has been called "sensory pageantry"?[119] Indeed, what are the semiotic ideologies of these megachurches? The data collected by Wheeler is rich semiotic data, an analysis of which might prove instructive in understanding the rituals and symbolism associated with succession and thereby the succession itself. In Parts IV and VI, I will show the importance of interpreting symbolic enactments to understand founder succession and related theologies.

CONCLUSIONS

In this chapter, we have looked at how successions, particularly founder successions, within Christian organizations have been studied, with a view to

115. Wheeler, "Leadership Succession Process," 340.

116. Wheeler, "Leadership Succession Process," 181.

117. Wheeler, "Leadership Succession Process," 147.

118. Yelle, "Semiotics," 355.

119. McCauley and Lawson, *Bringing Ritual to Mind*, 114, cited in Yelle, "Semiotics," 357.

learning methods that might produce good data for analysis, and then how appropriate analysis might take place to understand the subject better. My conclusions include that there is a lack of methodological rigor in this field, often with confusing aims; methods are furthermore poorly applied, which then leads to unreliable data and conclusions. How the matter of reflexivity affects our studying this topic has been poorly understood; omission of reflexivity affects the reliability of the data and means that conclusion must be viewed with caution; in one case (Peterson), it facilitated the study's becoming part of the official discourse of the institution under study. Furthermore, despite multiple theological statements and references in the data, all studies to date largely ignore any exploration of the religious beliefs of the subjects on the successions. In studying this topic, theological exploration is needed in order to gain a fuller understanding of how Christian groups enact succession.

Chapter Eleven ————————————————————

A Fresh Approach to the Study of Succession in Christian Organizations and Movements

IN THIS CHAPTER, I set out an approach to the study of succession within Christian movements and networks. I state the question I wished to answer from the research material for this book, and I outline the types of data I wished to collect, the likely sources of such data and the sources' characteristics, the type of analysis I wish to undertake, and thus the methods to obtain such data analysis.

To begin my study of succession, I defined focused questions to drive this research:

> What are the processes which Christian movements construct and enact in transferring leadership from the founder to a successor? What are the theoretical and theological influences on the construction and enactment of such processes?

The data required to answer the research questions of processes and theological and conceptual influences on founder succession were of several types: factual data about decisions made and the adoption of plans; descriptions by key stakeholders of such decisions, phases, and plans; comment and reflection by key actors on such decisions, phases, and plans, including evaluatory comments; personal feelings, experiences, and reactions to the decisions and processes, that is, POBA (perceptions, opinions, beliefs, and attitudes) categories of data;[1] and descriptions and interpretations of the theological and theoretical frameworks, whether espoused or operant, in which these successions took place.

The data required to answer the research questions fall, therefore, into a number of categories. Quantitative or highly structured methods are less likely to produce such data. An approach is needed which activates a deeper level than facts and occurrences in order to ascertain the perceptions, worldview, and theology which shaped them and to explicate how such processes and "facts" are interpreted by the key stakeholders. The aim of this research, therefore, is not superficial or thin description; it aims for the "*noema* ["thought," "content," "gist"] of the speaking. It is the meaning of the speech event, not the event as event."[2] In this chapter, I propose a specific method which will facilitate the production of such experiential accounts and theological understandings.

DATA SOURCES

Documents

The findings in this book rely primarily on two types of sources, namely documents and interview-generated content. In broad terms, documents helped determine facts, processes, and the institutional discourse of the organization being studied. Interviews elicited feelings, reactions, evaluations, and theological reflections. Documents included artifacts such as books, magazines, articles, and video recordings. Documentary analysis was a complementary approach rather than "stand-alone";[3] the main research method was the interview. Documents were viewed not as receptacles of information but, following Wolff, as "*eigenständige methodische und situativ eingebettete Leistungen*,"[4] or, as Flick describes them, as "methodologically

---

1. Potter and Hepburn, "Eight Challenges," 555–70; Puchta and Potter, *Focus Group Practice*; Puchta and Potter, "Manufacturing Individual Opinions," 345–63. Space does not permit a full treatment of the complexities around POBA questioning in interviewing, such as whether people have immediate access to their opinions. However, it is acknowledged that POBA questioning tends to elicit relevant data in ways that other questioning does not. (See Potter and Hepburn, "Eight Challenges," 555–70.)

2. Ricoeur, *From Text to Action*, 146.

3. Flick, *Introduction to Qualitative Research*, 353.

4. Wolff, "Dokumenten- und Aktenanalyse," 504.

created communicative turns."[5] They were considered in terms of "their content, context, production and function in society."[6] Due cognizance was taken of their discursive formations, their "conditions of existence";[7] they are situated products[8] and social products which may have been received differently by different constituencies. They are not static but were considered "in terms of fields, frames and networks of action. In fact, the status of things as 'documents' depends precisely on the ways in which such objects are integrated into fields of action, and documents can only be defined in terms of such fields."[9]

Interview-Generated Content

"The qualitative research interview attempts to understand the world from the subjects' points of view, to unfold the meaning of their experiences, to uncover their lived world prior to scientific explanations."[10] It is most often used in qualitative research for "the purpose of obtaining descriptions of the life world of the interviewee in order to interpret the meaning of the described phenomena."[11] There are many forms of interview, the selection of which is dependent on the research purposes.[12] Each of Roulston's six types has a different purpose, structure, and relational dynamics and produces different types of data. Classically, there are three structures that are determined by the nature of the questions asked: structured, semi-structured, and unstructured. Each structure lends itself to a certain type of data collection and analysis. The highly structured interview is often of the survey variety, which lends itself to quantitative study due to the vast amount of data that may quickly be collected and to the often binary nature of the data. Much qualitative work has used the semi-structured interview, but with the increasing use of narrative approaches to research, what has been called the "fifth moment" in qualitative research,[13] the unstructured interview is now widely employed.

5. Flick, *Introduction to Qualitative Research*, 357.

6. Davie and Wyatt, "Document Analysis," 151.

7. Foucault, "Politics and the Study of Discourse," 61.

8. Scott, *Matter of Record*, 34.

9. Prior, *Using Documents in Social Research*, 2.

10. Brinkmann and Kvale, *InterViews*, 3.

11. Brinkmann and Kvale, *InterViews*, 6.

12. Roulston, *Reflective Interviewing*, 51.

13. Denzin and Lincoln, *Handbook of Qualitative Research*.

METHODS

Which Type of Interview Is Optimal for This Research Project?

Determination by Sample Population Characteristics

The determination of the interview type will be made by considering the characteristics of the sample population and how this specific population might be interviewed to produce optimal data and by providing evaluation of the analytical methods available to interpret such data. A decision was made to seek to obtain data from those closest to and most affected by the successions. Such a sample would, therefore, need to be of the founders who had started a movement or organization and those who succeeded them. Rather than interviewing a large population, if theological reflection on succession was needed, it was more appropriate to spend considerable time with those close to the succession processes and decisions.

In considering such a population and how best to obtain data from them, I reflected on their characteristics. What were the likely characteristics of such a sample and which form of interviewing might enjoin the optimal participation and data production from them? To answer these questions, I drew from five areas of study: theology of leadership, sociolinguistics, trait-based leadership theory, organizational psychology, and qualitative studies on elites and experts.

1. Theology of leadership

    As the interviewees were to be leaders in Christian ministry, it was likely that they would have skills in spoken communication. In Clinton's research on Christian leaders, he maintains that of all the lessons a leader must learn and all the gifts he or she may have, the ability to use words and discern the significance of words is both paramount and ubiquitous.[14] Such gifts are often "vested gifts," appearing "repeatedly in a person's ministry and can be repeated at will by the person."[15] Given this, it seems appropriate to allow them considerable latitude in how they choose to respond in the interview, as they are likely to provide clear and high quality data on leadership succession.

2. Sociolinguistics

    In turning to sociolinguistics to understand better the capabilities of the sample, Christian leaders have high levels of "communicative

14. Clinton, *Making of a Leader*, 143.
15. Clinton, *Making of a Leader*, 233.

competence."[16] By this, it is meant not simply the original Chomskyan sense of the word as the ability to produce an infinite number of grammatical sentences from a finite set of syntactic rules, but also the "proficiency in use of its indexical properties"; that is, competence in knowing which expression may be used under which circumstances to convey which meanings.[17] Briggs is clear that understanding an interviewee's communicative competence involves not just their ability to encode and decode referential meaning alone, but also the proficiency in indexical properties; both factors must be taken into account in any analysis of interview data. Founders of Christian agencies are likely to have higher levels of linguistic communicative competence, honed through textual exegesis training of biblical and theological education. This assertion was tested in the pilot study. Such competence means that the interviewer should be aware that verbal fluency might provide established discourse or good impression management.[18] However, such fluency means that this population sample will be capable of responding well in a very open-ended form of interview. Indeed, their communicative competence might be better activated by unstructured interviewing.

3. Trait-based leadership theory

Trait-based theories of leadership may also assist in understanding my interviewees.[19] Kirkpatrick and Locke's study articulates the six traits which distinguish leaders from others: drive, motivation, integrity, confidence, cognitive ability, and task knowledge.[20] Stevens details the entrepreneurial behavior of nonprofit founders, finding fourteen entrepreneurial behavior patterns.[21] Many of those interviewed are people of high cognitive ability and entrepreneurial orientation. They will also have high levels of "sunk costs" in the ministries they founded.[22] This may mean that they desire to project a good image

16. Briggs, *Learning How to Ask*, 43.

17. Briggs, *Learning How to Ask*, 43.

18. Burris and Navara, "Morality Play—or Playing Morality?" 67–76.

19. For trait approaches to leadership, see Jung and Sosik, "Who Are the Spellbinders?," 12–27, and Northouse, *Leadership*.

20. Kirkpatrick and Locke, "Leadership," 48–60.

21. Stevens, "In Their Own Words."

22. Kets de Vries, "Dynamics of Family Controlled Firms," 58–71. "Sunk costs" is a phrase from economics referring to costs already occurred in an endeavor and which may not be recouped. Zeelenberg and van Dijk show a positive relationship between successors' high levels of sunk costs and risk-averse decisions in assuming leadership (Zeelenberg and van Dijk, "Reverse Sunk Cost Effect," 677–91).

of the organization which they founded and will provide discourse with this aim in mind. This should be duly taken into account during data analysis; an open-ended, unstructured interview method will provide an opportunity to observe such traits and to ascertain how such leaders perceive succession.

4. Organizational psychology

Schein,[23] from the discipline of organizational psychology, has shown specifically how founders create an organizational culture. In determining how a new endeavor is shaped with regard to the external environment and internal integration, Schein shows how founders embed cultural elements in the new endeavor in ten ways (also see chapter 3 for a fuller treatment of this matter). Thus, founders established the mission, structures, values, and the eventual prevailing discourse of the organization which they founded. A form of interview which allows such people to speak freely of their founding of a ministry and of discourse establishment would be appropriate. A structured approach would provide responses based on the categories predetermined by the interviewer. Giving such entrepreneurial people latitude to recount processes and reflections in their own words may yield rich data relevant to the question of determining the conceptualization of succession. It will show what they judge to be narratable and thus important.

5. Qualitative studies on elites and experts

A fifth point of reflection is that this sample is constituted of "experts" in the field of Christian leadership. I use the term "expert" as this is commonly used in other fields of study to apply to those who have considerable experiences in their field, usually with broad networks of relationships and high status functional responsibility.[24]

Consideration of the expert characteristic of the interview sample is significant for this interview approach. First, the interviewer needs to be well informed on the subject of their expertise, for experts tend to share more freely with those who possess knowledge of their field.[25] Secondly,

---

23. Schein, "Role of the Founder," 13–28.

24. Welch et al., "Corporate Elites," 613. Extensive definitions of "expert" from the research literature on interviewing experts are to be found in Meuser and Nagel, "Expert Interview," 19, and Bogner and Menz, "Theory-Generating Expert Interview," 54.

25. Beckmann and Hall, "Elite Interviewing," 196–208; Meuser and Nagel, "Expert Interview," 32.

and especially with regard to religious leaders, there may be an openness to participate in qualitative research, not so much out of kindness but due to clergy seeing their work and that of social researcher as similar in terms of social status; applying Coxon et al.'s analysis of social stratification, both professionals (researcher and clergy) are in the same quadrant—high formal education and high people content profession.[26] However, Aldridge's experience in studying Anglican clergy in England is that this understanding of mutual social status is not a given but rather needs to be negotiated in order to gain full access.[27] Issues of social standing, deference, and power are, therefore, relevant. A third and related point is that clergy are used to leading discussion rather than being led in discussion.[28] A more highly structured interview might be perceived as counter to their usual role and professional status self-perception. A less structured interview, therefore, might elicit better responses and data, as this places clergy in a habituated position, one consistent with their role self-perception. This is supported by Meuser and Nagel's epistemology of expert knowledge being "tacit or pre-theoretical experiential knowledge"; such knowledge is better elicited by open interviewing.[29] Fourthly, all professions have a corpus of sacred discourse which is guarded by licensed practitioners.[30] Key words typically signal the boundary between sacred discourse of the profession and the profane discourse accessible to laypeople. Aldridge, in his research with Anglican clergy, found that the word "theology" was a signal that the ensuing discourse would be of such a "sacred" nature; the word "theology" serves as a linguistic marker that the following responses would be an important argument and one to which they claimed expertise and authority. In analysis, I was, therefore, aware of such linguistic markers that change the relational position between the interviewee and interviewer; in the interview, I needed to elicit such utterances and the data which ensued, as this was indeed the data sought in this research.

Conclusion from Sample Characteristics

In summary, interviews are likely to be conducted with those who have word gifts, are accustomed to spoken communication, and are experts. Given this, a

26. Coxon et al., *Images of Social Stratification*.
27. Aldridge, "Negotiating Status," 111–23.
28. Aldridge, "Negotiating Status," 121.
29. Meuser and Nagel, "Expert Interview," 31.
30. Aldridge, "Negotiating Status," 111–23.

form of unstructured interviewing was proposed in order to produce optimal data (accounts of succession and theological reflection thereon).

Determination by Analytical Methods

The second matter to determine the interview type is the selection of analytical method. Any interview must produce data suited to the intended analysis. Three approaches could have been employed in this research, namely discourse, content, and narrative analysis.

DISCOURSE ANALYSIS

It could be possible to employ a discourse analytical approach, which pays attention to the social phenomena around the text, the "social systems of relations."[31] Language is not viewed as representing a given reality but is formative and constitutive of reality. It is thus about the significations of the language. Discourse concerns "practices that systematically form the objects of which they speak";[32] it is "the structured totality resulting from the articulatory practice."[33] Secondly, discourse often focuses on issues of power—what power is behind and in the discourse, who has the right to say and who does not (mechanisms of exclusion), and who is advantaged or disadvantaged by the discourse. Thirdly, discourse analysis is interested in the generation of social identities; it reduces consideration of people as agents.

Discourse analysis may, of course, be beneficial. In certain contexts, it can make manifest power dynamics; it can show inclusion and exclusion, and why some are marginalized; it assists studying debates, as it highlights "antagonisms," that is, the struggle for meaning creation on a linguistic level.[34] This is related to a fourth benefit, namely that it makes more evident changes in social viewpoints on the discourse topic.

Discourse analysis would have been helpful in my research were the primary goals the broader understanding of leadership within Christian communities, analysis of power relations, or a study of the debates within Christian leadership and management on succession by analyzing the articulatory practices of the non-crystallized "moments" in Christian leadership

---

31. Howarth, *Discourse*, 8.

32. Foucault, *Archaeology of Knowledge*, 49.

33. Laclau and Mouffe, *Hegemony and Socialist Strategy*, 105.

34. Laclau and Mouffe, *Hegemony and Socialist Strategy*; Bergström et al., "Discourse Analysis," 216.

discourse.[35] A discourse analytical approach, however, was not selected, as the research goal was not to study the broader sociological discourse of Christian leadership but the specific conceptualizations and enactments of certain leaders and agencies. These may reflect broader discourses, yet each organization to be studied is a new foundation seeking to develop its own discourse, and, as shown above, the participants are likely to be highly articulate leaders who have in multiple ways established a new discourse. The aim of this research was to understand succession processes and the actors' reflections thereon, not broader social discourses or the nature of hegemony in leadership discourse.[36] In my research project, while aware of both the institutional and broader evangelical discourses, focus is on other aspects (enactments and theological reflection thereon).

Content Analysis

Content analysis was considered but eschewed. Content analysis is often quantitative. Many of the standard and oft-cited reference works, such as Krippendorff[37] and Neuendorf,[38] are works on quantitative research, defining content analysis in purely quantitative terms: "Content analysis may be briefly defined as the systematic, objective, quantitative analysis of message characteristics."[39] Quantification will not produce the rich description for processual and theological reflection needed to answer my research question; nuanced understanding of theology and relational processes is provided in a thick description, which requires a qualitative approach.

Secondly, while it is possible to employ qualitative content analysis rather than quantitative, both quantitative and qualitative approaches are often employed when large quantities of text are to be studied. This relates, of course, to the first point, that larger quantities of material lend themselves to quantitative analysis; thus, many of the standard works such as those by Krippendorff and Neuendorf come from the field of mass media studies.[40] Content analysis has been employed in empirical theology, but often even

---

35. Laclau and Mouffe, *Hegemony and Socialist Strategy*, 134.

36. For a fuller treatment of the role of hegemony in discourse, see Laclau and Mouffe, *Hegemony and Socialist Strategy*, especially 134–45.

37. Krippendorff, *Content Analysis*.

38. Neuendorf, *Content Analysis Guidebook*.

39. Neuendorf, *Content Analysis Guidebook*, 1. For a fuller definition, see Neuendorf, *Content Analysis Guidebook*, 10.

40. Krippendorff, *Content Analysis*; Neuendorf, *Content Analysis Guidebook*.

here using data from mass media.[41] This research project did not have such large amounts of data.

In thus eschewing a quantitative approach, further consideration is given to qualitative content analysis (QCA). I suggest, however, that this approach can be highly problematic and, even if employed well, would not answer the research questions in the way I intend to answer them. There is confusion as to the nature of QCA. "Qualitative content analysis is a method of systematically describing the meaning of qualitative material. It is done by classifying material as instances of the categories of a coding frame."[42] This is a definition from a standard textbook, yet all we learn from it is that it is systematic and it categorizes. Secondly, standard works on qualitative research such as those of Flick[43] and Mayring have but a few pages.[44] More recent works, such as that of Boréus and Bergström,[45] are synopses of Schreier, *Qualitative Content Analysis in Practice*, one of the few books dedicated to qualitative content analysis. Thirdly, attempts to describe qualitative content analysis, moreover, develop into descriptions of quantitative content analysis, thus showing either confused methodological thinking or the ambiguity and fluidity of the method. Perhaps realizing such fluidity and ambiguity even in their own writing, Boréus and Bergström state that the difference between quantitative and qualitative is not one of kind but degree.[46] With its roots in quantitative studies and with a lack of clear differentiation, Hijmans questions whether QCA actually is a method.[47]

Content analysis does, of course, lend itself well to certain types of study. Nelson and Woods see the benefits of content analysis as follows: for tracking specific data to identify and understand a direction of, or change in, specific phenomena over time; for identifying patterns or commonalities within a particular genre; for identifying difference by drawing comparisons; for assessing the image of a particular group in society; for measuring a specific phenomenon against some standard in order to classify the

41. Driel and Richardson, "Categorization of New Religious Movements," 171–83; Abelman and Pettey, "How Political Is Religious Television?," 313–59.

42. Schreier, *Qualitative Content Analysis in Practice*, 1.

43. Flick, *Introduction to Qualitative Research*.

44. Schreier, "Qualitative Content Analysis," 170–83, is a short overview in a general work and is based on the more extensive book Schreier, *Qualitative Content Analysis in Practice*. Mayring, "Qualitative Content Analysis," 266–69, is a very brief English language entry, which is slightly expanded in a German version, Mayring, "Qualitative Inhaltsanalyse," 468–75.

45. Boréus and Bergström, "Content Analysis," 23–52.

46. Boréus and Bergström, "Content Analysis," 24.

47. Hijmans, "Logic of Qualitative Media Content Analysis," 93–109. For more on this debate, see Schreier, *Qualitative Content Analysis in Practice*, 14–15.

phenomenon; and in order to relate certain message characteristics to the variable.[48] Boréus and Bergström see it as advantageous for comparisons and for making evident changes in corpora over time.[49]

In this research, even qualitative content analysis was eschewed, however, as it often reduces data (unlike most qualitative methods which open up the data for more nuanced interpretations). It handles large amounts of text well. Reductions can be helpful in comparing categories across data, but it is unable to analyze data that is "not there." Moreover, even a qualitative approach must select categories; it does not allow for a more holistic approach to the data and it cannot analyze connotative meanings or the symbolic.[50]

The goal of theoretical and theological reflection on the processes cannot be achieved from quantitative data. I did not intend to make comparison, to study broader corpora of text, nor to examine longitudinal changes, all of which may benefit from a content analytical approach. Indeed, a contextual understanding of the interview responses is crucial to understand the nuances around the personal data; theologies require a more qualitative approach in order to gain a "thick description."[51] Such descriptions are less likely to come from the classic units of analysis used in content analysis, which are the physical (e.g., number of pages), syntactical (number of words, phrases, sentences), referential (presence or absence of objects), propositional (statements/arguments), and thematic (repeating patterns of ideas or treatments).[52]

Narrative Analysis

"Innombrables sont les récits du monde."

—Barthes[53]

The characteristics of the interviewee sample lead to an open, unstructured form of interview. This section considers the eventual analysis to be

48. Nelson and Woods, "Content Analysis," 109–21.

49. Boréus and Bergström, *Analyzing Text and Discourse,* 7.

50. Schreier, *Qualitative Content Analysis in Practice,* 52.

51. Geertz, "Thick Description," 3–30.

52. Krippendorff, *Content Analysis.*

53. "The narratives of the world are numberless." The need to cite the original French is explained above. A fuller definition of "narrative" is provided in the following section. This epigram is found in Barthes, "Introduction à l'analyse structurale," 7. I have not been able to find the original 1966 edition.

undertaken so that the interview can be conducted appropriately to provide the best data for such analysis. In turning from both discourse analysis and content analysis, it seemed clearer that a narrative approach would yield the targeted rich description.

Barthes's opening sentence (above) to his seminal work on narrative ushered in a new place for narrative in academic research. His use of anastrophe in this sentence brings not just a declarative intent but a hortatory tone to which we should pay heed, something lost in the standard, pedestrian English "the narratives of the world are numberless."[54] The ubiquity and universality of narrative is established; it appears in multiple genres, substances, forms, and in all cultures. It is as if *"toute matière était bonne à l'homme pour lui confier ses récits"*;[55] that "all material" or "all matter" (*toute matière*) can be used for narrative must of course include conceptualizations of leadership succession. In seeking to select definitively and with specificity the form of analysis intended and thereby the mode of interview to be adopted to facilitate that analysis, the subject of narrative is now addressed in further detail.

What Is Narrative?

For an understanding of narrative, I adopt the following definition:

> Narratives are stories with a beginning, a development, and a state of affairs at the end about an event or process. Typically, they involve a complex structure that links facts and details to an overarching whole. . . . Using narratives for collecting verbal data should take the structure of the narrative into account instead of isolating single statements from it.[56]

Narratives are produced by people usually in the following ways:

> First the initial situation is outlined ("how everything started"), then the events relevant to the narrative are selected from the whole host of experiences and presented as coherent progression of events ("how things developed"), and finally the situation at the end of the development is presented ("what became").[57]

---

54. Barthes, "Introduction to the Structural Analysis of Narrative," 79.

55. Barthes, "Introduction à l'analyse structurale," 7.

56. Flick, *Introduction to Qualitative Research*, 199.

57. Hermanns, "Narrative Interview," 183, cited in Flick, *Introduction to Qualitative Research*, 265.

Narrative functions as a "fundamental interpretative frame, helping us to organize our experiences and make the world comprehensible."[58] Narrative provides details of processes and events—what happened but also "insights into how individuals imbue those events and actions with meaning."[59] This speaks to the dual aspect of narrative, namely *histoire* (the "what," such as content, "existents," characters) and *discours* (the "how," the means by which the content is communicated.)[60] It provides a more detailed and nuanced understanding of the text, in part because narrative analysis allows for an analysis of both denotation and connotation; content analysis, for example, does not allow for connotation. Furthermore, a study of narrative provides the opportunity to note what is absent from or taken for granted in a text,[61] for omissions may be just as useful interpretative data as commissions.[62] A narrative analysis stresses human agency rather than broader sociological discourses (while not denying their influence). Indeed, narrative might provide insights into something larger or more general: "Such generalization can only take place if specific micro-level narratives are related to accumulated or macro-level and recurrent narrative themes."[63]

The above advantages of a narrative approach lend themselves well to answering the research questions. Narratives can provide data to show the processes of succession (*histoire*) and the meaning imbued by key actors (*discours*). Narrative research will allow for a nuanced interpretation of the topic, making manifest both connotations and denotations. It may, furthermore, make manifest leadership identity creation during narration which will help show theological and theoretical understandings of leadership. A narrative approach to analysis will, therefore, be employed. The interviews must, therefore, produce appropriate narratives. There are many methodological approaches within narrative research. A well-practiced approach is that of "narrative inquiry." Such practitioners tend to eschew functional definitions,[64] preferring to approach the method by asking what narrative inquirers do. Perhaps the closest that we may come to a definition is that:

> Narrative inquiry is a way of understanding experience. It is collaboration between researcher and participants, over time, in a place or series of places, and in social interaction with milieus.

58. Robertson, "Narrative Analysis," 123.

59. Robertson, "Narrative Analysis," 124.

60. Chatman, *Story and Discourse*.

61. Robertson, "Narrative Analysis," 136.

62. Feldman and Almquist, "Analyzing the Implicit in Stories," 207–28.

63. Robertson, "Narrative Analysis," 143.

64. Clandinin and Connelly, *Narrative Inquiry*, 49.

> An inquirer enters this matrix in the midst and progresses in the same spirit, concluding the inquiry still in the midst of living and telling, reliving and retelling, the stories of the experiences that make up people's lives, both individual and social.[65]

Such an approach could be attempted where the narrative is to be co-produced from close empathy and rapport between researcher and participant and particularly where "temporality" is the key concept to this approach, for things are better studied over time to understand the deeper experience upon experience of the narrators. For a closer examination of this method, the reader is referred to Clandinin and Connelly.[66] In this book, I eschew narrative inquiry in this tradition, as I did not intend to conduct a longitudinal study but two interviews with each participant. This means, furthermore, that joint life narratives produced from close relationship will also not be possible. To distinguish from "narrative inquiry," for the method employed in this book, I will employ the term "narrative analysis." This approach relies less on ethnography, is applicable in shorter term research, and does not examine the interplay between the researcher's own biographical narrative and that of the participants; it relies heavily on the interview as the main method of narrative elicitation. This latter point, however, requires greater specificity of interview genre, something to which we now turn.

Specificity of Narrative Interview Type

In deciding the narrative analytical approach, a determination still remains to be made concerning the type of interview to be conducted to elicit the narratives. There are a number of interview approaches within narrative interviewing, the details of which need not detain us here.[67] Such interview methods include the biographic interpretive method.[68] A further method, one which has no title, is espoused by Flick.[69] This is where an interview begins with a "generative narrative question."[70] I have, therefore, called this

---

65. Clandinin and Connelly, *Narrative Inquiry*, 20.

66. Clandinin and Connelly, *Narrative Inquiry*.

67. For fuller treatment of varieties of narrative interviewing, see Bunton, "Founder Succession," 102–9.

68. Chamberlayne et al., "Introduction," 1–30; Merrill and West, *Using Biographical Methods*; Riessman, *Narrative Methods for the Human Sciences*.

69. Flick, *Introduction to Qualitative Research*.

70. Riemann and Schütze, "Trajectory as Basic Theoretical Concept," 353, cited in Flick, *Introduction to Qualitative Research*, 266.

method "Generative Interview," taken from the first question, namely the "generative narrative question."

For this project, I developed a philosophy of interview for which I coined the term "Generative/Dialectic." This decision was shaped by the need to obtain narratives not just about the processes of succession, but also the theories and theologies shaping the succession enactments, as well as by the above mentioned characteristics of the participants (those who founded and were successors in leading Christian organizations), namely their high levels of linguistic competency, leadership, and entrepreneurial gifts. Interviews were used to stimulate free-flowing data production in a manner of telling that the participants choose. Thus, an unstructured, narrative analytical approach to interviewing is advocated. This approach is supported by the literature on interviewing experts, particularly as it is narrative which provides "insight into the tacit aspects of expert knowledge, which she or he is not fully aware of and which, on the contrary, become noticed only gradually in the course of the narration."[71] The macro-structure was in three main parts, in two interviews. Parts I and II comprised Interview I; Part III comprised Interview II. Part I consisted of a "generative narrative question" (taken from Flick)[72] to release "full extempore narration."[73] This was similar to the openings of both the biographic interpretive method and the Generative Interview. Part II was narrative probing, seeking further narrations from the interviewee on matters pertinent to the research question which the interviewer believes could be developed with great specificity. Part III raised matters omitted in earlier narrations. For example, if theological reflection was not volunteered in Parts I and II, then theory and theology were raised at this point. Furthermore, the researcher posited alternative interpretations or explanations for evaluations volunteered in Parts I and II, adopting the subject position of *advocatus diaboli*, thus making Part III maieutic or dialectic, seeking to test the viewpoints previously proffered with the aim of eliciting "synthetic" understandings.[74] Part III is not the received semi-structured interview (where the same interview protocol is put to each participant); the question will be predetermined by the researcher, but such protocols will differ in each second interview; they are contingent on the data procured in each first interview. I found this generative/dialectic

71. Meuser and Nagel, "Expert Interview," 32. Tacit knowledge transference is a crucial factor in leadership (Kikoski and Kikoski, *Inquiring Organization*), and in successful succession and organizational generativity (Peet, "Leadership Transitions," 45–60). This matter was previously mentioned in chapter 1.

72. Flick, *Introduction to Qualitative Research*, 266.

73. Rosenthal, "Reconstruction of Life Stories," 59.

74. "Synthetic" is taken from dialectic terminology.

method produced many free narrations which allowed participants to articulate the content that they feel is important and in a narratological manner, which itself may reveal data about the perceived significance of the topics being narrated. It also, however, allowed further probing and debate. Before fully utilizing this approach, a pilot study was conducted to confirm, reject, or refine this suggested approach.

Chapter Twelve ─────────────

Pilot Study
Testing the Fresh Approach

AS STANDARD IN RESEARCH interviewing,[1] a pilot study was conducted prior to the main research phase. The aims of this pilot study were to evaluate my conceptualization of the "Generative/Dialectic" interview method supported by documentary analysis and to reflect upon a priori assumptions about the sample's characteristics.

The sample used in the pilot study was a founding pastor and successor of an American megachurch.[2] The interviews confirmed that the sample had high logo-functionary capabilities and "vested" word gifts.[3] Indeed, the four interviews confirmed that the Christian leaders of the sample displayed the characteristics of "experts" in their field[4] and responded freely. My own knowledge of the subject seemed to enhance their facility of narration, a further characteristic of experts.[5] The decision to elicit data through narrative interviewing was confirmed by the pilot study, as was the fruitfulness of probing the interviewee further, namely a dialectic approach. The pilot study confirmed many of the questions included in

1. Gilham, *Research Interview*, 53–57.

2. Details in Bunton, "Founder Succession," 110–16.

3. Clinton, *Making of a Leader*, 143, 233.

4. Welch et al., "Corporate Elites," 611–28.

5. Beckmann and Hall, "Elite Interviewing," 196–208; Meuser and Nagel, "Expert Interview," 32.

the pre-study protocols, but also made clear certain aspects which would require further questioning.[6]

It became clearer that the nature of the post-transition dyadic relationship between predecessor and successor was significant in understanding the succession; thus, further questions on this topic were included. Furthermore, the pilot interviews made evident the gendered nature of succession. As a male researcher, I was interviewing men, and from my initial unsuccessful attempts to find cases with female subjects, I was becoming aware that all my cases solely contain interviews of men. Being aware of "gynopia"[7]—the inability to see women, something which is relevant to gendered interviewing[8]—led to an inclusion in Interview II protocols of at least one question which activated gender considerations.

The pilot study was, furthermore, helpful in showing how documentary analysis could be a key part in research, bringing forth data for analysis that was not procured using the interviews. The pilot study led to a conceptualization of a philosophy of documentary analysis.[9]

6. For a fuller consideration of the pilot study's findings on matters such as content, rapport, interviewer and interviewee subject positions, and transcription philosophy, see Bunton, "Founder Succession," 110–16.

7. Reinharz, "Feminist Distrust," 153–72.

8. Reinharz and Chase, "Interviewing Women," 73–90; Schwalbe and Wolkomir, "Interviewing Men," 55–72.

9. Explained more fully in Bunton, "Founder Succession," 115–17.

PART III

Cases of Succession

Chapter Thirteen

Introduction to the Use of Case Studies

CONSISTENT WITH PUNCH'S APPROACH,[1] a goal of producing ideographic findings was established, from which I could both describe the phenomenon of founder succession but also allow initial exploration and interpretation of the concomitant themes. Furthermore, I pursued "horizontalization imaginative variation"[2] in an attempt to see and interpret the phenomenon from different perspectives, using an interdisciplinary analysis which draws on understandings of succession not just from theology, but also from social sciences: "The secrets of both the sacred and the secular are often revealed more in their adumbrations and interpenetrations than in their separation."[3] Studying religion is not a question of materialism *or* theology, for "institutions are symbolic systems which have nonobservable, absolute, transrational referents and observable social relations which concretize them."[4]

To obtain such ideographic knowledge pertaining to succession, a case study approach was pursued, more specifically "exploratory" case studies (according to Yin's typology of cases).[5] An "exploratory" case study is one which describes and attempts tentative explanation and interpretations.

1. Punch, *Introduction to Social Research*, 33.

2. Merriam, *Qualitative Research*, 199; Moustakas, *Phenomenological Research Methods*, 97–98.

3. Demerath et al., *Sacred Companies*, vi.

4. Friedland and Alford, "Bringing Society Back in," 249.

5. Yin, *Case Study Research*.

Given the anticipation of longer narrative interviews, and with a desire for deeper analysis and presentation of the cases with imaginative variation, a decision was made to include only three cases.[6] Maximum variation of cases within that small population was pursued in an attempt to explore diversities of approach to succession. In particular, identifying cases in different nations was a high priority in this maximum variation. Purposive sampling was thus pursued, particularly maximum variation sampling.[7] Recent studies supported my goal, showing that maximum variation is feasible and productive.[8]

Delimitation, particularly temporal, was established. A succession that had taken place too recently might find participants still in the throes of transition, either unduly overwhelmed or still with an idealized view of succession. Transitions enacted too far in the past could turn the cases into historical research rather than current practice. Attempts were made to locate cases of succession within the range one to fifteen years prior to the research.

The three identified cases allowed for maximum variation on many aspects including impetus for succession, power and decision-making, planning, theologies of leadership, exogenous environment, and country of origin (Sweden, United Kingdom, and US). Variation was not achieved in two noteworthy areas, namely successor origins (all were internally appointed successors) and gender (all three founders and all successors were male). This was despite multiple efforts to locate external appointments and female founders or successors; finding no examples of either is interesting in itself. This study may be narrower for only finding cases of internal succession. There could be correlation between internal succession and flourishing rather than struggling organizations, and this may limit the applicability of any findings.[9] However, as seen in chapter 15, Christian ministries tend to insist on internal succession; my case studies are thus in this regard representative of a broader population of Christian ministries.

---

6. Patton, *Qualitative Research*, 245.

7. Punch, *Introduction to Social Research*, 162.

8. Vohra, "Using the Multiple Case Study Design," 54–64.

9. Cannella and Lubatkin, "Succession," 763–93; Allgood and Farrell, "Match between CEO and Firm," 317–41.

Chapter Fourteen ——————————

Setting the Scene

Three Cases of Founder Succession

BEFORE LOOKING MORE CLOSELY at a number of themes and issues to consider when reflecting upon succession within Christian organizations and movements, this chapter seeks to outline several processes that organizations underwent when considering succession. Much of the content of the succession themes which follow in Part IV derives from these three examples, which formed case studies in my research. An overview of how succession was enacted will prove helpful, as knowledge of the processes as well as the underlying issues, themes, and theologies is important in itself.

THE CASE OF A SWEDEN-BASED INTERNATIONAL DEVELOPMENT AGENCY: INTERNATIONAL AID SERVICES

International Aid Services (IAS) was an international nongovernmental organization (NGO) founded in 1989 by Leif Zetterlund (born 1952, Swedish, white, male) and a team of workers with the purpose of assisting conflict-affected populations in South Sudan. Zetterlund and his family had worked for several years in government-controlled Juba and had seen the plight of the people. Sudan's Peoples Liberation Army was fighting for independence, while the Lord's Resistance Army was active toward the Ugandan border kidnapping children and forcing them to become soldiers. Local people lacked necessities such as water and food, but many aid agencies left Juba. In these circumstances, Zetterlund launched IAS on New Year's Eve 1989 (the original acronym stood for International Aid Sweden, which was later changed to International Aid Services as it grew from being a solely Sweden-based organization). Leif Zetterlund led the ministry for twenty-five years, from its inception until 2014.[1]

IAS's vision was stated as a "godly transformed society." Its mission is articulated as "to save lives, promote self-reliance and dignity through human transformation, going beyond relief and development."[2] This is a Christian ministry "abiding by Christian values."[3] The core values are expressed as missions, integrity, relational leadership and teamwork, empathy (compassion), and equality.[4]

By 2015, the ministry was working in ten countries, primarily in the Horn of Africa and Eastern Africa, supported by four offices in Europe and the US. The alliance's head office is located in Stockholm. The organization had some 350 employees, of which 95 percent in the program countries were indigenous, not expatriate. By that time over six million people had been assisted by IAS, with, for example, over five thousand wells having been drilled. IAS's annual budget was around that time approximately US$9.5 million. Income was largely through donations and grants from individuals, churches, businesses, and governmental agencies (Sida[5] and USAID) as well as international agencies (UNICEF, UNHCR).[6]

As a general preparation for new leadership, all original members of the international board relinquished their board positions. The founder saw this as "phase one" of the succession. Subsequently, some two years prior to the succession, there was a general sense among the leadership of the ministry that new leadership structures and vision might be needed given the changing political and donor environment in which the ministry functioned. In 2012, Douglas Mann, chair of the IAS international executive

1. Much of this information was taken from content on the International Aid Services website. Since my research, and prior to publishing this work, the content has been archived. The website now takes readers to the web page below, which contains contact details. It is suggested that any reader requiring access to the archived data contact the organization. https://sites.google.com/ias-intl.org/lakarmissionen-ias-together.

2. International Aid Services, *2015 Annual Report*, 4.

3. See note 1 above.

4. See Appendix A for full statement of values.

5. Sida is an acronym for Swedish International Development Cooperation Agency (*Styrelsen för Internationellt Utvecklingssamarbete*), the overseas aid department of the Swedish government.

6. See note 1 above.

board, raised the matter of succession with the founder. There was no specific activating event, but "I think it was more seeing the fact, the old man is getting old and one day he will not be around. Why wait until it is getting late. Let's do something before it is too late."[7] The founder asked Mann to lead the succession planning. Candidates were considered and interviewed. Daniel Zetterlund (son of Leif, born 1981, Swedish, white, male) had grown up within IAS, often as a child volunteering to assist the mission. Between 2007 and 2012 he was the director of IAS Sudan. While in Khartoum, in May 2013, at this point working at the Swedish embassy, Daniel received a call from the president of the IAS international board stating that the board was considering a successor, that they would prefer to find an internal candidate. Consultations ensued, resulting in February 2014 with the Executive Board unanimously offering the position of CEO to Daniel Zetterlund. Wider consultation took place with field workers. The Executive Board's recommendation was approved by the General Assembly in May 2014. Daniel served the following six months as deputy CEO.[8] There was no specific training or successor socialization. Daniel Zetterlund became CEO on January 1, 2015, and a celebrative ceremony of installation was held in March 2015 in Yei, South Sudan.

The successor instituted what he calls a "rebirth process"[9] with restructuring to increase capacity to reach objectives; it was a framework which allowed for geographic expansion. A new partnership alliance was crafted to build capacity; legal changes were made. The previous board was dissolved; a new legal board was put in place. The Swedish office became the international office. Audits took place to clarify the financial status of the organization. Having led IAS to change its global governance structures, Daniel Zetterlund developed a five-year strategic plan entitled "Fit for Purpose."[10] As a successor to an entrepreneurial founder, Daniel Zetterlund hoped that "I'm harnessing the positive energy that is there and elevating that in a more structured way . . . That's what I would like," adding, "It's a different time now."[11]

---

7. Leif Zetterlund Interview I, 17. The interview transcripts used as data in this research project are not publicly available. Requests to the author to access such data may be made by contacting the publisher.

8. IAS Press Release, June 23, 2014, available as Appendix B.

9. Daniel Zetterlund Interview I, 19.

10. International Aid Services, *Fit for Purpose*. Available at http://www.ias-intl.org/wp-content/uploads/2016/05/Fit-for-purpose_a-strategy-for-sustained-growth_2016–2020_FINAL.pdf.

11. Daniel Zetterlund Interview II, 24.

The founder, Leif Zetterlund, and successor, Daniel Zetterlund, were each interviewed twice in Stockholm, Sweden, in March 2018. Documents examined included: the IAS website, especially the report (written, photographic, and video) of the transition ceremony in South Sudan; the June 23, 2014, press release announcing the appointment of Daniel Zetterlund as CEO (Appendix B);[12] and the *2015 Annual Report*.[13]

NEW APOSTOLIC NETWORK OF CHURCHES INITIATED IN THE UNITED KINGDOM: NEWFRONTIERS

Newfrontiers is a network of churches begun in the United Kingdom, which developed into a large international network. The founding leader, or apostle, is Terry Virgo (born 1940, British, white, male).[14] Beginning evangelistic ministry in the late 1960s, Virgo started churches in southern England, which became a base for broader and eventually extensive international ministry. When it became clear that nomenclature was important, the name "Coastlands" was adopted, becoming officially registered as a charity in 1982. The growing movement was renamed "New Frontiers International" to express the practice and desire to be doing new things in new places.[15] In 2002, the network was rebranded as "Newfrontiers," which ameliorates the negative connotations of the word "frontier" in some languages.[16]

The numeric growth of both churches and attendees was sustained. At their first Downs Bible Week in 1979, some 2,700 attended, growing to around 10,000 in ten years. This annual summer gathering later relocated to the showground at Stoneleigh, Warwickshire. By 2001, thirty thousand people came for the summer camp of Bible teaching and workshops. Such growth began to receive the attention of scholars; Smith's title "An Account

---

12. http://www.ias-intl.org/se/?author=1&paged=3.

13. International Aid Services, *2015 Annual Report*. It should be noted that since 2019 and therefore since some the research for this book was undertaken, IAS is "an integral part" of another Swedish agency, although former IAS Alliance members in other nations continue to exist as independent and legal entities and IAS country offices continue to exist as IAS branded country offices (see https://sites.google.com/ias-intl.org/lakarmissionen-ias-together).

14. A fuller account of both Virgo's life and the development of Newfrontiers is available in Virgo's autobiography (Virgo, *No Well-Worn Paths*). A briefer account of the network appears in Kay, *Apostolic Networks*, 64–81.

15. New Frontiers International was officially registered with the Charity Commission in December 1991, but had in effect been in existence before that time (see Kay, *Apostolic Networks*, 71).

16. See Aune, "Postfeminist Evangelicals," 31.

of the Sustained Rise of New Frontiers International within the United Kingdom" was telling of what was being observed.[17] By the time of founder succession in 2011, Newfrontiers numbered some 850 churches in sixty nations.[18]

To understand better the founder succession of this movement and frame the analysis, three descriptive points regarding its theology and ecclesiology are made at this point, namely that the network was evangelical, Calvinistic (yet charismatic), and restorationist. Newfrontiers possessed the classic four "special marks" of evangelicalism, known as the "Evangelical Quadrilateral": conversionism, activism, biblicism, and crucicentrism.[19] Within evangelicalism the network is more specifically Reformed or Calvinistic in theology.[20] Walker, however, believes that Virgo's Calvinism is not that of the mainline Reformed tradition: "Terry's Calvinism is in the spirit of the great Puritan leader John Owen, mediated through the separatist tendencies of Martyn Lloyd-Jones and the earlier evangelicalism of C. H. Spurgeon."[21] The theology of Newfrontiers is, furthermore, unusual in that it combines Calvinism with a belief in the ongoing existence and use of the charismatic gifts of 1 Cor 12.[22] Thirdly, Newfrontiers is restorationist. "Restorationism" has been elucidated by Walker in his now classic work[23] and subsequently studied by Kay.[24] According to Walker, "restorationism" describes those movements of churches desiring to

17. Smith, "Account," 137–56.

18. Newfrontiers, *Forward Together*, 4.

19. Bebbington, *Evangelicalism in Modern Britain*, 16 (digital version). Bebbington's 1989 printed original has become a classic study of British evangelicalism. I have used the 2005 digital version (Bebbington, *Evangelicalism in Modern Britain*). There has been much scholarly discussion on this quadrilateral, but, as Bebbington writes in 2015, none has yet "challenged the fourfold description" ("Evangelical Quadrilateral," 87).

20. According to the entry "Reformed Theology" in *Westminster Dictionary of Theological Terms*, "key aspects include God's initiative in salvation, and election, and union with Christ" (McKim, "Reformed Theology," 234). Letham cites the five characteristics (from the Canons of Dort) generally accepted as descriptive of reformed theology: total depravity, unconditional election, limited atonement, irresistible grace, and perseverance (Letham, "Reformed Theology," 570).

21. Walker, *Restoring the Kingdom*, 332.

22. Newfrontiers is "exceptional, if not unique, in combining Calvinism with charismatic theology" (Kay, *Apostolic Networks*, 334), although the following case study of Grace Network is also of a network similar in its theological tenets.

23. Walker, *Restoring the Kingdom*. I used the 4th ed. (1998).

24. Kay, *Apostolic Networks*.

restore or return to the New Testament pattern (as they see it) of the Early Church. The restoring of the Church as it was in its pristine form is to restore a charismatically-ordained church, and one in which Christians are seen as living in a kingdom run according to God's order and rules.[25]

Walker continues that restorationism "refers to a recognizable cluster of doctrines and practices adhered to by a considerable number of churches which nevertheless prefer to see themselves as non-denominational."[26] Walker believes that there are two types of restorationism in Britain, namely R1 and R2, designations which are widely used, even by Virgo himself.[27] For Walker, R1 types are the more conservative and most like the ideal type; R2 groups are more liberal and fluid.[28] Newfrontiers is R1. A particular feature of restorationism, and one which is pertinent to this study on succession, is that of the role of modern-day apostles.

> Restorationism in essence argues that the power and pattern of the early church can be restored to the contemporary church. Along with a belief in charismatic gifts is the belief in 21st century apostles. The two are intimately linked because apostles may be recognised, among other things, by their exercise of charismatic gifts.[29]

Virgo states that the key themes of the restorationist church are "body ministry, a committed community, grace, spiritual authority and a prophetic hope,"[30] while Devenish, the leading missiologist within Newfrontiers, sees two components, namely the restoration to New Testament truth and to New Testament practices.[31] As these two are restored, *we put our hope in the prophetic promises of an end-time glorious church affecting every people group.*[32]

In 2011, with 850 churches, Newfrontiers underwent founder succession—not by replacing Virgo with another international director or lead apostle, but by dividing the international movement into fifteen autonomous "apostolic spheres," each with its own name and leadership. Newfrontiers ceased to exist as one church-planting movement. This unusual, bold,

---

25. Walker, *Restoring the Kingdom*, 39–40.
26. Walker, *Restoring the Kingdom*, 41.
27. See Virgo, *No Well-Worn Paths*, 82.
28. Walker, *Restoring the Kingdom*, 39.
29. Kay, *Apostolic Networks*, 318.
30. Virgo, *No Well-Worn Paths*, 80.
31. Devenish, *What on Earth Is the Church for?*, 9.
32. Devenish, *What on Earth Is the Church for?*, 10 (italics in original).

and controversial act provides important data for understanding a different approach to succession than many enact; indeed, multiple church leaders, including a representative from the Evangelical Alliance, the body representing two million UK evangelicals, either wrote to Virgo or met with him to urge Newfrontiers not to enact succession in this way.

I conducted interviews with Virgo in March 2018; transcripts, online articles, and sermons as well as some of his multiple books were also used to gain a deeper understanding of the succession (see bibliography for a list of Virgo's publications). Due to the multiplication of successors, there was no single successor to be interviewed. To interview all fifteen, in Australia, India, South Africa, and elsewhere, was prohibitive. The decision was made to interview one, namely David Devenish (born 1948, British, white, male). He was one of the fifteen successors and subsequently became the coordinator for any collaboration between those spheres. His apostolic sphere is "Catalyst."[33] He was interviewed in March 2018. He also has authored several books that are used in this analysis.[34]

Newfrontiers had no written plan for succession. At the annual international leadership conference (2008), a visiting preacher, Mark Driscoll, publicly stated that Virgo needed to find a successor from the next generation in the next four years: "Are you going to honour your future, not over-honour the founder?"[35] This was followed by reference to a photograph Driscoll had seen of the wedding of Virgo's daughter. Driscoll posited that a young man had to be found to "marry" Terry's spiritual "daughter"—that is, a younger man to become the leader of Newfrontiers.[36] Virgo announced, "This is from God,"[37] to ensure that the congregation knew that he accepted Driscoll's forthrightness.

The international leadership team of Newfrontiers subsequently deliberated this message. The team approved the four-year period and began thinking of who that successor might be, assuming it would be a man in his forties. During these years of deliberation, Virgo became aware, however, of friends in other networks for whom succession had been problematic. One network had transferred leadership from its founder to a much younger man; other church leaders within that network spoke to Virgo that it had

33. https://catalystnetwork.org/. In 2017, Devenish transitioned from leading this sphere but remained leading Newfrontiers Together.

34. Devenish, *Demolishing Strongholds*; *What on Earth Is the Church for?*; *Fathering Leaders*; *Succession or Multiplication?*.

35. Virgo, "Honouring the Future."

36. For Newfrontiers, church government and apostolic leadership are exclusively male. In chapter 21, we will return to this matter in greater depth.

37. Virgo Interview I, 10.

not progressed well, largely because they could not relate to the successor as a spiritual father, although admiring this younger leader's gift and integrity. A second leader in this movement wrote Virgo a long document explaining this. The effect was to cause the Newfrontiers leaders to "stop in our tracks."[38] Virgo's chief concern was that in appointing a new younger man, others might not look to the successor as a spiritual father.[39] Virgo stated that final clarity came through a reading of Ps 45 concerning sons becoming fathers. Although he did not provide a specific verse reference or quote verbatim, Virgo was referencing Ps 45:16: "Your sons will take the place of your father; you will make them princes throughout the land."

Observations received from others, as well as this fresh understanding of Ps 45:16, caused a paradigm shift in Newfrontiers' conceptualization of succession; the "international team" adopted a model of multiplication of apostolic leaders and spheres. This was processed with a wider group, the "apostolic forum," where apostolic leaders were already meeting for training and deliberation.[40] The international team appointed a transition team (chaired by Devenish) to discuss and advise on the precise way forward; the international team made the decisions concerning whom to appoint as sphere leaders, but with considerable deference to Virgo.[41] Virgo asked fifteen people to consider such an appointment. The transition plan was announced in June 2011; Terry Virgo retired from executive responsibility on December 31. At that year's annual leadership conference (with some five thousand present), the fifteen men stood and groups gathered around them to pray for them. These fifteen, although now autonomous, stated a desire for some (limited) ongoing collaboration across the spheres; Devenish was appointed to lead a team to investigate how such a desire might be implemented.

Between announcement of the succession plan and its execution, Virgo had been shocked at reactions from those in other British churches who expressed concern that the voice of Newfrontiers, so influential within British evangelicalism, would be dissipated, to the detriment of British evangelicalism as a whole. Indeed, others saw Newfrontiers as having pioneered new ways of church which helped those in other networks.[42] Newfrontiers stayed its course. Indeed, Virgo believes that the values of Newfrontiers have been amplified within the British church.

38. Virgo Interview I, 25.
39. Virgo Interview I, 25–26.
40. Devenish Interview I, 7.
41. Devenish Interview I, 8.
42. Virgo Interview II, 23–25.

Not all matters proceed smoothly, however. Virgo narrated three principal difficulties with the succession: It took two years for churches and leaders to know fully where to locate themselves in the post-succession structures; one leader was pained, feeling overlooked in the new leadership appointments (who subsequently has acknowledged that decisions made were correct); and one of the fifteen sphere leaders struggled with there no longer being one movement with one name. This leader withdrew from joint meetings with the other fourteen. Devenish added that the fifteen leaders were not well prepared for administrative and legal matters. This, as well as the placing of each church in the new spheres, was an issue of greater difficulty in the United Kingdom than other countries.

Subsequent to succession, Devenish led the sphere leaders to clarity on ongoing matters of "togetherness," particularly in matters of accountability, training, participation, and concomitant financing. These processes led to formalization and documentation including, for the first time, a written doctrinal statement. By 2016, Devenish believed that such discussions were concluded; any collaboration needed to move beyond knowing a common past and set of values to a common future vision and direction. He stresses that this was "a vision for our togetherness, not a vision for each individual sphere. That's their own autonomy. But if you want to be involved all together, this is what we're about."[43]

In retrospect, the transition, after two or three years, resulted in increased church-planting around the world. According to Devenish, there were by 2018 some two thousand churches in the combined spheres.[44] There is now clarity concerning autonomy of spheres, as well as mutual (and documented) agreement on matters in which the spheres still desire cooperation.[45] Indeed a brief account of Newfrontiers' succession and the initiation of Newfrontiers Together (as part of the institutional discourse of Newfrontiers Together) is publicly available online, cited in full here:

> As a result of another message at one of our leaders' conferences, the international team began to consider whether Terry Virgo should now hand over executive responsibility for the Newfrontiers family to a younger generation. We resisted the idea

43. Devenish Interview I, 17.

44. Devenish Interview I, 33.

45. "Newfrontiers is a group of apostolic leaders partnering together on global mission, joined by common values and beliefs, shared mission and genuine relationships" (https://newfrontierstogether.org/.) The fuller documentation details the nature of the mutual collaboration and accountability as well as doctrine. Subsequent to my interviews with Virgo and Devenish, much of this documentation has been published and is available in Devenish, *Succession or Multiplication?*, particularly 75–94.

of appointing a next generation successor to Terry and instead felt God leading us to multiplication of apostolic ministry. We treasured the fact that we were a family of churches and families grow into the next generation, not by appointing a new leader but by "sons" becoming "fathers." We therefore recognised a number of brothers who had already become like fathers to other churches and who also had a clear apostolic calling, and it was agreed that Newfrontiers would multiply into autonomous but interdependent apostolic spheres. Those who were leading these spheres did not want to move apart from each other even though they appreciated the freedom given to develop their own apostolic call and their own apostolic family. They therefore invited David Devenish to lead what Newfrontiers continued to be together in its interdependence. So from January 2012 David took on that role with a team that became known as the New-frontiers Together Team. We therefore continue to have international conferences in some form or other bringing the leaders of the spheres together once a year.[46]

Documentation concerning the succession is located in four categories: Virgo's and Devenish's books; the Newfrontiers Together website; Virgo's online articles and sermons; and the magazine issue *Forward Together* (2011) which communicated the succession to adherents around the world. A list of such documentary sources is provided in Appendix C.

Some of Virgo's final written comments prior to the succession event were a call to the future and to change:

The time has come to redefine Newfrontiers. Through 2011, Newfrontiers will begin to take on a new identity. It will be the name given to multiplied apostolic spheres who plan to work together interdependently, owning the same values, retaining the same Newfrontiers title and aspiring to fulfil the prophetic promises given to us.

Virgo concludes this message:

Some decades ago, God told us that there are no well-worn paths ahead. More recently, He has promised us multiplication and exponential growth. We are not following traditional patterns, but we know that he who calls himself "the Way" will continue to provide us with his guidance and grace.[47]

46. Newfrontiers Together, "About Newfrontiers."

47. Virgo, "Newfrontiers Redefined." http://www.terryvirgo.org/articles/transition -into-multiplication-newfrontiers-redefined/.

INTERNATIONAL NETWORK OF CHURCHES
INITIATED IN THE US: GRACE NETWORK

Grace Network was founded in the US in 1980. The three founders, Jimmy Hollandsworth (Roanoke, Virginia), John Manzano (Charlottesville, Virginia), and Dick Blackwell (Harrisonburg, Virginia), each provided guidance and oversight to churches in the US and overseas. In 1980, they agreed to formalize meeting together and to invite churches to be part of a network. By 1988, the founders registered their network as a charity under the name "Grace Presbytery and Ministry International," later becoming "Grace Network International" (but usually referred to as "Grace Network"). The purposes of the network were to provide assistance, accountability, and biblical teaching and to start new churches and ministries in the US and overseas.[48] Churches were self-governing; the leadership team of the network provided advice, support, and training to those churches and leaders desiring it and wishing to be part of a broader network of fellowship and voluntary collaboration than is possible in a single congregation.

The by-laws of the ministry articulate belief in twelve statements, broadly in line with the Lausanne Covenant[49] and similar to many evangelical churches.[50] These by-laws more narrowly defined the network's spirituality with the acronym "CARE" (Charismatic, Apostolic, Reformed, Evangelical).[51] Over time, the leadership employed the acronym "I CARE," having added the "I" for "inclusion." The leadership and member churches (in the US) were largely white; the accretion of "inclusion" expressed their desire to collaborate with black and Hispanic American churches. Indeed, three Spanish-speaking congregations in the US were admitted to membership. The founding leadership governed as a triumvirate, with co-equal authority. When one founder retired, Jack Groblewski was appointed as director and then later as executive director (successor to founders) in 2005.

Grace Network International had member churches and para-church ministries in a number of nations. Their work in Uruguay, for example, developed when a Christian leader from Uruguay visited Grace Covenant Church in Harrisonburg. The American church then supported the church and a large orphanage led by this Uruguayan leader. This work grew to

---

48. Grace Network, *Constitution*, art. II.

49. See https://www.lausanne.org/content/covenant/lausanne-covenant.

50. Grace Network, *By-Laws*.

51. Grace Network, *By-Laws*, sect. III-B. See this part of the by-laws, attached as Appendix D, for further understanding of these four foundational doctrines. Grace Network, like Newfrontiers, is both charismatic and reformed. Such a combination of theologies, as previously mentioned, is rare.

seventeen new churches in Uruguay. Blackwell's role was to provide spiritual oversight to the Uruguayan leader who in turn would oversee the churches in his nation. The "mother" church in Uruguay was part of Grace Network, even adopting (in Spanish) the nomenclature of Blackwell's Harrisonburg church (*Pacto de Gracia*). Similarly, the network helped establish and support churches in Haiti. While an independent, self-governing network, Grace Network International also sought to establish good working relationships with other similar networks around the world. This led to the forming of a loose affiliation with Ground Level (United Kingdom)[52] and The Christian Network (TCN) in South Africa.[53] Through this affiliation, Grace Network began to collaborate with the other two on matters of training and international ministry, using the name "Partners For Influence" (PFI) for such collaborative efforts.

The overseas churches in Grace Network were considered full members. Representatives would attend network conferences in the US; there was much cooperation and considerable financial support to works in Haiti, Uruguay, and later in Africa. Furthermore, other types of ministry could be members of Grace Network. Betel is both an international network of ministries to those suffering addiction and a church-planting ministry. Representatives of Betel attended Grace Network conferences in the US. Some Betel missionaries were ordained through churches within the Grace Network in the US.

In 2017, Grace Network merged with others to form One Focus; Grace Network as a separate movement now no longer exists. Given this, there are few documents currently available (the former website is no longer extant). The website of One Focus provides the sole online statement on Grace Network's ministry, history, founding leadership, and succession.[54]

Dick Blackwell (born 1941, American, white, male) was chosen as the founder for the purposes of the research interviews. One of the other founders is now deceased; the other was unable to be interviewed on grounds of health. The successor, indeed, the first person actually given the title "executive director," was Jack Groblewski (born 1948, American, white, male). The two interviews with Blackwell were conducted in Virginia, US, in May 2018. Research interviews with Groblewski were conducted in June 2018 in Pennsylvania.[55]

---

52. https://www.groundlevel.org.uk/. For more on Ground Level, see Kay, *Apostolic Networks*, 135–42.

53. http://www.tcn.co.za/site/.

54. https://onefocus.global/about/, also attached as Appendix E.

55. In the interviews, Groblewski is referred to by his nickname "Grubby."

Grace Network was led by a "three-headed leadership team,"[56] which Blackwell believes operated well due to mutual respect and lack of any "grasping for leadership."[57] There was no succession plan for Grace Network. In 2005, Van Niekerk, the South African leader of TCN, articulated difficulty in relating to a triumvirate; he challenged Grace Network to appoint a "representative"[58] who could speak on behalf of Grace Network in PFI matters. Blackwell and Manzano proposed that Jack Groblewski be appointed as a new executive director. Network members were consulted. At a regular network meeting, less than six months after the PFI leaders articulated the need for an executive director, Groblewski absented himself so that discussion and voting could take place. A unanimous vote followed; Groblewski, at the same conference, was installed into office through prayer, *cheirotonia*,[59] and anointing with oil. At the induction event, the scriptural passage of Num 27:18–20, was read; these verses describe God saying to Moses to take Joshua, on whom God had put his spirit, and to lay your hands upon him, and some of the power on Moses would transfer to him. There was little discussion as to role or expectations and no specific training provided. In Groblewski's words, it was similar to Joshua saying to the people, "Get up. You have not been this way before."[60]

Groblewski narrates that succession was problematic in two significant ways. Firstly, it raised unrealizable expectations among the churches with regard to his role. His precise role was not clearly articulated or communicated. Secondly, his role with the other two leaders was not clarified; that is, the leadership decision-making process and the amount of authority he had was unclear. For him, the model was unsustainable over time.[61]

Groblewski believes that he instigated changes in leadership methodology and conceptualizations, seeking to be a more directive leader. When significant pressure came upon the movement years later, the leadership, however, reverted to their prior understanding of co-equality. That external pressure was the grave failings within the leadership of TCN, which led to addressing many painful pastoral issues. The role of PFI waned, and the Grace Network leadership reverted to a former modus operandi (although Groblewski was still executive director). These exogenous factors brought

56. Blackwell Interview I, 2.

57. Blackwell Interview I, 2.

58. Blackwell Interview I, 3.

59. "Laying on of hands." I have found no reference to such action, or indeed to anointing with oil, in the interviews or documents of my other two case studies.

60. Groblewski Interview I, 11. This is a reference to Josh 3:4.

61. Groblewski Interview I, 5.

the co-equal Presbyterian leadership model into unavoidable view and catalyzed criticism from within the network from those desiring a more decisive leadership. Faced with such comment, with which Groblewski agreed, the three directors saw that there was no one else wanting to take leadership in this manner. A decision was made (2016–17) to disband the network and offer the churches the possibility of joining One Focus, a new network merging several church networks. Despite such difficulties, Groblewski nonetheless viewed his tenure as a "very fond time of my life."[62]

CHAPTER CONCLUSIONS

The above three accounts provide details concerning the processes enacted and key decisions made in each case of succession. A close analysis of these successions from the various documents available as well as the transcripts of my interviews with the founders and successors in the organizations reveals complexities surrounding the successions, as well as multiple themes related to succession. Part IV follows and draws attention to a number of these themes which merged from the research data.

62. Groblewski Interview II, 20.

PART IV

Aspects of Succession

Chapter Fifteen ─────────────

Succession Origins
Insider or Outsider?

IN CHAPTER 2, ATTENTION was drawn to the matter of succession origins. This theme was the founding theme of succession studies in the modern era,[1] a topic which occupied a good deal of print (see Kesner and Sebora for a review on some thirty pieces of research on succession origins,[2] and see specific studies such as Cannella and Lubatkin[3] and Collins and Porras).[4] More specifically, research from the organizational world shows that organizational success and longevity are positively correlated with internal succession;[5] yet, at times of forced departure, however, external appointments may be needed.[6] Indeed, Collins and Porras found that successful, visionary companies appoint internally six times more frequently than less successful companies.[7]

A detailed understanding of why successor origins became the dominant theme in the earlier years of succession studies is beyond the scope of this book. However, I posit the notion that it remained a focus during the

1. Grusky "Corporate Size," 261–69; "Effects of Succession," 83–111.

2. Kesner and Sebora, "Executive Succession," 327–72.

3. Cannella and Lubatkin, "Succession," 763–93.

4. Collins and Porras, *Built to Last*.

5. Collins and Porras, *Built to Last*; Ocasio, "Institutionalized Action," 384–416; Shen and Cannella, "Revisiting the Performance Consequences," 717.

6. Allgood and Farrell, "Match between CEO and Firm," 317–41.

7. Collins and Porras, *Built to Last*, 10.

1970s and 1980s when leadership studies and theory in general was placing great emphasis on the leader as person.[8] More recently other conceptualizations of leadership have focused on matters such as environment. Contingency theory, for example, states that leadership effectiveness depends on leader/context fit.[9] Other approaches to leadership emphasize the dyadic relationship between leader and followers, such as leader-member exchange theory,[10] which draws attention away from origins as the most significant factor in succession.

Whether influenced by "leader as person" theories or other concerns (see below), Christian organizations place great importance on origins; they almost universally desire internal succession, as the following selection shows: New Covenant Ministries International (NCMI) (South Africa),[11] Salt and Light (United Kingdom),[12] Cure International (US),[13] Operation Mobilization (United Kingdom),[14] Youth With A Mission (US),[15] Global Advance (US),[16] Edify (US),[17] Life Impact Ministries (US),[18] International Aid Services (Sweden).[19] This raises the question of why Christian agencies prefer or even limit their understanding of succession to the internal. Conclusive findings should, of course, be reserved for a further and more far-reaching study. It is possible, however, to attempt a few tentative explanations. In writing about founder succession in Edify, Christopher Crane, founder, when speaking of his successor, highlights the successor's history of high performance and his demonstrated long-term commitment to the organizational mission.[20] The appointment was thus due to high levels of trust for future performance, something that would have been more difficult to assess with an external candidate. For Shibley at Global Advance, the decision of whom to appoint as successor was made over a five-year

8. Jago, "Leadership," 315–36; Lord et al., "Meta-Analysis," 402–10; Bennis and Nanus, *Leaders*.

9. Northouse, *Leadership*, 123–36; Fiedler and Chemers, *Improving Leadership Effectiveness*.

10. Northouse, *Leadership*, 161–84.

11. https://www.ncmi.net/.

12. https://www.saltlight.org/.

13. https://cure.org/.

14. https://www.om.org/int/home.

15. https://www.ywam.org/.

16. https://www.globaladvance.org/.

17. https://www.edify.org/.

18. https://lifeimpact.care/.

19. http://www.ias-intl.org/.

20. Correspondence from Crane, Feb 20, 2018 (cited with permission).

period of reflection. Shibley writes concerning the (internal) successor that it "became obvious to everyone he was God's choice."[21] This speaks to the preference for a long period of reflection and observation before appointing, something almost impossible with an external candidate. For Life Impact Ministries, the successor, David Knauss, writes that the founders desired an internal successor because of a "strong desire that the core values of the mission be carried on. Those values are often not seen in mission agencies and one of the reasons Life Impact Ministries exists in the first place."[22] In this example, strong emphasis is being placed on maintenance and continuation of organizational values, for which an external candidate would not be qualified.

In placing such comments from three organizations together, it would seem that these international evangelical organizations proceeded slowly and cautiously over the appointment of a successor, preferring to see demonstrated high performance and commitment to the ministry and its values as crucial qualifications. Such emphases favor internal appointments.

It is also likely, furthermore, that this preference for internal succession as a means to perpetuate values and organizational spirituality is due to concern that in the future, the organization will depart from its founding Christian values and become a humanistic, philanthropic organization. Greer and Horst posit (with examples) that "mission drift" is due to the persuasive pressure of secularization: "Functional atheism is the path of least resistance" for a Christian ministry; taking such a path is to be resisted.[23] This seems to be a widely held belief among Christian leaders, evidenced in a survey of hundreds of Christian leaders at the Q conference in Los Angeles (April 2013) at which 95 percent said mission drift was a challenging issue to faith-based nonprofit organizations.[24] Such a view was also echoed by Crane, who recently led the organization he founded through (internal) succession: "It's the exception that an organization stays true to its mission. The natural course—the unfortunate natural evolution of many originally Christ-centered missions—is to drift."[25] Internal succession is one means, it is believed, to maintain the Christian nature of an organization's calling and purpose.

21. Correspondence from Shibley, Aug 17, 2018 (cited with permission).

22. Correspondence from Knauss, Oct 29, 2018 (cited with permission).

23. Greer and Horst, *Mission Drift*, 42–43.

24. Greer and Horst, *Mission Drift*, 20. Q is a ministry which "educates church and cultural leaders on their role and opportunity to embody the Gospel in public life" (http://qideas.org/).

25. Interview with Greer, Feb 2013, in Greer and Horst, *Mission Drift*, 19.

It is interesting, indeed noteworthy, that all three detailed case studies in this research, International Aid Services, Newfrontiers, and Grace Network, engaged in internal succession, as is common in Christian organizations. To illustrate internal succession, detail on this succession theme will be provided by comment on the succession within Grace Network.

Grace Network would not have made an external appointment to the position of executive director: "No, we wouldn't. We believe, any way possible, to do it from within. I mean we had—we didn't even need to think about external."[26] This reluctance to search external to the organization may be seen in the more general organizational characteristic of needing to know potential leaders over time. This is typified in the constitutional provision that one had to be a member of the movement for at least five years before one could be admitted to the board of directors.

What lies behind the organizational culture of caution and reluctance to make external appointments? According to Groblewski, there were a number of factors, including the following: organizational culture preservation—"So I think that provision [five-year membership] was put in so that no one would come in and really eviscerate the culture of Grace Network";[27] the desire for doctrinal fidelity—"But, as time went on, we became, I believe, more parochial, more focused on maintenance, more focused on, uh, doctrinal tidiness, uh, which is always a pitfall of Reformed groups";[28] and concern for maintenance of Christian ethics and morality:

> Well, to maintain, I think, to maintain order, doctrinal tidiness
> . . . the—the charismatic movement . . . These are charismatic
> Reformed churches. And so, you've got a tension right there.
> The charismatic movement has just seen so much, uh, ineptitude
> as far as its moral—its moral and ethical posture has gone, you
> know, the televangelist controversies, all those kinds of things
> . . . And I, uh, think it was just caution and, uh, not wanting our
> churches to suffer . . .[29]

This citation also manifests a fourth point, that of protection of the churches.

The successor's understanding of the reasons for an internal appointment is confirmed in the founder's narratives. These show a motivation of conservatism: "It was—it was natural, and it was easy for us to do because we didn't feel like Grubby was going to take it—take it places we weren't

---

26. Blackwell Interview II, 4.

27. Groblewski Interview I, 13.

28. Groblewski Interview I, 13.

29. Groblewski Interview I, 14.

comfortable with."[30] This is related to a desire to preserve the organization's culture and values:

> Unless you wanted it to have radical change, turn it over to somebody with similar DNA who has similar values and mode of operation. I think, if the organization is good the way it is . . . has good values to begin with that you want to continue, then you have to have someone come along who has similar vision, values.[31]

The founders of Grace Network conceptualize organizations as having a DNA: "You make radical changes to that and you mutate into something."[32] Any such mutation was to be avoided.[33]

It has already been suggested that Grace Network's belief in internal succession was framed within cultural, doctrinal, and ethical preservation. The use of emotive vocabulary such as "mutate"[34] and "eviscerate"[35] underlines the conservative and preservative nature of the succession.

There are three main points of analysis which lead toward a critical evaluation of the focus and emphasis on internal succession in Grace Network. First, conservatism obscured focus on future goal orientation, environmental challenges, or a broader contextual evaluation for leader-situation congruence. Second, there was a strong yet unacknowledged espousal of leadership theory. A focus on the person of the leader rather than other factors (as seen in contingency theory or leader-member exchange theory) indicates that Grace Network espoused a trait-based leadership theory, not even other person-orientated theories of leadership such as leadership as skills. Thus, a strong, yet unacknowledged, theoretical understanding of leadership emerges, that of trait and character-based leadership.[36] This may lead to an overlooking of other crucial aspects to be considered in transition, such as skills and environmental match: "The natural tendency is to think about succession in terms of specific people rather than skills and talents. But even strong internal candidates will have strengths and limitations, and when 'working backward' from the person to

30. Blackwell Interview I, 4.

31. Blackwell Interview II, 14.

32. Blackwell Interview II, 15.

33. The implications of this biological metaphor are treated more fully at the end of this chapter.

34. Blackwell Interview II, 15.

35. Groblewski Interview I, 13.

36. Bass, *Handbook of Leadership*; Kirkpatrick and Locke, "Leadership" 48–60; and others.

the job, the limitations often get overlooked."[37] Focusing on the successor's origins and traits, furthermore, may displace attention from the need for a change in communication strategy, something that Kondrath identifies as important in founder succession in religious ministries.[38] Emphasis tends to be placed on the replacement of the founder and the successor's provenance, not on the broader interpersonal dynamics with other leaders in the process and the general depth and breadth of intraorganizational communication.

A third potential problem is that internal succession may be seen as panacean. Internal founder successions in organizations may, however, and indeed do, fail, both in business[39] and in Christian ministries.[40] This speaks to the possibility that emphasis on successor origins may obscure other vital matters in the succession process, such as skill and style similarity, the transmission of tacit knowledge, and the extent to which the predecessor had already led the organization through strategic change. Dyck et al. reached a number of conclusions concerning founder succession: The greater the similarity between the skill sets and managerial styles of incumbent and successor, the more likely it is that the succession will be successful; and the greater the level of agreement between incumbent and successor on the mode of succession, the more likely it is that the succession will be successful.[41] Kikoski and Kikoski found that high functioning organizations are influenced by the tacit knowledge of their leaders,[42] while Linde suggests "new leaders adapt to the roles by learning the stories of their organization."[43] Knowledge sharing is therefore a critical component of leadership succession.[44] Furthermore, Zúñiga-Vicente et al. found that long-tenure leaders could perform extremely well in the area of change. Indeed, "long tenure may reflect leaders' ability and willingness to continuously initiate appropriate strategic change. As a result, new leaders following long-tenured predecessors may find their firm better aligned to the environment than new leaders following short termed predecessors, reducing the need for post-succession strategic change."[45] An emphasis on successor origins may obscure the matter of whether the

---

37. Garman and Tyler, "What Kind of CEO," 3.

38. Kondrath, "Transitioning from Charismatic Founder," 83–115.

39. Dyck et al., "Passing the Baton," 143–62.

40. Owens, *Never Forget!*; Lavietes, "Rev. Robert Schuller"; Lobdell and Landsberg, "Rev. Robert H. Schuller."

41. Dyck et al., "Passing the Baton," 143–62.

42. Kikoski and Kikoski, *Inquiring Organization*.

43. Linde, "Narrative and Social Tacit Knowledge," 160–70.

44. Peet, "Leadership Transitions," 45–60.

45. Hutzschenreuter et al., "How New Leaders Affect Strategic Change," 741.

predecessor has produced the optimal environment for succession. Such considerations reduce the significance of the person of the successor and increase that of the preparatory role of the founder.

In conclusion, Grace Network's succession was suboptimal due to conservatism, an overemphasis on trait-based leadership theory (strongly advocated yet unacknowledged), and an over-attention to successor origins. All three are, of course, interdependent and produce a conceptualization of leadership succession which will be shown to produce problems in later organizational life.

To complete this analysis of successor origin perceptions in Grace Network, a final matter to be considered is that of metaphorical corporate self-conceptualization. Analysis of a rhetor's metaphors reveals much about conceptualizations and actions.[46] Metaphorical analysis may help provide an interpretation of a subject's theology;[47] this is because the characteristics associated with the vehicle of the metaphor are used to organize conceptions of the tenor of the metaphor.[48] Tenor and vehicles index how the rhetor sees the world. The structure of a metaphor contains assumptions; it prescribes how to act. It does not merely support an argument; the structure of the metaphor itself argues.[49] Metaphors structure how we think and what we do.[50] Metaphors also thus suppress and obscure. In foregrounding the vehicle of "DNA" and the need for new leadership to have that DNA to the tenor of Grace Network as an organization,[51] the ministry is seen as something that, once conceived, cannot (naturally) be changed, for metaphors lead us to see their entailments as true.[52] Other conceptualizations of the organization (hierarchy, bureaucracy) are suppressed, even concealed;[53] the organic, biological nature is privileged. Such a metaphorical understanding must lead to internal succession, for an appointee must have the DNA of the founders and others within the organic structure. To believe and apply the metaphor consistently thus leads inexorably to internal leadership

46. For a deeper understanding of metaphor and its analysis see Boroditsky, "Metaphoric Structuring," 1–28; Lakoff and Johnson, *Metaphors We Live By*; and Boréus and Bergström, "Metaphor Analysis and Critical Linguistics," 146–73.

47. Graves, "Functions of Key Metaphors," 364–78; Adams, "Linguistic Values," 58–68.

48. Foss, *Rhetorical Criticism*, 299.

49. Foss, *Rhetorical Criticism*, 301.

50. Lakoff and Johnson, *Metaphors We Live By*, 4.

51. Blackwell Interview II, 14.

52. Lakoff and Johnson, *Metaphors We Live By*, 159–84.

53. Boréus and Bergström, "Metaphor Analysis and Critical Linguistics," 149.

appointments and excludes external appointments; internal succession is privileged by the network's metaphorical corporate self-identity.

Given the desire for little change, the trust of internal leadership, and the desire to preserve organizational culture and doctrinal purity, together with the metaphoric self-identity, Grace Network could only appoint from within the movement. This is common in new Christian movements. The advantages of such appointments are supported by much empirical literature from other fields of study. Emphasis on successor origins, however, may obscure other factors to be taken into consideration in founder succession. Internal succession in itself is not a panacea, nor is it a guarantee that all will go well in the next season of organizational life.

Chapter Sixteen —————————————

Succession as Change from
an Entrepreneurial to a
Professional Leadership Style

It HAS ALREADY BEEN stated (chapter 7) that some Christian writers, indeed scholars, seem to believe that there are normative models of succession and that the successor needs to be a reproduction of the founder. This seems to be the implicit position of writers such as Fountain.[1] This may lead to the assumption that a successor leader must be very similar to the founding leader whom he or she is to replace. I have already mentioned this to some extent in the matter of internal rather than external succession (chapter 15). Christians can have considerable concern about a dissolution of the vision and values of the ministry, especially the spiritual and decidedly Christian nature of that mission.[2]

A further concern pertaining to succession matters can be that of seeking to avoid "routinization of charisma," as previously explained (chapter 3). Christians seeking to maintain the spiritual and charismatic nature of their new movement can be troubled by the fear that such routinization will take place; they will, therefore, seek to avoid it.[3] Such understanding is, how-

1. Fountain, "Investigation," 187–204.
2. Greer and Horst, *Mission Drift*.
3. See, for example, Owens, *Never Forget!*; Habib, "New Paradigm in Leadership

ever, moderated by Andelson, who shows that charismatic leadership may continue beyond the founder where there was a theology which allowed for multiple *charismata*.[4] Furthermore, Melton shows that in the modern world, founders often establish vast international organizations and bureaucracies which perpetuate their mission, regardless of any one individual. While initially a new movement is an extension of the founder's ideas and dreams, once the vision has been enunciated and teachings imparted, it exists independently of the founder and develops a life of its own.[5] Indeed, as many modern organizations will need legal registration (often in multiple countries) with concomitant boards and structures, Melton argues that today there is far less focus on founding charisma and power concentration.

Rather than becoming too mired in the debate over routinization of charisma itself, it might be more helpful to consider succession from the dynamic of change of leadership style, and thereby to adopt other terminology, now broadly accepted within organizational studies, namely that of "entrepreneurial" and "professional" styles of leadership. One of the case studies, International Aid Services, shows that such style changes may indeed take place with founder succession in international Christian agencies.

My approach here, to examine succession from the perspective of leadership style change, draws on the work of Tashakori and Schein from business studies[6] and Kondrath from practical theology.[7] Schein explores the ways and means by which founders embed organizational culture.[8] He shows that founder-owners and professional managers tend to differ in four key areas: motivational and emotional orientation, analytical orientation, interpersonal orientation, and structural/positional perspectives. Entrepreneurs subconsciously embed non-economic assumptions into the culture, which a professional manager will want to rationalize. This can create conflict as such rationalization may challenge perceived organizational culture.[9] Tashakori specifically employs the terminology of "entrepreneurial" and "professional" leadership style to posit that succession is not merely a change of person but invariably a change of leadership style.[10] Entrepreneurial style displays characteristics such as the leader's regular involvement in detail,

---

Development."

4. Andelson, "Postcharismatic Authority," 29–45.

5. Melton, "When Prophets Die," 1–12.

6. Tashakori, *Managerial Succession*; Schein, "Role of the Founder," 13–28.

7. Kondrath, "Transitioning from Charismatic Founder," 83–115.

8. Schein, "Role of the Founder," 13–28. Explained in chapter 3.

9. Balser and Carmin, "Leadership Succession," 185–201.

10. Tashakori, *Managerial Succession*.

little planning, reactive financial planning, little input from others, informal reward systems, and few formal control systems. If plans are devised and laid out, they are not followed or are often changed. Tashakori believes that the core characteristic is the involvement in detail which is the founder's "delegation contract."[11] Conversely, successors employed a professional leadership style, with characteristics such as written plans, fewer changes to plans, delegation to others, formal evaluations, a change from oral to written reporting, decisions based on empirical data rather than intuition, and formal structures: "The core characteristic of professional management is the professional manager's involvement in operations decisions by exception (that is to say, when there is a deviation from plan) rather than on a routine basis."[12] That founder succession is about change of style and not just person was confirmed by Kondrath in his study of founder succession in three Christian ministries.[13]

LEADERSHIP STYLE CHANGE WITHIN INTERNATIONAL AID SERVICES

The appointment of Daniel Zetterlund as successor to the founder of IAS may be viewed in a similar light to the analyses of Schein, Tashakori, and Kondrath, namely that of succession as transition from entrepreneurial to professional leadership. This assertion stems from seven factors.

First, Daniel Zetterlund applies an understanding of organizational life cycles to discern the stage of development and thus which actions were needed to allow not merely for continuation but "rebirth."[14]

> So this organizational rebirth, after 20, 25 years, very typical as well, I think in organizational development basis. You have that defining moment. Whenever you want to speed up into the next gear, if you don't address these issues that you've identified, you will probably start to decline. But if you do address them properly, you, maybe, will probably have rebirth and you can shoot off again in a new shape and form.[15]

11. Tashakori, *Managerial Succession*, 15.

12. Tashakori, *Managerial Succession*, 23.

13. Kondrath, "Transitioning from Charismatic Founder," 83–115.

14. For further understanding of organization life cycle, see Adizes, *Corporate Lifecycles*.

15. Daniel Zetterlund Interview I, 17.

Second, and in response to discerning the life cycle stage, Daniel Zetterlund embarked upon organizational audits to assess IAS's strengths and weaknesses. This showed strengths such as esprit de corps and strong relational connections between workers, but also significant deficiencies in "infrastructure and hardware. . . . But this exercise helped us to see why. Because we simply didn't like it! It was not part of our DNA as an organization necessarily."[16] Seeing such organizational resistance, external consultants were introduced, itself a move toward greater management professionalization. Such steps show professionalization as posited in Schein's change in analytical and motivational orientations and Tashakori's emphasis on empirical data in decision-making. There is, furthermore, a turning from an implicit agency theory, often prevalent in founder-led businesses. Agency theory states that there is a natural alignment of founder and agents (managers, staff) which decreases the need for formal supervision and governance mechanisms, thus reducing agency costs.[17] Daniel Zetterlund's stance, however, follows the contrary understandings of those who revealed that the lack of supervision in such alignments actually increases agency costs.[18] Daniel Zetterlund's change is a sign of professionalization through a different interpersonal orientation.[19]

This relates closely to a third professionalization marker, the emphasis of financial clarity and restructuration. The successor felt that due attention to such matters had been lacking. This had resulted in the impossibility of gaining a comprehensive understanding of the financial status of the global organization. This led to the realization that existent audits would henceforward be inadequate for the procurement of grants from the Swedish International Development Cooperation Agency (Sida) and the European Union. A decision was made to conduct a "fully consolidated audit"[20] and to pay a considerable fee for this to be completed. The founder balked at such expenditure, thus showing a value difference between founder and successor, and a shift in analytical orientation and structural perspectives (Schein). Rather than a mere pragmatic professional rationale, however, for the successor this was part of his service to God: "I want IAS to prosper; not for IAS's sake. But I think the Gospel, you know, deserves it. I think the Lord deserves better."[21]

16. Daniel Zetterlund Interview I, 16.

17. Poza, *Family Business*, 14.

18. Gomez-Mejía et al., "Role of Family Ties," 81–96.

19. Schein, "Role of the Founder," 13–28.

20. Daniel Zetterlund Interview I, 25.

21. Daniel Zetterlund Interview I, 28.

For Daniel Zetterlund, greater professionalization honors God, thus providing a theological rationale, not merely a managerial one.

A fourth marker was organizational culture shift. This may be seen in a number of matters: greater globally centralized leadership; increased reliance on and consolidation of procedures and documents;[22] and formalization of a truly international office rather than only national offices. This reflects Schein's structural/positional perspectives[23] and Tashakori's comments on both greater formality and the transition from oral to written reporting.[24]

Professionalization led, moreover, to change in corporate governance structures. IAS branches in the US, Denmark, Norway, Germany, and Sweden were each legally responsible for various matters, yet the implementation and decision-making in actuality resided with the Swedish office. This status was changed to provide the Swedish branch full legal ownership of IAS (international). The successor clarified that his status was as an employee of the organization, accountable to the board.[25] This change reflects Kondrath's recommendation that in order for Christian ministries to weather succession successfully, others must be involved in the change process, with a greater dissemination of ownership of the ministry. I suggest, furthermore, that Daniel Zetterlund's enhancement of board power is also a noted feature of founder succession power distribution change. Block and Rosenberg discerned that founders of charities led in different ways from non-founders; a larger percentage of founder leaders exercise greater influence and power than non-founders, including in matters such as reduced board meeting frequency and higher frequency of founders establishing board agendas and approving minutes before distribution.[26] Daniel Zetterlund's views on board authority are in accord with the professionalization in founder succession found by Block and Rosenberg.

A sixth marker of professionalization is the refined and focused strategy, evidenced in the *Fit for Purpose* document. The strategy sought to emphasize core values, which facilitated strategic decision-making:

> So, that strategy is framing the vision. It's not saying we will go to Libya tomorrow, but we're putting the framework of a

---

22. Daniel Zetterlund Interview I, 17–18. See also *Fit for Purpose*. For other documents, contact the organization.

23. Schein, "Role of the Founder," 13–28.

24. Tashakori, *Managerial Succession*.

25. Daniel Zetterlund Interview I, 18.

26. Block and Rosenberg, "Toward an Understanding of Founder's Syndrome," 353–68.

geographical expansion, we're putting the priorities here and those kinds of things. It means also we need to say "no" to things. If people want us to start programming in Zambia, we will say "thank you, but no thank you." Because our heart and passion and drive is for this region because in terms of spiritual needs, humanitarian needs, human rights needs, development needs, this is the area that we should focus on.[27]

A seventh and final factor in professionalization was the implementation of a corporate communications strategy in order to ensure that the global vision was clear and decisions were made in accordance with the strategy. The successor believed the prior lack of communication was a classic trait of new, entrepreneurial organizations:

> IAS, as an organization, has grown very organically. It is driven by a strong vision, but the vision is not necessarily communicated . . . It's been up to everyone to run their own thing, essentially. All these little countries popping up like mushrooms and little kingdoms, running their own bookkeeping systems, all their procedural stuff. And then, along the way, and this I think is very classical for organizations coming from a very strong family spirit into something, okay, you need to do something in order to enhance further growth.[28]

The development of enhanced communications was seen by Kondrath as a crucial need in second-generation leadership.[29]

While it is this book's position that IAS's succession was an enactment of greater professionalization, there are, however, a number of ways in which my study contradicts or extends current understandings of the change from entrepreneurial to professional leadership style. The literature might imply that the two styles are mutually dichotomous.[30] This seems particularly the case with Tashakori's findings that entrepreneurial founders are unstructured, lacking in clear plans and policies to achieve their goals, and especially likely to generate problems through over-involvement.[31] In the case of IAS, the founder had, however, created a functioning organization, with written goals, which had achieved much. Tashakori also found that founders were reluctant to relinquish leadership.[32] In the case of IAS, Leif

27. Daniel Zetterlund Interview I, 19–20.
28. Daniel Zetterlund Interview I, 16–17.
29. Kondrath, "Transitioning from Charismatic Founder," 83–115.
30. Tashakori, *Managerial Succession*; and Schein, "Role of the Founder," 13–28.
31. Tashakori, *Managerial Succession*, 30.
32. Tashakori, *Managerial Succession*, especially 35–40.

Zetterlund was aware of the need to do so, acknowledging that the cultural and political environments of 2014 were different from those of 1989:

> So, and I think if you talk a structural—I think this is where you have a difference between a well-organized organization that doesn't have this kind of background as ours. Uh, everything is in writing. Everything is very structured, well worked on, well, well, well documented. I—I think that is part of our weaknesses under my leadership, that everything was not documented, and he has picked up on that and put it in proper systems.[33]

Indeed, for his founding creation to expand and be more effective, Leif Zetterlund knew a different leadership approach was necessary:

> So, I could see that bringing in somebody from that point of view, now when bureaucracy is becoming a number one thing for donors and partners and systems must be in place, it might be a very healthy thing for the organization in order to grow forward, grow both in depth and what also be able to—to—to actually spread out to other countries as well.[34]

In two further areas, moreover, IAS succession did not reflect the findings of other succession literature, namely that the post-succession relationship between founder and successor was absent of the many problems in other post-succession relationships,[35] and that an internal appointment resulted nonetheless in change of style. This is contrary to findings that "longtime executives have a propensity to adopt the owner/founder's style of management."[36]

A closer examination of the successor shows, furthermore, that professionalization need not imply an undue reliance on bureaucracy and administration. Daniel Zetterlund was appointed precisely because he also possessed visionary insight.[37] Daniel's faith, including belief in God's speaking to Christians today through thoughts, ideas, and even specific intervening prophecies, is a constitutive factor in Daniel Zetterlund's vision. This matter is treated by Edwards with his thesis that bureaucracy is violence and that the Christian message of peace runs contrary to bureaucratic totalizing[38] and subverts the controlling norms of bureaucracy. While there

33. Leif Zetterlund Interview I, 16.
34. Leif Zetterlund Interview I, 9.
35. Tashakori, *Managerial Succession*, 64–70.
36. Tashakori, *Managerial Succession*, 107.
37. Leif Zetterlund Interview I, 5, 19; Daniel Zetterlund Interview II, 18.
38. Edwards, "Violence of Bureaucracy," 211.

is much in Edwards which shows the negative impact of bureaucracy, Edwards, however, overly reifies bureaucratic structures as inherently evil, for there is "an unquestioned expectation that formal procedures are the best imaginable means of solving particular issues. In all such processes, there is an invalid application of the principle which veers towards pervasive formal control."[39] In the case of IAS, I argue that increased professionalization enhanced their ministry.

The successor's clear belief in God's speaking to his people motivates his enthusiasm for his work as well as provides ideas for specific strategies:

> I'm looking at Lebanon, Syria, Libya, Sudan. And I live in Morocco now. That's a different story. But there are so many visions and dreams and prophecies on how the whole region will just be swept across from the far west, which is Morocco, to the Far East, probably somewhere down in Indonesia, right? So very exciting times.[40]

The spiritual and visionary nature of Daniel Zetterlund's leadership may also be seen in his receiving a prophetic utterance from an intercessor concerning how IAS should "dig deeper" in its ministry. The prophetic *ipsissima verba* were used to frame and title a funding campaign for borehole drilling in Africa called "We Dig Deeper."[41] The successor's vision is not merely to continue the work of IAS but to become a significant organization within the international development and evangelical missionary sector, bridging both organizational fields.

While stating that IAS's founder succession enacted entrepreneurial to professional leadership style change, this should not be perceived in terms of binary opposites but that both founder and successor find their place on a continuum, where both display aspects of entrepreneurial as well as professional leadership style.

The change of leadership style has, moreover, served IAS well. Applying Greiner's widely supported theory of evolutionary and revolutionary stages in an organization's development, Daniel Zetterlund's markers of professionalization comport with Greiner's "coordination" stage (for example, more centralized governance and coordination of decision-making).[42] An organization in such a phase tends to require the kinds of changes Daniel Zetterlund introduced in management style. That such professionalization was necessary may be seen in the changing nature of Sida funding, no

---

39. Edwards, "Violence of Bureaucracy," 199.

40. Daniel Zetterlund Interview I, 11.

41. See chapter 14, note 1.

42. Greiner, "Evolution and Revolution," 350–51.

longer to individual organizations but to "framework organizations" who, in turn, redistribute funds. The Swedish government now grants funds to the Swedish Missionary Council, of which IAS is a member. Indeed, it was not long before IAS began to receive more money from the Swedish Missionary Council than any other group.[43] The greater professionalization of IAS has meant that the ministry may take advantage of such funding opportunities.

I have stated that Christian organizations tend to fear a loss of spiritual values and of becoming overly routinized, replacing their founding charisma with a more bureaucratized management. The case of IAS shows that, at times, a greater professionalization of leadership can benefit the organization and enable it to take advantage of fresh opportunities.

43. Daniel Zetterlund Interview I, 32.

Chapter Seventeen

Succession as Apostolic Multiplication

THE TITLE MIGHT APPEAR odd to some, wondering why an examination of contemporary organizational succession might reflect on apostles. Perhaps those with some theological education may be familiar with the term "apostolic succession." A simple definition can be found in the *Oxford Encyclopedic English Dictionary*, for example, as "the uninterrupted transmission of spiritual authority from the Apostles through successive popes and other bishops."[1] Vastly more complicated definitions may be found elsewhere, and multiples volumes have been written on this topic; these, however, may not detain us here. For a brief yet fuller understanding of the doctrine of apostolic succession as a central tenet of, for example, the Roman Catholic Church, the reader is referred to Neuner.[2] In this chapter, however, we are not dealing with this doctrine as usually understood as legitimating the authority of contemporary popes and bishops. This chapter reflects on those new church movements, called restorationist, who believe that the gift of apostleship is still valid and extant today. For groups holding to such an understanding of apostles, leadership succession, especially from the founder of a movement, can be seen as an act of continuing and multiplying apostles. This chapter seeks briefly to outline this theological perspective, before examining how one of the case studies, namely Newfrontiers, enacted succession according to

1. *Oxford Encyclopedic English Dictionary*, 62.
2. Neuner, "Apostolic Succession," 335–39.

the belief that they were multiplying apostolic appointments. Such theology affects how succession is conceived, planned, and executed. For those restorationist networks which began in the 1970s and 1980s, founder succession is a recent phenomenon. Kay, in his work on apostolic networks in Britain, writes, "The next major challenge facing almost all the networks is to find the right person to fill the shoes of their founding apostle."[3] As if following Kay's cue, Newfrontiers planned and enacted founder succession in the following years. It is restorationist theology that shaped and defined Newfrontiers' understanding of leadership and therefore of succession; it is more specifically the theology of apostleship that is crucial for an analysis of that succession.

Within the broader church, apostleship is a disputed doctrine. Many churches have no official doctrinal position on whether the office of apostle continues today.[4] In contrast, most churches in the reformed tradition are adamant that this gift was extinguished after the first apostles of Scripture: "The officers which Christ hath appointed for the edification of his church, and the perfecting of the saints, are, some extraordinary, as apostles, evangelists, and prophets, which are ceased."[5] Catholicism since Vatican II, however, addresses the matter in stark contradistinction to both reformed theology and restorationism. In Catholicism, all lay people are part of the apostolate,[6] and the laity have the "right and duty to be apostles."[7]

In the last few decades, however, the new networks of churches have reintroduced the doctrine of the ongoing apostolic gift but with a more restricted understanding than Catholicism; indeed, it is almost the primary doctrine around which much else in restorationism coalesces: "Sociologically and theologically what is distinctive about the networks is their concentration upon the ministry of the apostle."[8] This coincides with and is indeed part of a broader global phenomenon of newer networks propagating the ongoing office of apostle. Wagner presents cases of eighteen new networks (thirteen in the US, five in other nations) under the title, *The New Apostolic Churches: Rediscovering the New Testament Model of Leadership and Why It Is God's Desire for the Church Today*.[9] Indeed, so crucial is the theology of apostleship that of the nine factors which Wagner believes to

3. Kay, *Apostolic Networks*, 350.

4. See McNair Scott, *Apostles Today*, for an analysis of the conceptualizations of the apostolate throughout history.

5. This example is from the Free Church (Continuing), http://www.freechurchcontinuing.org/about/government.

6. Second Vatican Council, *Lumen Gentium*, 33.

7. Paul VI, *Apostolicam Actuositatem*, 3.

8. Kay, *Apostolic Networks*, 292.

9. Wagner, *New Apostolic Churches*.

be characteristic of the new apostolic churches, it is the concept of apostleship which is the primary defining characteristic: "In my judgment, views
of leadership and leadership authority constitute the most radical of the
nine changes from traditional Christianity. Here is the main difference: *The
amount of spiritual authority delegated by the Holy Spirit to individuals*."[10] He
states, "We are seeing a transition from bureaucratic authority to personal
authority, from legal structure to relational structure, from control to coordination and from rational leadership to charismatic leadership."[11]

This cardinal point of restorationist doctrine has not merely influenced
other denominations but also, to varying degrees, it has been adopted by
them. It is advocated in influential works on contemporary church planting
and mission from multiple church and theological traditions.[12] McNair Scott,
in his study of the charismatic apostolate in the United Kingdom, concludes

> In summary, the charismatic apostolate is becoming a feature of
> the church scene in Britain; this will not be a short-lived fad, but
> rather something that will remain commonplace in the inde-
> pendent churches and become more so in the older mainstream
> ones. The desire for mission, for a new shape of leader, for more
> organic expressions of church life will make it inconceivable
> that the charismatic apostolate in its various guises will disap-
> pear from the scene.[13]

APOSTLESHIP WITHIN NEWFRONTIERS

What is apostleship within Newfrontiers, and how can succession occur
from the founding apostle? These questions frame this analysis of Newfrontiers' succession. It should be noted that, even within restorationism,
Newfrontiers has the most monolithic belief in contemporary apostolic
ministry. Based on Kay's quantitative research on British networks, Newfrontiers adherents were "significantly more likely to accept the importance
of apostle" than other restorationist networks; in particular, moreover,
they "were significantly more likely to accept the importance of apostolic
networks."[14]

10. Wagner, *New Apostolic Churches*, 19–20 (italics in original).

11. Wagner, *New Apostolic Churches*, 19.

12. McNair Scott in his work *Apostles Today* cites the following examples: Gibbs,
Leadership Next; Frost and Hirsch, *Shaping of Things to Come*; Murray-Williams,
Church after Christendom.

13. McNair Scott, *Apostles Today*, 219.

14. Kay, *Apostolic Networks*, 319.

For Virgo, the movement's founding apostle, this theology developed through praxis. In describing his work in the early years, he writes that he was involved in the "planting and overseeing of scattered local churches, laying foundations of truth, and providing ongoing love and care. I was increasingly gathering a team of men who also served those churches. In the New Testament this was what apostles did."[15] Virgo dedicates a chapter in his work on church restoration to apostleship.[16] My analysis of this writing is that there are six key characteristics. First, Virgo sees three classes of apostle: Jesus, the twelve, and others belonging in the class referred to in Eph 4:8–11 ("He gave some as apostles").[17] Secondly, with regard to drawing upon Scripture, Virgo refers to his being a "master builder and foundation layer," citing 1 Cor 3:10.[18] This leads to a third observation, namely that a primary purpose is to hold churches to correct doctrine: "One of God's great provisions to safeguard his church from going astray is a continuing apostolic ministry."[19] Fourthly, Virgo states that such a gift can only operate if there is relationship with those being overseen; there can be no imposed authority. Fifthly, apostolic ministry transcends boundaries, including national boundaries; and sixthly, apostles emerge as "they are brought out by the sovereign choice and anointing of God."[20]

Concerning specific roles of apostles, Virgo posits the following: helping church leaders apply truths and providing wisdom in decision-making; recognizing and installing leaders in a church, which is enacted by recognizing others' gifts and the respect in which these men are held in their congregation;[21] going to new places to pioneer new works;[22] and bringing others onto "apostolic teams." Such teams can facilitate others utilizing their spiritual gifts and providing experience for other "embryonic apostles."[23]

Devenish, one of Virgo's successors in apostolic ministry, defines the roles of the apostle in the New Testament in similar terms: planting and

15. Virgo, *No Well-Worn Paths*, 98. In the theology of Newfrontiers, apostleship and other gifts of church government are exclusively male. Such gender issues will be treated more fully in chapter 21.

16. Virgo, *Restoration in the Church*, 125–36.

17. Virgo cites on more than one occasion, and seems particularly influenced by, J. B. Lightfoot (Lightfoot, *St. Paul's Epistle*) in his understanding of the continuance of the apostolic gift (see, for example, Virgo, *Restoration in the Church*, 126–27).

18. Virgo, *Restoration in the Church*, 128.

19. Virgo, *Restoration in the Church*, 129.

20. Virgo, *Restoration in the Church*, 132.

21. Virgo, *Restoration in the Church*, 131.

22. Virgo, *Restoration in the Church*, 131–32.

23. Virgo, *Restoration in the Church*, 135.

laying foundations in churches; appointing elders in churches; moving to unreached areas and involving the church in mission; bringing wisdom in difficult situations. To this, however, he introduces the conceptualization that apostles must ensure that the poor are served.[24] Devenish writes of the fathering heart of the apostle. As with Virgo, he cites 1 Cor 3:10; the conceptualization therefrom of apostles as builders is a main theme: "By the grace God has given me, I laid a foundation as an expert builder, and someone else is building on it. But each one should be careful how he builds."[25]

APOSTOLIC SUCCESSION

The complexity of the succession with Newfrontiers is made more evident in considering a number of matters concerning apostleship. First, Newfrontiers' theology does not allow for the "creation" of apostles by humans; it is a "sovereign choice and anointing of God."[26] Secondly, and following from this first point, thus "there is no apostolic succession."[27] This leads to a belief that in a sense there is no second generation; the future of Newfrontiers must always be God's raising new apostles who will always be their first generation of God's fresh work. As Devenish states,

> My contention is that "apostolic succession" in the traditional sense is not the way forward, but rather that each generation should be like a first-generation church in its life and organization, while maintaining the foundation built on the truth laid down by the original apostles and prophets or what Jude, as we have already seen, described as "the faith that was once for all entrusted to the saints."[28]

A third crucial perspective is that there is no scriptural framework for succession: "The original apostles, it seems, envisaged the body of New Testament doctrine being passed on to subsequent generations, but they give no specific instructions as to how any succession to their apostolic

---

24. Devenish, *What on Earth Is the Church for?*, 65–66.

25. Devenish, *Fathering Leaders*, 87. Discussion on further complexities surrounding an understanding of the apostle as builder and how such a conceptualization affects succession appears in chapter 26.

26. Virgo, *Restoration in the Church*, 132.

27. Virgo, *Restoration in the Church*, 133. It is difficult to know if at this point Virgo states this position against the backdrop of the Roman Catholic understanding of succession as a negative example. He certainly states this explicitly in Interview I, 28.

28. Devenish, *Fathering Leaders*, 335.

office should take place."[29] Thus, Newfrontiers could approach the decision and structuration of succession with freedom, not looking to follow biblical models. While not viewing their succession as normative for others,[30] but contingent on contextual factors, particularly that of organizational size,[31] others have proffered Newfrontiers' approach as an ideal type.[32]

Fourthly, it is in succession in particular that the role of apostle as "father" is activated:

> In practice, leaders today need not only a written record of the example of fathering leadership in the first century, but actual spiritual fathers. And each church needs to express Christian family relationships and to be joined with those who can serve them both by caring for them and by involving them in world mission. This needs to take place dynamically and relationally in each generation, through those anointed by the Holy Spirit for this task. The apostolic and prophetic foundations need to be laid dynamically in each generation, always consistent with the truth set out in the pages of the New Testament but contextualized in each generation and location.[33]

Succession in Newfrontiers is thus familial, pioneering, and not wedded to the founding generation's contextualized structures.

Fifthly, while succession does not seek a man or men to replace the founder, it must, however, include recognition of new apostles: "We need to recognize those with an apostolic call who will need to function in the next generation, because churches will continue to want to be related to and served by such ministries."[34] It was this recognition of "new" apostles which led to the appointment of fifteen men, each with his own autonomous sphere:

> We aim to imitate the New Testament practice of travelling ministries of apostles and prophets, with *apostles having their own spheres* of responsibility as a result of having planted and laid the foundations in the churches they oversee. Such ministries continue the connection with local churches as a result of fatherly relationship and not denominational election or appointment.[35]

---

29. Devenish, *Fathering Leaders*, 335.
30. Devenish Interview II, 26.
31. Virgo Interview II, 20.
32. Pugh, "Succession Plans," 129.
33. Devenish, *Fathering Leaders*, 335–36.
34. Devenish, *Fathering Leaders*, 336.
35. Devenish, *Fathering Leaders*, 33 (italics mine).

To summarize, founder succession within Newfrontiers took place from founding apostle to other apostles, but not as direct apostolic succession as understood through church history. Succession was the recognition of men who were planting and overseeing churches, teaching biblical doctrine and "building" the church across boundaries. While they may be trained, they were not "made" by Virgo and team; all the founder and team could do was to recognize and announce those already engaged in apostolic ministry. Thus, succession in Newfrontiers was a form of apostolic succession but one reconceptualized through contemporary restorationist understanding of the apostolic gift and ministry.

DISCUSSION

There is much around the Newfrontiers conceptualization of apostleship that is problematic. Several aspects on this will be discussed more fully in chapter 26, including the power in the installation of apostles that Virgo and others yielded to congregants, without so knowing. Here I wish to draw attention to the lack of clarity concerning the characteristics which identify a man as apostle. Newfrontiers' theology suggests we are to look for a "father" and a "master builder," but there is no definition of what these terms mean and how a master builder is to be recognized, except perhaps later when there is an obvious edifice. There is, furthermore, a lack of clarity on the difference between an apostle and the more general term "leader." Are all leaders apostles? We presume not, but what exactly is the difference? Surely, there are many characteristics that might apply both to someone viewed as an "apostle" and the more general term of "leader," such as setting goals, communicating direction, and seeking to take people with him/her on a venture. There is a lack of definition concerning the differences between apostle and leader, even more in reflection on the term "father," for it is possible to be a spiritual father, to love and nurture people, and not be an apostle. Perhaps the emphasis on "foundation" might be one aspect that provides a crucial distinctive characteristic. Indeed, the lack of differential definition between "apostle" and "leader" is in line with one of the main criticisms of charismatic theory; Sashkin asks the question whether charismatic leadership is a different Gestalt from other "ordinary" leadership, as this is theoretically unclear.[36]

A second problematic characteristic of apostolic multiplication by recognition is the overlooking of the role of the founder. For an emerging apostle to have the opportunity for recognition by the people, he may need

---

36. Sashkin, "Structure of Charismatic Leadership," 217.

to receive training and be allowed a place to exercise his gifts.[37] It is possible that there were gifted but not known apostles and for whom an environment was not created for their gifts to be recognized. This speaks to the crucial role of the founder in the model of apostolic multiplication by recognition. This critical nature of the founder's role in ensuring transference of charismatic authority was clearly seen in the groundbreaking study of Trice and Beyer, who showed the necessity for the founder to diffuse charisma among the members through rites, to produce written and oral traditions that sustain the leadership's message over time, and to establish norms and reference points for use in testimonies and the rearticulation of the vision.[38]

Thirdly, the concept of "apostle" does not take into account environmental and contextual factors. Is it as possible for the people to recognize the apostolic gift in a society where the church is latent and perhaps does not even meet publicly compared to a nation where there is freedom of religion and large conferences at which those with apostolic gifts are seen by many? Furthermore, charismatic leadership theory suggests that such leadership is more likely to be enacted and recognized in times of distress.[39] The founding of Newfrontiers by Virgo came at a time of retrenchment in much of the British church, with declining attendance and where the context facilitated the articulation of a compelling and competing vision differentiated from broader social trends. During less turbulent times, the recognition of an apostolic/charismatic leader may be more difficult.

For those who believe in the contemporaneous gift of apostleship, leadership succession is less about an organizational leader; succession is constructed in almost exclusively theological terms. Successful leaders of the movement must be recognized by current apostles as having the gift of apostleship, and this is to be endorsed and confirmed by the fruit of the gifts, namely others following them. With such a theology, Newfrontiers was able to move beyond the need to find a single replacement for Terry Virgo, but to appoint and release many new apostles. This, however, was not without its problems, as shown in chapter 20 and elsewhere.

---

37. Conger and Kanungo, *Charismatic Leadership*, 32.

38. Trice and Beyer "Charisma and its Routinization," 125–38.

39. Weber, *Theory of Social and Economic Organization*; House, "1976 Theory of Charismatic Leadership," 203–4.

Chapter Eighteen ───────────

Keeping It in the Family
Founder Succession from Father to Son

IN MANY AREAS OF life, succession is an intrafamilial phenomenon. This is perhaps most obviously in the world of business, where family businesses and their successions are all around us. According to figures available from the Family Owned Business Institute of Grand Valley State University in the US, there were (in 2011) 5.5 million family businesses in the US, which contributed some 57 percent of the US's Gross Domestic Product and employed 63 percent of the workforce.[1] The outperformance of family firms globally is demonstrated by a 6.65 percent difference in return on assets in the US, and at least an 8 percent difference in Europe and Chile, compared to businesses which are not family owned. Many family businesses enact succession from parent to child or children, traditionally from father to son,[2] although there are now also many cases of father-daughter succession.[3] Father-child leadership succession is also often replicated in churches and Christian ministries, particularly in the US. However, patterned after such American examples, intrafamilial leader and founder succession is also found in Pentecostal movements outside the US.[4]

1. All statistics in this paragraph from Family Owned Business Institute, "Family Firm Facts."

2. Ward, *Keeping the Family Business Healthy*; Poza, *Family Business.*

3. Halkias et al., *Father-Daughter Succession.* A fuller reflection on issues related to gender and succession is found in chapter 21.

4. Tushima, "Leadership Succession Patterns."

This chapter will seek a tripartite examination of the paternal-filial nature of a succession: first, by suggesting an interpretative framework drawing on business studies, ethics, theology, and psychology; second, by providing an exogenous and endogenous problematizing of the father-son succession enacted in one of the detailed case studies, namely International Aid Services; and third, by seeking to understand and evaluate that specific succession in light of the framework proposed above.

INTERPRETATIVE FRAMEWORK

Family Business

IAS was an organization in which several family members were involved, including occupying paid positions within the charity. As family business is common in many societies, research into family business succession may help inform the familial nature of IAS's succession. While larger companies may well look outside the organization for succession, as fewer people have the skills needed for larger corporate leadership, father-son succession within family enterprises is common.[5] Indeed, father-son succession is often expected by the family and employees.[6] Within a family business, succession may, nonetheless, be problematic. Contributing factors may include incongruent hierarchies between business and family;[7] poor intrafamilial communication;[8] founders remaining in post too long;[9] disharmonious relationship between father and son,[10] of which the life stage of the protagonists may be influential;[11] and lack of acknowledgment that title, power, control, and responsibility should transfer simultaneously.[12]

Notwithstanding the above, paternal-filial succession within business may be successfully navigated when certain factors are present: the business enacts resource-based strategies, where there is realistic understanding of and

5. Ward, *Keeping the Family Business Healthy*; Cabrera-Suarez et al., "Succession Process," 37–47; Poza, *Family Business*.

6. Poza, *Family Business*, 122–24.

7. Poza, *Family Business*, 58; Barnes and Kaftan, *Organizational Transitions*, 119–26 and 134–47.

8. Poza et al., "Changing the Family Business," 311–23; Habbershon and Astrachan, "Perceptions Are Reality," 37–52.

9. Barnes and Kaftan, *Organizational Transitions*, 153; Daily and Dollinger, "Empirical Examination," 117–36.

10. Dyck et al., "Passing the Baton," 143–62.

11. Davis and Tagiuri, "Influence of Life-Stage," 47–76.

12. Dyck et al., "Passing the Baton," 149.

exploitation of strengths;[13] appropriate professional governance structures;[14] the fortuitous age of the founder (for example, founders in their forties tend not to see company problems they have created, but they do when they are older);[15] the age-affected dyadic relationship between father and son (Davis and Tagiuri show that the relationship tends to be most harmonious when the father is in his fifties and the son between twenty-three and thirty-three, but more problematic when the father is in his sixties and the son thirty-four to forty);[16] mutual agreement concerning timing of transference;[17] and role of founder. Sonnenfeld and Spence provided researchers with a fourfold typology of founder role in succession (monarch, general, ambassador, and governor),[18] to which Poza has added "inventor" and "transition czar."[19] Literature concurs that the monarch and general role do not provide for good succession (that is, not releasing responsibility or even regaining power subsequent to succession).[20] I will later suggest that in the case of International Aid Services, Leif Zetterlund's conduct was of the ambassador type.

Public Ethics

A second matter which may contribute to a framework in which to analyze IAS's father-son succession is that of public ethics. In modern liberal democracies, there may be a suspicion of father-son succession, commonly viewed as nepotism; that is, "the practice of appointing relatives to situations of emolument, in disregard of the claims of others better fitted for the offices."[21] A meritocratic society values appointments according to talent rather than familial connections. Prevailing suspicion of familial appointments by public officials has, furthermore, led to such appointments being unlawful in public offices in many countries.[22] Indeed, such was international concern about nepotistic appointments that when, in 2018, Turkish

13. Cabrera-Suarez et al., "Succession Process," 37–47.

14. Poza, *Family Business*, 25.

15. Poza et al., "Family-Business Interaction," 99–118.

16. Davis and Tagiuri, "Influence of Life-Stage," 47–76.

17. Dyck et al., "Passing the Baton," 149.

18. Sonnenfeld and Spence, "Parting Patriarch of a Family Firm," 355–75.

19. Poza, *Family Business*, 27–33.

20. Daily and Dollinger, "Empirical Examination," 117–36; Poza, *Family Business*.

21. *Webster's Dictionary*, 1205.

22. In the US, for example, it is forbidden under US code 5 USC 3110 (b). Available at https://www.govinfo.gov/content/pkg/USCODE-2010-title5/html/USCODE-2010-title5-partIII-subpartB-chap31-subchapI-sec3110.htm.

president Erdogan appointed his son-in-law as finance minister, the national currency lost 3 percent of its value;[23] the interfamilial appointment was still causing problems years later.[24]

Empirical and Systematic Theology

Despite concerns about nepotism in government, father-son founder succession in large and in international Christian ministries is common (certainly in the US). The following table shows some well-known international ministries or megachurches where a son succeeded his father in leadership.

Organization	Father	Son	Year of Succession
Crystal Cathedral Ministries, California[25]	Robert H. Schuller	Robert A. Schuller	2006
Oral Roberts Ministries, Oklahoma[26]	Oral Roberts	Richard Roberts	2006
Global Advance, Texas[27]	David Shibley	Jonathan Shibley	2010
Liberty University, Virginia[28]	Jerry Falwell Sr.	Jerry Falwell Jr.	2007
Lakewood Church, Texas[29]	John Osteen	Joel Osteen	1999
Bethany World Prayer Center, Louisiana[30]	Roy Stockstill	Larry Stockstill, who in turn transferred leadership to his son, Jonathan	2011 (latest transition)
Christ Fellowship Church, Florida[31]	Tom Mullins	Todd Mullins	2011

Father to Son Successions

23. BBC, "Turkey's Erdogan Son-in-Law."

24. Deutche Welle, "Erdogan's Son-in-Law Resigns."

25. Lavietes, "Rev. Robert Schuller"; Lobdell and Landsberg, "Rev. Robert H. Schuller."

26. Richard Roberts Ministries, "Our History"; Richard Roberts Ministries. "Our Mission."

27. Global Advance, "Global Advance President and Founder;" correspondence with founder, August 27, 2018 (cited with permission).

28. Peterson, "Case Study."

29. Lakewood Church, "Our History."

30. Hunter, "Bethany Church Grows."

31. Mullins, *Passing the Leadership Baton.*

Many fathers such as Mullins[32] and Shibley[33] as well as the successor sons such as Osteen[34] claim that their succession was successful. Mullins asserts that the son being known to key stakeholders is helpful in that his strengths may be released, but the organization will know his limitations and how to mitigate them; the son is likely to be committed to the mission and culture of the organization.

Paternal-filial transitions in Christian ministries are not, however, immune from difficulty, even painful failure. Those enacting father-son successions within Christian ministries may benefit from awareness of the following factors. There should be a similar vision and way of operating, a factor seen in the aborted succession of Charles Stanley, senior pastor of First Baptist Church, Atlanta, to Andy Stanley. The father had announced that he would be succeeded by his son; during the transition preparations, the son noted that he had both a different directional vision and way of operation from his father; he thus aborted the succession,[35] causing pain to many.[36] Full authority, furthermore, must be transferred from father to son. The lack of authority transference has notably been problematic when Robert H. Schuller in 2006 transferred leadership of the Crystal Cathedral and associated *Hour of Power* broadcasting to his son, Robert A. Schuller. In 2008 the father reasserted his own leadership of the ministry, stating, "For this lack of shared vision and the jeopardy in which this is placing this entire ministry, it has become necessary for Robert and me to part ways."[37] The son's explanations were that his father did not release power, there was no formal agreement, and that sibling rivalries complicated the matter.[38] These explanations seem little different from the findings of Barnes both on fathers resuming power and sibling rivalry complicating succession in family businesses.[39]

Robert A. Schuller's comments point, furthermore, to the need for a clear plan accepted by all key stakeholders. Moreover, theological assumptions are better articulated and agreed. Due to the prevalence of many well-known Christian leaders transferring leadership to children, Schenck, a well-known leader in American evangelicalism, believes father-son

32. Mullins, *Passing the Leadership Baton*.

33. Correspondence with founder, Aug 27, 2018 (cited with permission).

34. https://www.lakewoodchurch.com/about/history.

35. Mullins, *Passing the Leadership Baton*, 73–74.

36. Blake, "Two Preaching Giants."

37. Associated Press, "'Hour of Power' Preacher Removed by Father," para. 3.

38. Mullins, *Passing the Leadership Baton*, 8–9.

39. Barnes, "Incongruent Hierarchies," 212.

transition may be viewed as a sign of God's special blessing. This may, however, cause painful reactions within a son who does not wish to follow his father. Such an expectation, Schenck admits, caused "rupture" in his own family.[40]

Even if the son wishes and is qualified to succeed his father, it does not necessarily entail that the succession is free of problems. Sons may feel they need to be like their father, and indeed others may expect that of them. This may hamper effective leadership unless the son is able to enact healthy differentiation and individuation. This is illustrated by Joel Osteen, successor to his father at the megachurch Lakewood Church in Texas:

> When I first started preaching, I thought I had to have a long opening text with forty support scriptures, like my dad. And during the week I thought I had to walk the halls and talk to everyone like he did. These things didn't suit my personality, though, and I struggled to find a balance between who I really was and who everyone expected me to.[41]

Eventually Osteen needed to individuate in order to lead: "Some people didn't stand with me, but I had a strength from God to say, 'You will not pigeon-hole me into being who you want me to be: I will be who God wants me to be.'"[42] Jerry Falwell Jr. at Liberty University speaks in similar terms: "I had to break everyone of the notion that everything would be done just the way Dad did it. You have to be yourself . . . don't try to copy other people."[43] Similarly, in family business research, Barnes found that successor children, in order to flourish in their new roles, needed to develop both a new self-identity as well as a new identity in the eyes of others around them.[44]

Despite the number of Christian organizations enacting father-son transition, there seems to be relatively little theological, rather than organizational, reflection on this matter. Tushima provides, however, one such theological reflection. He studied contemporary leadership succession patterns in Pentecostal and charismatic churches and movements. Tushima believes that succession to a son, or indeed other family members including a spouse, is common in such movements, focusing his work on the African context, which he believes took American Pentecostal succession as its model. Indeed, American Pentecostalism is replete with father-son

40. Schenck, *Costly Grace*, 46–47.

41. Interview, Feb 19, 2013, cited in Mullins, *Passing the Leadership Baton*, 109.

42. Interview, Feb 19, 2013, cited in Mullins, *Passing the Leadership Baton*, 109.

43. Interview, Feb 18, 2013, cited in Mullins, *Passing the Leadership Baton*, 110.

44. Barnes, "Incongruent Hierarchies," 215.

transitions[45] such as Kenneth E. Hagin to his son, Kenneth Hagin Jr.[46] African examples cited are the succession in the Church of God Mission International in Nigeria from Benson Idahosa to both his wife and son (1998) as well as succession within New Anointing Ministry from Godwin Ikyernum, first to his wife and then to his son, Joshua.[47] Tushima posits that much of Pentecostalism has a social inferiority complex. He sees the emphasis of the prosperity gospel and the amassing of wealth as an attempt by Pentecostals for social advancement; when this is successful and ministries acquire significant assets, financial concerns induce leaders to place confidants around them. This environment leads toward only trusting family members and hence family preferment. This is supported by Ngomane who shows the extent to which African charismatic movements concentrate on fundraising rather than the development of leaders.[48]

Tushima's conclusions are that Jesus established collegial leadership based on the gifts of his followers; others in the New Testament were appointed to lead on the basis of doctrine, character, and the traditions handed down by the apostles (1 Tim 3:1–13; Titus 1:5–9) and not "familial affiliation."[49] He sees no evidence that either Christ or the early apostles and sub-apostolic leaders made familial appointments.[50] He believes that a change from collegial leadership to "sole proprietary managerial leadership patterns" correlates with family succession.[51] In summary, "Following in the example of Jesus, familial affiliation should not be the criterion for advancing in the leadership hierarchy, leading to succession in a Christian ministry setting."[52] What Tushima does not explore, however, is whether appropriate character or gift and family connection are mutually exclusive categories; this leaves ambiguity in his position. While not explicitly stating their exclusivity, his reiteration of comments on finding no family connections in biblical and apostolic successions and by juxtaposing this with stating that family connection was not the criterion for appointment leaves a putative interpretation that family membership is an exclusionary characteristic per se. It could be, on the other hand, that he does leave open the possibility that a family member may be a successor as long as the relationship is not the

45. Robins, *Pentecostalism in America*, 131.

46. Tushima, "Leadership Succession Patterns," 6.

47. Tushima, "Leadership Succession Patterns," 7.

48. Ngomane, "Leadership Mentoring."

49. Tushima, "Leadership Succession Patterns," 6.

50. Tushima, "Leadership Succession Patterns," 6.

51. Tushima, "Leadership Succession Patterns," 7.

52. Tushima, "Leadership Succession Patterns," 7.

ratio decidendi for the succession. While Tushima is unclear in this regard, I argue that it is indeed possible for a son also to display the qualities for Christian leadership that Tushima advocates as the criteria for succession; thus, relationship and character are not mutually exclusive categories.

Psychoanalytical Perspectives—Oedipus or Orestes?

In seeking to draw from theoretical understandings of father-son succession to be able better to analyze IAS's succession, attention is also turned to the field of psychoanalysis, particularly the work of Eisold, previously outlined in chapter 2 and repeated here.[53] Eisold attempts a psychoanalytical reflection of the dynamics of succession, noting that, since Freud, succession has been seen in the light of the Oedipus drama of father-son conflict and power usurpation; successors are destined to live in guilt about overcoming their predecessors and not to go beyond their achievements. Eisold suggests that we have been interpreting succession with an inadequate metaphor (Oedipal)[54] and ignored the more helpful one of Orestes,[55] where there is a communal and political element to the succession development, as seen in the establishment of the first court of law and jury to judge the deeds of Orestes and discern who is to succeed. Thus, succession and justice are determined not by the predecessor and successor but by a more dispassionate organ from the community. Eisold applies this to modern institutional succession, suggesting that we consider three matters: the creation of a mechanism to permit others to make impartial judgments on behalf of the community; the recognition of the emotions of those involved in succession, which necessitates the above mechanism so that irrational emotions do not dominate the succession process; and that we take into account the broader social and economic milieu in which the organization undergoing succession locates itself. Eisold suggests one practical application of the establishment of a search committee for an institution's successor that represents the interests of different stakeholders. For Eisold, the Orestes model "offers a more complex and promising view of the intergenerational transfer of leadership and authority" with the introduction by Athena of the first court of law to decide intrafamilial matters.[56]

53. Eisold, "Succeeding at Succession," 619–32.

54. Sophocles, *Oedipus the King.*

55. Aeschylus, *Eumenides.*

56. Eisold, "Succeeding at Succession," 619. While not a classicist, Eisold's interpretation of the establishment of impartial mechanisms for justice and decision-making is consistent with renowned classicists such as Thomson, *Aeschylus and Athens*, 259, and

EXOGENOUS AND ENDOGENOUS PROBLEMATIZING OF THE ENACTMENT OF IAS FATHER-SON SUCCESSION

Having framed this topic with reference to business, ethics, theology, and psychology, an attempt will be made at both an exogenous and endogenous problematizing of the paternal-filial succession enacted within IAS, before seeking evaluation according to the aforementioned framework.

Exogenous Problems

The most significant exogenous problem the ministry faced was that of judgment from others concerning nepotism. The leadership of IAS took this potential, imputed nepotism into account through a number of strategies.

There was full recognition of potential accusations. Referring to father-son succession, Leif Zetterlund remarks, "And uh, in America, it's not very unusual, but in Sweden, it is almost a crime. . . . So it's extremely sensitive and we wanted to avoid any kind of nepotism here, as much as it was ever possible."[57] This sensitivity continues post-succession:

> We have always tried to kill the kind of rumor of family orga-
> nization because it is not, but it could be seen as that. We, of
> course, have been a hundred percent aware of this. So, a . . . we
> are very careful in how to handle that . . . So it should not be seen
> as a family issue still.[58]

Such concerns were not without foundation, as evidenced when a representative of the Swedish government raised the matter subsequently (see below). It is indubitably with imputed nepotism in mind that the press release announcing Daniel's appointment stressed how the board had evaluated "numerous qualified candidates."[59]

A second strategy was Leif Zetterlund's recusal from the appointment, as well as communication of this recusal: "And today I'm glad it was on that level because it was not a father-son kind of issue. It was on a completely different level. And I was not actually involved in the decision-making process

---

with understandings of the Athenian *nomophulakia* (Cawkwell, "ΝΟΜΟΦΥΛΑΚΙΑ," 1–12). To this, I would add that the Aeschylean drama is not proposing a one-time expediency but establishing a good governance principle: "The people of Athens shall have this council forever" (Aeschylus, *Eumenides*, line 683).

57. Leif Zetterlund Interview I, 7.

58. Leif Zetterlund Interview I, 9–10.

59. Appendix B

at all here."[60] Further strategies include that a body of people (the international board), not the founder/father, led the process and made the decision. There was, moreover, agreement from staff in many nations, which mitigated suspicion of this being a family matter.

Further to the above strategies, attention is drawn to the post-succession strategy that good governance practices were confirmed and communicated, so that the management of the ministry was not seen as intrafamilial but according to recognized good practice. That this was indeed a strategy and was boldly communicated may be seen when the matter of imputed nepotism was raised by a representative of the Swedish government. This related both to Leif Zetterlund and Daniel Zetterlund but also to Daniel's brother, Andreas, who also worked for IAS:

> The head of internal audits for *Sida*, the Swedish government ... They were sitting in a high-level meeting with us, evaluating our programs and stuff. And he started pinpointing at family issues. And he didn't get to the point. He spoke very indirectly. And I was sitting next to my brother. He said, "You're handling government money. You need to be careful." I said, "What are you talking about? Are you talking about me and my brother?" And I just laid my hand around my brother and said, "Yeah, he's my brother. You can't take that away from us. We're in the same organization."
>
> But then I tried to say, "We have these policies in place. This is how we structure our work in order to safeguard that we're not making decisions that, you know, our family ties tie into."
>
> And he said, "Okay, good."[61]

Despite the above strategies and statements, a critical evaluation of IAS in this regard still reveals inadequacies. The appointment was made by the board and not the founding father, but nevertheless the board may have still been influenced through the founder's power. Board members had worked with the founder over years and may not have been fully independent from the founder; Block and Rosenberg show how great a founder's power over a board of a charity may be.[62] Furthermore, IAS may have left itself open to charges of nepotism by not enacting a fully transparent and public application process where other candidates also had the opportunity officially to apply for the post rather than simply being considered by the board. A greater

---

60. Leif Zetterlund Interview I, 3–4.

61. Daniel Zetterlund Interview I, 45.

62. Block and Rosenberg, "Toward an Understanding of Founder's Syndrome," 353–68.

degree of corporate reflexivity may have led to such actions, which would increase transparency and thus further counter suspicions of nepotism.

Endogenous Difficulties

Further to the exogenous problem of imputed nepotism, father-son succession raised matters endogenous to IAS, including an assumption of successor knowledge (and thereby lack of successor socialization), the complexities of a multilayered dyadic relationship between founder and successor, where work decisions and family relationships might be mutually affected, and the difficulty for a son to lead a father.

Daniel Zetterlund believes successor socialization was inadequate. There were no documents or a written brief concerning issues that he was to address as he began his tenure. In short, there was no customary socialization for an incoming CEO; the father-son dynamic was partly responsible for that.[63] The second endogenous problem might have been the successor needing to challenge, criticize, or confront the decisions of the founder. Daniel's assessment is that "it adds some complexity because we're father and son . . . But I think we've been handling that quite well."[64] The successor feels that he has asked his father not to be involved in some matters and is making the changes he feels the organization needs. In this, he appreciates the support of his chief financial officer, a neutral colleague who enforces certain policies and does not allow any interference from the founder.

INTERPRETATIONS—APPLYING THE FRAMEWORK

Given how paternal-filial succession was enacted, especially in light of imputed nepotism and potential endogenous intrafamily problems, how might this succession be interpreted in light of the frameworks provided by business, ethics, theology, and psychology? Several interpretations are suggested.

Regarding the broader ethical concerns of potential nepotism, the actual strategies implemented by IAS have already been enumerated. Following Eisold's model, I suggest these strategies form part of an adoption of the Oresteian approach, namely the establishment of an independent body to guide the process (board of directors). Not only is this helpful in terms of external communications to a suspicious society, but it does also address the three matters recognized by Eisold in succession: the need for

---

63. Daniel Zetterlund Interview, I 37–38.
64. Daniel Zetterlund Interview I, 39.

an impartial body; the removal of interpersonal subjective emotions from the process; and the representation of broader society. I suggest Eisold's three factors were duly addressed when the board made the decision. In taking these factors into account, the board reduced intrafamilial pressures, and furthermore, duly recognized the interests of stakeholders (donors, intercessors, worldwide staff, and especially grant-making institutions and public bodies). At a personal psychoanalytic level, it assisted the founder and successor to have confidence in the appointment and not feel guilt over family advancement.

The enactment of succession, furthermore, avoided some of the pitfalls of intrafamily succession in business. IAS deployed the appropriate professional governance structures necessary in family enterprises.[65] The initiation of the board on this matter, furthermore, ensured that the potential problem of the founder's remaining in post too long was avoided,[66] and that the findings of Dyck et al.—that title, power, control, and responsibility need to transfer simultaneously—were enacted in the transition.[67] Even protagonist age shows us that the founder leaving office in their sixties tends to allow for smoother transitions than when younger.[68]

While in some ways the succession corroborated previous findings, IAS succession did not, however, support previous research in two areas. According to Barnes[69] and Poza,[70] "incongruent hierarchies" between business and family are very problematic. I suggest that in the case of IAS such incongruent hierarchies existed; for example, the successor was not the oldest son. Yet, contrary to Barnes and to Poza, such incongruences were not causative of problems. This was due to such hierarchies being reified as separate entities and the determinative factor in appointment being the giftedness of the successor candidate. IAS's succession, furthermore, did not support Davis and Tagiuri's findings that the dynamics of a father in his sixties and son in mid-thirties are not conducive to a convivial relationship when working together. This was not problematic due to factors which include the founder's perception that it was the appropriate time to resign. Applying Sonnenfeld and Spence's typologies[71] and those of Poza,[72] Leif Zetterlund acted according to

---

65. Poza, *Family Business*, 25.

66. Daily and Dollinger, "Empirical Examination," 117–36.

67. Dyck et al., "Passing the Baton," 149.

68. Poza et al., "Family-Business Interaction," 99–118.

69. Barnes, "Incongruent Hierarchies," 212–21.

70. Poza, *Family Business*.

71. Sonnenfeld and Spence, "Parting Patriarch of a Family Firm," 355–75.

72. Poza, *Family Business*.

the "ambassador" role of departing founder. This type steps aside for others, transfers full authority, and does not seek self-reassertion but is available for "diplomatic or representational duties on behalf of the corporation."[73] Leif Zetterlund, with Daniel's agreement, remains active in a representational capacity and is available for advice if asked.

In turning to the framework of theology, particularly the five observations of paternal-filial succession within other Christian movements (above), a number of evaluations may be made. Both founder and successor were motivated by similar vision and led from a similar values system. There was full transfer of title, power, and authority, as recommended by Dyck et al.[74] This is seen very clearly at the succession ceremony in South Sudan, an event analyzed in greater detail in chapter 22. The transition was agreed on by all key stakeholders, including staff around the world (unlike succession of the Crystal Cathedral). There appear to be no unarticulated theological differences (see following section). Finally, as recommended by other son-successors in Christian ministry, the son was able to differentiate his leadership from that of his father, as seen, for example, in the greater professionalization of leadership.[75] While Tushima might not approve of the father-son succession, I suggest that Daniel Zetterlund does display the qualities which Tushima posits as qualifications for inheriting Christian leadership. The IAS succession is one of biblical and character qualities for leadership coalescing with familial relationships (contra Tushima).

The Positive Possibilities of Paternal-Filial Succession

While the chapter has sought to problematize paternal-filial succession, there may of course be advantages, including appointing one who already understands the organization: "I grew up, in many ways, with the organization."[76] The son, moreover, honored and admired the founder; his father was a "great source of inspiration."[77] With such honor, the successor was not going to embark on a significant change in direction or challenge organizational values. The son, furthermore, was already well known and respected within the ministry. The consultation and agreement of international workers meant that the whole organization could move forward in unity.

---

73. Poza, *Family Business*, 29–30.

74. Dyck et al., "Passing the Baton," 149.

75. Mullins, *Passing the Leadership Baton*, 109–10.

76. Daniel Zetterlund Interview I, 2.

77. Daniel Zetterlund Interview II, 21.

In turning to the pragmatic question, "Did it work?" three main comments will be made. The founder views the succession as positive: the successor has a "zeal in his heart . . . [and a] commitment . . . to serve,"[78] as well as commitment to the "unreached."[79] The founder believes the policy changes being implemented are necessary in this phase of the organization's life. There was, moreover, no attrition—the appointment was universally accepted. The organizational systems of the ministry have been changed by Daniel to meet the challenges of new governmental engagement; the organization is now receiving funds in new ways. In this case, paternal-filial succession was largely successful due to the engagement of an impartial decision-making body,[80] the correct timing in the organizational life cycle,[81] the role and character of the founder,[82] the successor's adherence to organizational vision and values, good relationships stemming from honor and respect, clear decision-making processes, and collaborative international consultation. Indeed, Daniel Zetterlund believes that the familial nature of the leadership is now viewed as an organizational strength:

> I think both my brother and me and Leif have realized this is actually something to be proud of . . . I sit in networks like ECHO,[83] . . . And they know I'm the son of the founder. I think they know I'm different, of course, but they know we're family . . . but I think their respect actually grows over time.[84]

78. Leif Zetterlund Interview I, 9.

79. Leif Zetterlund Interview I, 20.

80. Eisold, "Succeeding at Succession," 619–32.

81. Adizes, *Corporate Lifecycles*.

82. Poza, *Family Business*, 27–33.

83. European Civil Protection and Humanitarian Aid Operations. See https://civil-protection-humanitarian-aid.ec.europa.eu/index_en.

84. Daniel Zetterlund Interview I, 46–47.

Chapter Nineteen ————————————

When It's Expected of You
Succession as Coercive Isomorphism

THIS CHAPTER'S TITLE MAY seem strange to the reader. After all, everything that has been written thus far has an a priori assumption, not acknowledged until this point, that succession is something desired—desired by the founders and leaders as they get older or when they determine that they have completed their work, or desired by followers who wish to see the company or church continue and flourish in the future. But, what if you "kind of want to" appoint a new leader, but not really out of conviction? Can an organization enact succession simply due to the expectations of others?

This introduces a concept into our reflections on leadership succession, namely that of coercive isomorphism. It may surprise us to realize that often an organization will do things less out of conviction or enactment of core values but more because they feel they are forced to do so in some way, particularly because of the expectation of others, whether it be customers, other businesses in their field, constituents, or partners. In this chapter, I examine how this can influence leadership succession, even with Christian organizations or movements. I will particularly draw on an analysis of Grace Network and describe this case within the concept of coercive isomorphism. Following an explication of terms, Grace Network's succession will be set within the typologies of isomorphism and the theory of new institutionalism. I will show how, both at the theoretical and case level, new institutionalism may be applied to practical theological analysis. Founder succession in the case of Grace Network, however, will also be shown to be more complex than a simple reading of coercive isomorphic theory, as the succession showed both acquiescence and resistance to isomorphic pressures.

EXPLICATION OF TERMS

Borrowing from natural science, "isomorphism" is a term adopted by the social sciences since the seminal work of DiMaggio and Powell,[1] who posit that organizations tend toward homogeneity within their organizational field; a field being "organizations that, in the aggregate, constitute a recognized area of institutional life."[2] Fields have a structuration of parts including interaction among organizations within the field. Defined interorganizational structures of domination and patterns of coalition merge; mutual awareness develops among participants that they are involved in a common enterprise.[3] Within such a field, there is pressure toward homogenization; this is isomorphism, defined as "a constraining process that forces one unit in a population to resemble other units that face the same set of environmental conditions."[4] DiMaggio and Powell identify three types of isomorphic pressure: coercive, mimetic, and normative. Coercive isomorphism "results from both formal and informal pressures exerted on organizations by other organizations upon which they are dependent and by cultural expectations in the society within which organizations function."[5] Many studies support this concept, including Swidler on how organizations appoint leaders contrary to their own values of non-hierarchical decision-making so as better to relate to the exogenous environment inhabited by other bureaucracies.[6]

A second form of isomorphism identified by DiMaggio and Powell is "mimetic isomorphism," which is modelling after others due to uncertainty, and often becoming like others who are viewed as successful.[7] The third type of isomorphism, namely "normative," occurs when professions enforce certain norms and standards on the organization. DiMaggio and Powell extend their work to identify predictors of isomorphic changes, which include

---

1. DiMaggio and Powell, "Iron Cage Revisited," 147–60. Bolman and Deal found this article to be the most cited of the previous few decades in the area of organization studies and sociology, and the tenth most cited work of all academic fields (Bolman and Deal, *Reframing Organizations*, 439–41).

2. DiMaggio and Powell, "Iron Cage Revisited," 148.

3. DiMaggio and Powell, "Iron Cage Revisited," 148.

4. DiMaggio and Powell, "Iron Cage Revisited," 149.

5. DiMaggio and Powell, "Iron Cage Revisited," 150.

6. Swidler, *Organizations without Authority*.

7. DiMaggio and Powell, "Iron Cage Revisited," 152.

dependence on other organizations, exchange relationships, the extent to which an organization views its goals as ambiguous and others as successful, as well as the extent to which internal conflict is repressed in the interests of harmony. In this latter case, it is easier to mimic others than confront the hidden disagreements.[8]

Conceptualizations of institutional isomorphism are set within the broader theoretical frame of "new institutionalism," a perspective that stresses that it is the exogenous factors of an organizational environment which shape an entity's decision-making, structures, and procedures.[9] New institutionalism "is a theory of diffusion that provides ways to think about how an organizational structure or behavior goes from an artificial creation lacking legitimacy to being unconsciously accepted by all."[10]

An increasing number of scholars have applied concepts of new institutionalism and isomorphic change to religious studies.[11] Lindsay studied isomorphic pressures on evangelical elites,[12] while Chaves shows the extent of isomorphic pressures on positions adopted by denominations on the matter of women's ordination.[13] I am unaware of any research seeking to interpret founder or leadership succession in the frame of isomorphism, but suggest that, given the above citations, this is a logical extension of previous research in the practical theological field. Indeed, Dollhopf and Scheitle specifically study the isomorphic pressures in founding religious "noncongregational nonprofit organizations" during a period (in the US) of "explosive growth" of such ministries since the mid-1990s.[14] This growth in the last two decades, unless these organizations ceased, must mean there have been, or soon will be, many founder successions, which begs the question (unable to be answered without further research) whether the large number of isomorphic religious networks leads to isomorphic successions.

---

8. DiMaggio and Powell, "Iron Cage Revisited," 155.

9. Powell and DiMaggio, New Institutionalism.

10. Scheitle and Dougherty, "Sociology of Religious Organizations," 989.

11. Cormode, "Does Institutional Isomorphism Imply Secularization?" 116–31; Swartz, "Secularization, Religion, and Isomorphism," 323–39; Kondra and Hurst, "Institutional Processes," 39–58; Packard, "Resisting Institutionalization," 3–33; Zainiddinov, "Institutional Isomorphism," 346–62.

12. Lindsay, "Elite Power," 207–27.

13. Chaves, "Ordaining Women," 840–73; Chaves, Ordaining Women.

14. Dollhopf and Scheitle, "Explaining Variations," 261.

SUCCESSION IN GRACE NETWORK

Groblewski had replaced Hollandsworth as the third director. They continued a co-equal leadership model, which led to one of their external partners, Van Niekerk of The Christian Network in South Africa, to urge the appointment of one director who should be empowered to deal with international partnership matters. Groblewski, who was not a founder, was appointed to this new role; this was judged to have been a leadership transition with minimal change in vision or modus operandi.[15] Groblewski is clear that it was international pressure which caused the triumvirate to acknowledge that their leadership model was not understood or helpful to their partners:

> I'm mentioning that because that was the trigger that moved me from being, uh, part of a triumvirate, three—three leaders, to being an executive leader. And the reason was the other two networks had executive leaders. And since we had decided to partner, the other two leaders were kind of insisting that Grace needed an executive leader, someone with whom they would be able to, uh, negotiate and have relationship and have a face to Grace Network and so forth. So consequent to, uh, their urging . . . I became the executive director.[16]

This succession may be interpreted according to new institutionalism theory, that it was the external environment that most shaped the decision and process of succession within Grace Network. Grounded on a fivefold rationale, I suggest more specifically that founder succession was a case of coercive isomorphism. First, the initiative for the succession was external and the appointment was to acquiesce to exogenous "urging": "So my accession was, I think, of international necessity or partnership necessity."[17] Second, the pressure was to follow the leadership pattern and structure of the PFI constituent movements: "And those networks both had hierarchial [sic] leadership with a measure of collaboration. And that needed to be imitated to a certain degree in order to facilitate Partners For Influence."[18] While Groblewski used the word "imitate," normally associated with the term "mimetic," the epithet "mimetic" in new institutional theory is more usually reserved for voluntary or self-initiated isomorphism because the organization desires to become like the other (often due to uncertainty). While coercive isomorphism does lead to imitation, in this case I argue that

15. Blackwell Interview I, 4.
16. Groblewski Interview I, 2.
17. Groblewski Interview I, 3.
18. Groblewski Interview I, 15.

it was not a self-initiated and thus not mimetic isomorphism in the sense used by DiMaggio and Powell.[19]

A third reason for describing this succession as coercive isomorphism is that in the broader field of new apostolic movements, a single defined apostolic leader had become the accepted norm.[20] Grace Network's decision accords with the findings of Chaves[21] and Lindsay[22] that church leaders institute policies or structures when those become commonly understood as bringing further legitimation. A fourth and more specific reason is that research shows that primary sources of coercive pressure on churches are their collaborative relationships with other networks or denominations.[23]

A fifth and final reason for citing this as a case of coercive isomorphism is, moreover, not simply the collaborative relationships but more specifically the dependency of Grace Network on its international partnership. In their original definition of coercive isomorphism, DiMaggio and Powell state that it is coercive when there are "pressures exerted on organizations by other organizations upon which they are dependent."[24] While not being financially dependent, each of the three networks in PFI had a pooled interdependency and reliance on each other.[25] As the other two organizations were already agreed on leadership structures, Grace Network adapted to suit the majority in the partnership.

While describing Grace Network's succession as one of coercive isomorphism, it is a case more complex than an assignation of such an epithet would suggest. Such complexity is revealed in the succession's differing effects on different levels of leadership within the network, in resistance to organizational change, and in a generalized ambivalence to the appointment.

The differing effects are seen in that the change to an executive or apostolic leadership mode only applied to the area of international partnership matters. Within their ministry in the US, the triumvirate ignored the change; they continued as before. There was no change in theological beliefs about leadership appointments and structures. To appease external partners, there was an overt change of leadership structure, a legal appointment

19. DiMaggio and Powell, "Iron Cage Revisited," 147–60.

20. Wagner, *New Apostolic Churches*, 19–20.

21. Chaves, *Ordaining Women*, 33.

22. Lindsay, "Elite Power," 207–27.

23. Chaves, *Ordaining Women*, 10; Kondra and Hurst, "Institutional Processes," 39–58.

24. DiMaggio and Powell, "Iron Cage Revisited," 150.

25. Thompson, *Organizations in Action*.

of an executive director, but, in reality, on most matters the team of three continued as before.

There was, furthermore, latent resistance to such isomorphic pressures. Groblewski's appointment, for example, was actually intended *not* to produce change:

> It was natural and it was easy for us to do because we didn't feel like Grubby was going to take it—take it places we weren't comfortable with . . . So, it was probably the smoothest transition you can have. It just seemed natural, the thing to do [laughs].[26]

Although a succession appointment and concomitant installation ceremony did occur, many within the movement did not view this as succession. An official ceremony took place, after which Groblewski's position was now changed both in juridical terms according to the constitution as well as in terms of spiritual authority. This installation caused Groblewski to experience internal shift: "I felt the weight of more responsibility."[27] The network was, however, creating a problem at this very point, because many did not view this enactment in the same way that Groblewski did. Indeed, there existed a dissonance between theological beliefs and enactment due to external pressure. During the prior fifteen years of its ministry, Grace Network had not seen any need for an executive director. This failure to appoint manifests a deeper issue of leadership theology. Put simply, had they believed in a model of *"primus inter pares"* or an "apostolic" model of leadership, someone would have taken that role within the first fifteen years of ministry. Confusion over the appointment was compounded by there being no consideration of expectations on the appointee, the precise hours he was to give in service in this role, or of any financial remuneration. Over time, Groblewski felt this put him in a difficult position, especially with the church of which he was pastor, and which in effect was paying him for work outside of the church. Full commitment to the role of executive director could have been evidenced by clearer expectations and remuneration.

This matter was compounded yet further by the lack of change of leadership mode; the triumvirate (Blackwell, Manzano, and Groblewski) largely continued their previous modus operandi,[28] except with reference to external partnership negotiations. The organizational ambivalence toward the nature of the appointment is evidenced in the nomenclature and equivocal response to my questioning. Blackwell's report of Van Niekerk's

26. Blackwell Interview I, 4.
27. Groblewski Interview I, 39.
28. Groblewski Interview I, 3.

urging the appointment of one leader is narrated thus: "It's difficult relating
. . . uh, relating . . . uh . . . There are times you all three can't come to meetings or whatever. Why don't you just have a representative?"[29] In narrating
the discussion concerning whom to appoint, we hear, "But we said . . . we
talked and we said, 'Grubby, how about you taking the primary leadership,
especially with outside groups? And even when we meet with just our home
. . . with our churches, um, you know, you be the point person.'"[30] It is hard
to know whether Blackwell was appointing Groblewski to a different role
concerning international matters than American matters ("primary leadership" in contrast with "point person"), and also the precise denotations and
connotations of "point person" and "representative." Certainly, terms such
as "executive" or "apostolic" were not employed. When questioned further,
Blackwell responded, "We called him 'executive director' [laughs]."[31] The
vocabulary of the responses and indeed the laughter (showing discomfort
with the term) indicate ambivalence to the nature of the appointment.

That the appointment did not come from a *theologia ex corde* is seen,
moreover, with the installation ceremony being functional rather than high-
lighted as a significant development in the life cycle of the organization.[32]
Churches in the movement treated ordination ceremonies as epideictic;
that is, a time of celebration with appropriate speeches and words of commendation.[33] At such ordination ceremonies, the gatherings also prayed for
the spouses of those being ordained and performed symbolic enactments;[34]
yet the time of prayer at a conference for Groblewski's appointment was
not replete with epideixis, nor was his wife even present at the occasion. In
Groblewski's words, "It wasn't a big deal."[35]

Thus, an appointment was made and enacted, resulting in positional
and legal change for Groblewski, yet ambivalence and awkwardness are
revealed in the interviews. While the leadership agreed an appointment of
executive director was necessary to develop their work with others, it seems
that this signified little to the other leaders of the movement or domesti-
cally within the US. In retrospect, for Groblewski this "was a succession

29. Blackwell Interview I, 3.

30. Blackwell Interview I, 3–4.

31. Blackwell Interview I, 12.

32. A *theologia ex corde* is a theology of the heart, a belief which is heartfelt and
fully embraced. A *theologia ex mente* is a theology of the mind, a belief to which one
intellectually assents but which one does not necessarily passionately or fully embrace.

33. The notion of *epideixis* is borrowed from Aristotle. It is defined with greater
specificity in my analysis of succession transition ceremonies in chapter 22.

34. Groblewski Interview I, 35–36.

35. Groblewski Interview I, 36.

of sorts."[36] Indeed, although the founders were installing a new leader for the network, with the two founders continuing much as before, this succession was not even experienced as such by most of those concerned. Thus, espoused and operant leadership theology were not coterminous. To put this more sharply, the founders' appointing of a non-founder as the primary leader in name and with authority in some defined areas was not experienced as succession by many in the network. Exogenous acquiescence to isomorphic pressure led to the processes, decisions, and ceremonies of succession, but for many this was experienced as "non-succession." This matter would prove problematic years in the future: "It was the succession thing that was the fly in the ointment."[37]

In developing this analysis further, however, I suggest that even the resistance to the homogenization of leadership structures may itself be interpreted as a further marker of coercive isomorphism. When an entity succumbs to isomorphic pressures it may still seek to maintain an organizational cultural uniqueness.[38] Meyer and Rowan identify a phenomenon called "decoupling" which "enables organizations to maintain standardized, legitimating, formal structures while their activities vary in response to practical considerations."[39] This may result in "loose coupling" which suggests "the dependence of organizations on the patterning built up in wider environments—rather than on a purely internal technical and functional logic."[40] Chaves states that such loose coupling is a signal to the environment rather than a regulation governing internal operations.[41] Chaves shows how churches and Christian groups enact such loose coupling. Prichard provides details of such a difference between an official denominational stance and actual practice.[42] Such inner subversion or resistance is, therefore, a sign of existent isomorphic dynamics. It is also a sign of conflict repression, itself a predictor of isomorphic changes.[43] Such conflict suppression and its theological roots will be examined later in this book (chapter 23) in order to gain a fuller analysis of founder succession in the case study.

In summary, succession within Grace Network was due to isomorphic pressures which led to the outward adoption of a new leader but in practice

---

36. Groblewski Interview I, 4.

37. Groblewski Interview I, 5.

38. Pedersen and Dobbin, "In Search of Identity," 897–907.

39. Meyer and Rowan, "Institutional Organizations," 58.

40. Scott and Meyer, "Preface," 2.

41. Chaves, *Ordaining Women*, 5.

42. Prichard, "*Grandes Dames*," 49.

43. DiMaggio and Powell, "Iron Cage Revisited," 155.

made little difference. The transition was not fully discussed; a change of role and expectations for the executive director were not articulated. An exogenous request was met, but Groblewski's appointment was not viewed as a moment for change, including ways to empower its first executive director. This will be shown to have been problematic for the network's sustainability.

Chapter Twenty ——————————————

Succession as Dismantling
the Movement

IF THE PREVIOUS CHAPTER on a type of "coerced" succession seemed star-
tling to the reader, this chapter's content may prove positively shocking;
that is, the topic of organizational succession by the complete dismantling
of the existing organization or movement. Yet, I contend that this is exactly
what can happen and has indeed happened. To explain this, I will draw on
the founder succession enacted by the Newfrontiers network of churches.
At the time of succession, there were approximately 850 churches in many
nations. Their succession from their founding leader, Terry Virgo, in 2011
was an intentional destruction of what had been built, with the closing of
its support office and staff. As I have found no existing word for this phenomenon, I have coined a new term, namely "kinesisoclasm," a term taken
from the Greek words for "movement," both in literal and figurative sense,
and for "breaking." In support of this neologism, I cite lexicographers Liddell
and Scott[1] and Pring.[2] In 2011, Newfrontiers ceased to exist as one movement, when fifteen apostles were appointed each to lead their own movement, although the term "sphere" rather than "movement" is the preferred
Newfrontiers nomenclature. In this chapter, I will discuss this radical way of

1. Liddell and Scott, *Greek-English Lexicon*, 806.
2. Pring, *Oxford Dictionary of Modern Greek*, 98.

handling founder succession by focusing on two concepts, namely those of "routinization of charisma" and Terry Virgo's theology around the concept "movement."

ROUTINIZATION

Succession from the founder of Newfrontiers was an enactment to obviate routinization, contra Weber's theory of the routinization of charisma in the transition of authority in new movements and organizations.[3] Having so begun this section, immediately a number of explanations and qualifications must be made. Weber's theory is complex and classic. Given the vast nature of the scholarship, it remains beyond the scope of this book to treat this matter fully. Weber's notion has, however, sustained considerable criticism, with some viewing it as inadequate to understand founder succession.[4] As Weber's notion, has, however, been the predominant notion of understanding founder succession in charismatic-led movements for many decades, it has relevance, therefore, to ongoing conceptualizing of the dynamics involved. Many of the critics do not so much expunge the theory but add to it by showing the greater complexity of succession in the modern world. The leaders of Newfrontiers, furthermore, seemed aware of the dynamics which Weber was seeking to describe, while being unfamiliar with the terminology of "routinization"; indeed, it was those dynamics which occupied their deliberations on succession.[5] A brief statement will be made concerning Weber before seeking to analyze Newfrontiers on this matter.

Weber posited that there are essentially three types of legitimate authority: legal, traditional, and charismatic. It is the latter that Weber applies to new religious movements or organizations:

> The term "charisma" will be applied to a certain quality of an individual personality by virtue of which he is set apart from ordinary men and treated as endowed with supernatural, superhuman, or at least specifically exceptional powers or qualities. These are such as are not accessible to the ordinary person, but

---

3. This theory is taken from Part I of Weber's *Wirtschaft und Gesellschaft*, published in German in 1919, better known in the English-speaking world through its 1947 translation *Theory of Social and Economic Organization*.

4. Sasson, "Shakers," 13–28; Andelson, "Postcharismatic Authority," 29–45; Shields, "Latter Day Saint Movement," 59–77; and others.

5. Devenish Interview I, 45–46.

are regarded as of divine origin or as exemplary, and on the basis of them the individual concerned is treated as a leader.[6]

The crucial factor is the perception of such a person by followers or disciples. It is others' recognition of the one in authority that validates charisma.[7] Often there is no constitutional authority or regulation of powers. There tend to be few administrative structures, and others are appointed because they too have charismatic authority. This authority operates outside of routine, rational, and bureaucratic or traditional authority; it rests on charisma. For a movement to endure, however, it must pass from the reliance on personal gifts to some form of routinization (according to Weber). Importance becomes attached to the ideal and the material interests of the followers as they seek to continue the movement. It is the disappearance of the founder which brings such matters to the fore, if they have not been already addressed.

Weber emphasizes that charisma's anti-economic character must be altered in order for it to be routinized. Laity and clergy might be differentiated, with the latter receiving a stipend, or there is distinction between the taxpayers and recipients. A strong influence on routinization is the desire for security, both economic and in the sense that the movement will continue its mission. The issue is not only succession from the founder but more fundamentally making the transition from a charismatic administrative staff to one that is adapted to everyday conditions.

Newfrontiers leaders were aware that routinization was a possibility, although they employed the term "institutionalization." There was, for example, a negative view of hierarchal structures. Referring to new apostolic networks, Devenish states, "The last thing that the founding fathers of these movements would want is to see their living, relational leadership structures being institutionalized into something more rigid and hierarchical by a second generation of leaders."[8] The prevention of such institutionalization would be by means of maintaining "the biblical emphasis on family relationship, particularly the continuing need for fathers."[9] Routinization (at least in this context) is viewed as negative and antithetical to the values of Newfrontiers. When questioned, Devenish responded,

> We did talk about that. I don't remember us saying this sociological . . . but we did, that observation is something we debated a

6. Weber, *Theory of Social and Economic Organization*, 358–59.

7. This understanding was first articulated in Durkheim, *Elementary Forms*.

8. Devenish, *Fathering Leaders*, 12.

9. Devenish, *Fathering Leaders*, 12–13.

lot. We looked at organizations, Christian organizations, which in the first generation had no constitution. In the second generation have a very complex constitution.

We felt that, firstly, each new sphere needs to be a first generation sphere, if you see what I mean. It's only our togetherness in the second generation. And therefore, it's only our togetherness which that could apply to. But because our togetherness is probably 10–20 percent of who we are, you see, all the churches, they're not Newfrontiers churches, they're all in their sphere. Do you see what I mean? So, we, that's . . . we like to . . . in one sense, though we didn't do it precisely for this reason, we may be kidding ourselves, I don't know, but we're thinking this is one way of trying to avoid that. . . . So we debated that.[10]

This nuanced response shows that devolution to fifteen autonomous spheres was a way of avoiding routinization and in fact perpetuating a continual first generation, a range of fresh new networks rather than a continuing of the old. Devenish allows that the continued collaboration of the "togetherness" might involve routinization. Indeed, I maintain that it has done so. The paper *Definition of Newfrontiers for the Current Phase* documents the common values of the fifteen spheres and defines mutual accountability as well as codifies doctrine for the first time. For a good while this was not a public document, but the substance is now published.[11]

While admitting greater formality with regard to "togetherness," the main thrust of the apostolic spheres, however, should be the continual renewing of the church to be first generation and thus perpetually charismatic rather than routinized: "Each generation should be like a first-generation church in its life and organization."[12]

Virgo similarly wished to avoid such bureaucratization. He believes the succession occurred without producing it:

Yes, I think, I think even sometimes the difficulty I have in answering is because it is based on gifting, personality, relationship, rather than on documents and details. We have never gone that way. . . . When people wanted to say, "Can we join you?" at one point we said, "Shall we print our fifteen values?" And we felt uneasy about that because it's like, well, if you want, this is the list. And we didn't want people to meet a list. We wanted people to meet a person and feel, "Are we getting engaged relationally?"

---

10. Devenish Interview I, 45–46.

11. Devenish, *Succession or Multiplication?*

12. Devenish, *Fathering Leaders*, 335.

So, in fact, one of the ways we have tried to overcome that was, on my website, I did a question-and-answer. My son asked me, on every one of the fifteen points, he probed in a video format. "What do you mean by this? What do you mean by that?" And then he would ask questions around, "What does that mean then?" So, at least, it was a conversational thing, rather than, well, there it is on paper, do it . . . So, relationship came first.[13]

This narrative shows an attempt to convey important values but, through the medium of video, to attempt to do so in a less formal or bureaucratic way than a written document.

Subsequently, as the "togetherness" leaders have documented certain doctrines and procedures, Virgo sees the benefit of this for the second generation working together in their current and future contexts. Nonetheless, Virgo believes they have been successful in avoiding the pitfalls of routinization. The interview transcripts as well as documentary sources indicate, while not using such terminology, that Newfrontiers believes in ongoing recharismaticization. This resonates with Ukah's notion of recharismaticization, that routinization of charisma does not have to be inevitable, but that a movement might in some way be rebirthed with renewed charismatic authority.[14]

MOVEMENT

Succession from the founder of Newfrontiers was, moreover, not solely an act of anti-routinization; it was an act of resistance to and destruction of "movement." To introduce the notion of "movement" into the analysis is fraught with complexity, as in the literature of sociology, including the sociology of religion, its meaning is contested.[15] While absent in Newfrontiers literature, in the research interviews, Virgo introduced the notion multiple times (unprompted);[16] he does not, however, include any concomitant meaning. Yet, to understand Virgo's conceptualization of "movement" is crucial to analyze the Newfrontiers succession.

A dictionary definition of "movement" is of "a body of persons with a common object."[17] The field of sociology often speaks of "social movements" as "networks of informal interactions between a plurality of individuals,

13. Virgo Interview II, 16–17.

14. Ukah, *New Paradigm*, 83.

15. See, for example, Della Porta and Diani, *Social Movements*, 25–28.

16. Virgo Interview I, 28, 29, 30, 32, 39; and Virgo Interview II, 12, 13, 14, 34.

17. *Oxford Encyclopedic English Dictionary*, 949.

groups and/or organizations, engaged in political or cultural conflicts, on the basis of a shared collective identity."[18] Della Porta and Diani state, however, that such a term does not apply to a religious (or any other) formalized organization.[19] Others, however, would indeed see a religious sect or cult as a social movement.[20] Hadden, moreover, states that social movements are "organized efforts to cause or prevent change" and that "religious movements" are a "subcategory of 'social movements.'"[21] Hadden adopts a three-part typology of religious movements, namely, endogenous (desiring change internal to the religion), exogenous (attempting to alter the environment in which the religion resides), and generative (seeking to introduce new religion into an environment). Endogenous movements seek to change one or more of the beliefs, symbols, practices, and organization of the religion; they frequently result in schism. If the religious hierarchy adopts the objectives, reform rather than schism may result. If the environment is conducive to the survival, economic viability, status, and ideology of the religion, then there is often harmony between the religion and surrounding culture; such groups in harmony are usually defined as "church" or "denomination."[22] If there is disequilibrium between the religion and society, exogenous movements may result.

Without pausing unduly over the debates on terminology, I suggest that Newfrontiers was, and each of the fifteen apostolic spheres is, a "movement." They organize people around certain values and goals; they desire change—indeed the restoration of New Testament Christianity and the working toward the presence of the kingdom of God. Newfrontiers is a religious movement, partly of the endogenous type, seeking to change certain beliefs and practices of Christianity, yet also of the generative type, seeking to introduce the Christian faith to societies including those with little church presence. It could be that Virgo would not even dispute this assertion, if spoken solely in terms of sociology: "But we do have a name. You've got to in the modern world . . . bank accounts, etcetera."[23] Nonetheless, Virgo is "anti-movement" in terms of church. What does he mean by "movement," and why is this anathema?

I suggest five ways to understand Virgo's conceptualization of, and opposition to, movement. First, "movement" is to be resisted: "In a sense, I

18. Diani, "Concept of Social Movement," 1.
19. Della Porta and Diani, Social Movements, 25.
20. Robbins, Cults, Converts and Charisma.
21. Hadden, "Religious Movements."
22. Hadden, "Religion and the Construction of Social Problems," 103.
23. Virgo Interview II, 12.

always resisted the concept that we are a movement."[24] Secondly, the motive for such resistance is its lack of biblical warrant, noting Virgo's antithetical juxtaposition of "movement" and "biblical": "I knew other people who started movements, and I think 'what's a movement?' I'm trying to be a biblical Christian. I don't know what a movement is. So, I challenged it. 'What is a movement?'"[25] Thirdly, this lack of biblical warrant is based partly on the reification of the relationship between Christians working together, turning the matter to a human institution which one joins; in contradistinction, church networks are to be based on mutual agreement to receive the ministry of those displaying the gifts stated in Eph 4:11. This epistle states that Christ gave the church "the apostles, the prophets, the evangelists, the pastors and teachers." Virgo explains,

> For instance, I strongly resisted . . . And over the years, people, you know churches, can I join Newfrontiers? I would say, "That's really not a very good question. It is not a biblical question. Are you asking for Ephesians 4 ministries to help you? Do you want, uh, apostolic help? Do you want prophetic help?" Because we're to model it on biblical principles, we have to have a name, but the way that's, I think . . . can I join this club, or whatever, is a—is just an unhelpful way in. Because it is asking the wrong question and therefore you can have the wrong concept.[26]

Fourthly, for Virgo, "movement" is similar to, and in danger of fully becoming, "denomination": "So denominations, I have always resisted that concept, of a denomination."[27] He continues,

> Well, Paul, as a biblical example, had churches that he worked with. They weren't denominations in the modern sense. But they were what the theologians call the Pauline churches, the ones he fathered or cared for. So I thought, well, this is a biblical principle. Paul could say, "All are yours." You know, Peter's in and out of Corinth, but he does talk about our sphere. We're not overextending our sphere. We are not building on another person's foundation. So, we've tried to observe those principles. And I just hope . . . I have always felt that is very important. And I'm not quite sure whether everyone has grasped how important I felt that to be. Because I think you then hear of all sorts of movements. So you hear of Acts 29 or this or that, who

24. Virgo Interview II, 13.
25. Virgo Interview I, 30.
26. Virgo Interview II, 13.
27. Virgo Interview II, 14.

are not . . . They are happy to call themselves movements, but I have been a bit resistant of wanting that title. But trying to argue it biblically.[28]

For Virgo, what conjoins is fathering relationships; those are organic, not structural. Fifthly, the concept of "movement" is antithetical to the model provided by the New Testament networks (plural). The New Testament does not show the church as one movement under one leader:

> I remember one of the things that Chris put in his paper, when he talked about Peter on the day of Pentecost. He said it became Peter's moment, not Peter's movement, which I felt . . . is a phrase that I still remember, obviously.
>
> It's not like Peter, then in stark contrast to the Roman Catholics . . . it's not like he became the leader of. . . . It was his moment, the day of Pentecost, not his movement. And that was a helpful little phrase.[29]

To be a movement with a leader puts one in the same theological and organizational position as Roman Catholicism. Virgo's objection to being a movement is, therefore, a resistance based not on sociology but on theology from which organizational developmental decisions must flow. Thus, the succession is not merely "anti-movement"; the succession to fifteen sphere leaders is "kinesisoclastic," an intentional destruction of movement:

> So, if Terry is an apostle, who makes fifteen apostles . . . well, we realized we can't go there because no man can make an apostle. That's what we felt. So that . . . we talked the whole thing through. We're trying to stay biblical and not just become a movement.[30]

Yet, at the same time, Virgo desired that which he founded to continue into the future in some form, in a sense to "move" from what it was through a decentralizing and multiplying process.

The case of Newfrontiers is thus of interest to those considering succession, for it challenges any a priori assumption that a Christian network or organization *should* continue into another generation. Indeed, in a sense, the model adapted is *against* succession by ceasing the existing and thereby allowing multiple others to form new alliances and networks from its midst. Rather than being prescriptive, however, Virgo seems to admit that this method may not be appropriate for all networks, hinting that a more

---

28. Virgo Interview II, 14.

29. Virgo Interview I, 28–29.

30. Virgo Interview I, 32.

conventional one to one succession may be desirable in a network much smaller than Newfrontiers was at its point of succession.[31]

31. Virgo Interview II, 20.

Chapter Twenty-One

Succession and Gender

It is with some trepidation that I broach the matter of gender and succession. This is because gender studies and the many issues around gender roles, socialization, identity, and gender construction have recently become a vast field of study and vociferous debate. Yet, of course, succession is also a gendered topic. Stating this more obviously, men or women succeed other men and women; the decisions made concerning whom to appoint are made by gendered people as well. Some reflection on the gendered nature of succession is thus also of critical importance to understand how succession is handled within Christian organizations. This matter, however, is within a context where traditionally, in both secular and religious organizations, it was men who appointed other men, except in the case of intentional women's organizations (although even here it could be a man who had to agree to the appointment). Within many businesses and organizations today, however, issues relating to succession and gender are changing; Halkias et al. provide many cases from multiple countries where daughters succeed their father in the family business.[1] Yet, as reported earlier in the book (chapter 13), I could find no cases of succession to a female leader within the potential population of cases I examined when seeking to identify appropriate cases for my research. This in itself raises important issues: do women not aspire to become leaders of Christian organizations (and if so, was this because of

1. Halkias et al., *Father-Daughter Succession.*

role socialization which discouraged them), or were they precluded by others, whether due to assumed and implicit theologies of gender or espoused and overt theologies? Understandings of gender and theologies of gender thus influence succession.

In this chapter, I cannot of course do justice to providing a full understanding of such matters. I will, however, provide an example of one organization, Newfrontiers, and show how understanding of gender shaped succession. My purpose in writing will not be to provide a full critique of their theology of gender, but to point out how such matters are not adequately reflected upon and how such lack of reflexivity does affect appointments and succession processes. This is done within the context of examining succession, because, certainly in the case of Newfrontiers, it was succession which reinforced and reduplicated their theology of gender. Indeed, it was, in this case, succession which became a medium for the perpetuation of male hegemony, as power was transferred from Virgo to fifteen men. I seek to explain why founder succession in Newfrontiers had to be the appointment of men only, before moving to not a critique of Newfrontiers' theology of gender and their complementarianism but to an argument that the network was lacking in reflexivity on this matter, unaware of other matters which may have been impinging upon decisions and affecting their appointing only men as successors to Virgo.

GENDER AND LEADERSHIP IN THE CHURCH: AN INTRODUCTION TO THE DEBATE

Christians disagree on the issue of women in church leadership, whether it be congregational leadership or whether a woman may hold the office of apostle. This is a topic of considerable popular and academic debate, a full analysis of which lies beyond the scope of this book. A number of introductory comments, however, will be made.

In the last fifty years there has been a development of Christian feminist theology; Aune suggests a threefold typology of such theologies, namely reformist, revisionist, and revolutionary.[2] Some feminist theology is not evangelical,[3] but many within evangelicalism have constructed theologies of gender and leadership. British writer Elaine Storkey has been influential;[4] similarly, a well-known figure such as Loren Cunningham (male), founder

---

2. Aune, "Postfeminist Evangelicals," 117. For other typologies, see King, *Women and Spirituality*, and Clifford, *Introducing Feminist Theology*.

3. Bendroth, *Fundamentalism and Gender*, 36–37.

4. Storkey, *What's Right with Feminism?*

and, for many years, president of the global mission agency Youth With A Mission, has been an advocate for women in governmental leadership.[5]

Broadly speaking, evangelicalism divides itself into two theological camps on this matter, namely "egalitarianism" (those believing that women can exercise governance and apostleship) and "complementarianism" (those believing that each gender is assigned different roles by God, and thus that women are not to be in governmental roles).[6] Egalitarians, particularly evangelical feminists, hold some of the following tenets: that the curse of Gen 3:16, that a husband "will rule over" a wife, has been negated by Christ; that men and women are equal (Gal 3:28, which has been called the "Magna Carta" of Christian feminism);[7] passages such as 1 Tim 2:11–15 are seen as temporary culture-dependent guidance; egalitarians state that the meaning of "head" (1 Cor 11:3) is not "authority" but refers to "source" or "origin" as in the Genesis creation account. For complementarians, however, men's and women's roles are ordained in Gen 1 and 2; Christ only appointed men as apostles, thus the office is closed to women. Furthermore, complementarians believe that "male headship" is the correct interpretation of 1 Cor 11:3.

NEWFRONTIERS' COMPLEMENTARIANISM

As this book is not primarily a study of church and gender, I will limit my analysis of Newfrontiers' complementarianism to the data procured during the research interviews and to the following three texts which most clearly address the issue: Virgo's autobiography and history of Newfrontiers;[8] Devenish's work *Fathering Leaders*;[9] and the article of January 27, 2012, "The Presumption of Complementarianism."[10] For a more thorough treatment of Newfrontiers and gender, the reader is referred to Aune, from whom I have drawn for the broader framing of this issue.[11]

In his autobiography, Virgo only briefly comments on the issue of women in church government, stating that Jesus, who subverted the

5. Cunningham and Hamilton, *Why Not Women?*

6. See Aune, "Postfeminist Evangelicals," for a fuller account of the differences. The brief summary above draws from this work.

7. Aune, "Postfeminist Evangelicals," 118.

8. Virgo, *No Well-Worn Paths*, 235–37.

9. Devenish, *Fathering Leaders*.

10. Virgo, "Presumption of Complementarianism."

11. Aune, "Postfeminist Evangelicals," is a PhD thesis specifically on gender in Newfrontiers, with data gathered largely through the ethnographic and participant-observer method.

traditions and norms of the day, only appointed men as apostles. Women may engage in a variety of ministry and leadership (including breaking bread in communion), but they are not to exercise church government and the "authoritative teaching and leading of men" for "we would regard these as territory forbidden to women by Scripture."[12] Virgo believes that the New Testament "looks back to creation rather than forward to our ultimate heavenly state (see 1 Corinthians 11:8; Ephesians 5:31; 1 Timothy 2:13)."[13] Women are "to emulate the challenging and multi-faceted example set out in Proverbs 31 with maturity and security."[14] We are told, furthermore,

> Our desire has never been to belittle or underestimate over 50 per cent of God's created humanity and we don't aim to perpetuate a historic Victorian stance, dictating that women should be "seen and not heard." We simply and honestly believe that the Bible shows us that there are roles in the church that are gender-specific and that if these principles are correctly observed we shall see women blossom and flourish into the beautiful potential God has for them.[15]

Subsequently, in his 2012 article "The Presumption of Complementarianism," Virgo advocates for "women in ministry, prophesying, deaconing [sic], worship leading, preaching, teaching, leadership, missionary work, church planting"; only men, however, should be elders. Virgo provides several reasons. First, he locates his position within the hermeneutic of obedience to Scripture, unless it is clear that any commands or injunctions applied only to specific individuals or for a limited period. Thus 1 Tim 2:12, "I do not permit a woman to teach or exercise authority over a man," still applies as an injunction disbarring women from church government.[16] Secondly, he places the burden of proof on those who advocate for women in governmental roles, as church history has been overwhelmingly complementarian. Thirdly, Virgo stresses that greater weight should be accorded to New Testament passages which address an issue with specificity rather than generality (and he cites 1 Tim 3:1–7 and Titus 1:5–9 as so doing). His fourth argument is that of the hermeneutic of compatibility; if theological positions were compatible to the apostle Paul, they should also be compatible to

---

12. Virgo, *No Well-Worn Paths*, 236.

13. Virgo, *No Well-Worn Paths*, 237.

14. Virgo, *No Well-Worn Paths*, 236.

15. Virgo, *No Well-Worn Paths*, 237.

16. Brauch is representative of many proffering a differing interpretation (Brauch, *Hard Sayings of Paul*, 252–57).

us. Thus, Paul writes of gender equality, yet, for example, that wives should submit to husbands.

Devenish, one of the fifteen apostles commended as part of founder's succession within Newfrontiers, specifically addresses the question, "Are women able to serve as apostles?"[17] "I would argue that women do not hold the office of apostle in the New Testament, though it is clear that many women numbered among Paul's fellow workers and in that sense were part of apostolic teams."[18] Devenish makes his case based on "asymmetry" in the doctrine of the Trinity, namely that the three persons of the Trinity have equal yet asymmetrical relations and roles; therefore, such equality yet asymmetry in human relationships and roles is based on humans' being created in God's image.[19]

NEWFRONTIERS SUCCESSION

Such theology framed apostolic succession for Newfrontiers as a male-to-male transition. Women are precluded from such office on the basis of Scripture. Succession, therefore, ensures male hegemony within the networks which followed.

While not entering the scriptural debate over complementarianism per se, I suggest that a closer analysis, however, may reveal other influences on gendered founder succession, and that there is little evidence of reflexivity on such possible influences. First, there appears to be a gender-blindness or "gynopia"[20] when reading the very scriptures used both to support apostolic ministry and the model of multiple successors. Devenish titles his 2001 book *Fathering Leaders, Motivating Mission*, with chapter 4 titled "The Need for Fathers in Ministry and Mission." There is no mention that leaders might also need "mothering" or ministry from the feminine within the church. The work speaks of "fatherly leadership," "Paul's fatherly lifestyle," and "fathers for mission." It is ironic that one of the key texts cited to show the fatherly nature of apostleship is 1 Thess 2:6–7: "As apostles of Christ we could have been a burden to you, but we were gentle among you, like a mother caring for her little children."[21] These words of a male apostle use the simile of motherhood to express apostolic ministry. Devenish mentions this

17. Devenish, *Fathering Leaders*, 329.

18. Devenish, *Fathering Leaders*, 330.

19. Devenish, *Fathering Leaders*, 330.

20. Reinharz, "Feminist Distrust," 153–72.

21. Devenish, *Fathering Leaders*, 67. (Devenish does not state which version of the Bible he cites.)

in passing but does not provide any further exegesis on this point. The key text, therefore, cited to support "fathering" is one which explains apostleship with a feminine simile.

When speaking of succession, Virgo and Devenish cited Ps 45:16: "Your sons will take the place of your father; you will make them princes throughout the land." This was a scripture that for them provided clear direction on succession decisions. There is, however, no comment on the place of women in Virgo's or Devenish's citing of this psalm, despite the previous verses speaking of "daughter," and the princess being led to enter the palace of the king (v. 15). Yet the application of this psalm focused on the appointing of (multiple) males. There was no mention of how the women could be "led to the king" in Newfrontiers' application of this seminal scripture shaping their succession. It would have been possible to maintain a complementarian theology but also to refer in the narratives to the role of women.

Women, furthermore, are not mentioned in Virgo's texts; the language is often exclusively male, as seen in the following three citations. Virgo states that he gathered "men" to help him, yet women were part of his church-planting and ministry efforts.[22] Secondly, in his 2012 article "Newfrontiers Marches Forward into Multiplication,"[23] Virgo's account of a leadership conference in Turkey, where many women were present, includes the summation that "to meet with men from Bolivia to Mongolia, from Seattle to Sydney was a joy and delight." There appears to be no recognition of the women at the conference. Thirdly, in Virgo's 2011 interview "On the Future of Newfrontiers, Transition, but Not Retiring Just Yet," we read "I've seen guys I remember when they were starting and now I see 'Boy, look what he's built. Look at these men who look to him.'"[24] There is no acknowledgment of any role of women in this "building," despite Newfrontiers' theology allowing for women on apostolic teams.[25]

Further to this lack of acknowledgment of the role, at times even presence, of women, there are still other ways of reflecting on the correlation of gender and succession, upon which greater reflexivity may have been helpful as the network made a transition to a new phase. One such matter is that of the development of the "separate spheres" social practice of assigning men and women different societal roles stemming from industrialized capitalism, which separated work and home.[26] With men being to

---

22. Virgo, *No Well-Worn Paths*, 98.

23. Virgo, "Newfrontiers Marches Forward."

24. Warnock, "On the Future of Newfrontiers."

25. Devenish, *Fathering Leaders*, 330.

26. Davidoff and Hall, *Family Fortunes*; Aune, "Postfeminist Evangelicals," 168–89.

a greater extent away from home on business, an ideology was needed to reconceptualize home life and its importance. Evangelicals may think they have shaped culture, but Rosman shows that social context is a key driver in the shaping of evangelical attitudes to culture in England.[27] This, and the economic nature of evangelical "theology" on the matter may be seen in the writings of evangelical Congregationalist Ann Martin Taylor, publishing novels, letters, and pamphlets, writing that preserving domestic happiness is "an effectual, as well as simple means of increasing national prosperity."[28] "Separate spheres" in broader society drove "separate spheres" in church life, where women served in the home or in the nurturing areas of church, such as teaching children and visiting the sick.[29] If this is valid, then apostolic succession within the Newfrontiers movement may be an enactment of and is constructive of industrialized socialization. At best, "evangelicals may claim their gender ideals derive directly from the Bible, but these 'biblical' ideals are mediated through their cultural understandings."[30] Indeed, Aune would go beyond this understanding and assert that Newfrontiers is "substantially formed and informed by postfeminist discourse,"[31] and that, furthermore, a "backlash" against the feminism of the 1970s and 1980s may also be discerned within Newfrontiers. Thus, "NFI's public, congregational discourses and practices of gender are postfeminist, yet with a far stronger emphasis on separate spheres conservatism and its backlash reassertion."[32] While further work on this is necessary, it is my point, however, not to critique Newfrontiers' complementarianism but to suggest they lacked reflexivity on such matters.

27. Rosman, *Evangelicals and Culture*.

28. Ann Martin Taylor, *Reciprocal Duties*, 176, cited in Davidoff and Hall, *Family Fortunes*, 173.

29. See Aune, "Postfeminist Evangelicals," 113–15. See Davidoff and Hall, *Family Fortunes*, 107–18, for a fuller treatment on the development of "separate spheres" and evangelical teaching in the late eighteenth century and early nineteenth century.

30. Aune, "Postfeminist Evangelicals," 110.

31. Aune, "Postfeminist Evangelicals," 2. "Postfeminism" is a fluid and multivalent term (see Aune, "Postfeminist Evangelicals," 82–88). For Aune, "postfeminism" refers to "attitudes and practices of gender that amalgamate feminist and traditionalist ideologies within a postindustrial context. It is a sometimes-contradictory adherence to both gender traditionalism (manifested in the late-eighteenth and nineteenth-century notion of separate spheres and the post-1970s backlash against feminism) and feminist discourse, enacted within a late-modern context" ("Postfeminist Evangelicals," 92).

32. Aune, "Postfeminist Evangelicals," 143. As with any church or network, the official doctrine may not be believed in the same way by the multiple adherents: "In at least one local setting . . . NFI is less conservative and more feminist than the wider and national settings suggest. Conservative gender ideologies, therefore, despite their rhetoric are sometimes weakened in social practice" ("Postfeminist Evangelicals," 2).

In seeking to relate the implications of gender theology to succession, I also draw from Bendroth's attempt to trace the history of gender within evangelicalism and fundamentalism. She draws attention to Calvinism as a theology more likely to produce complementarianism, for Calvinists believe in the "natural order" of genders related in the Gen 1 and 2 accounts. Newfrontiers is Calvinistic. Certainly, other non-Calvinistic British restorationist networks seem more inclined to place women in governmental leadership.[33] Bendroth notes, furthermore, that during periods of growth, churches use and rely more on the gifts and energy of women, but that, conversely, during times of retrenchment they become more concerned with male status.[34] Newfrontiers has recorded sustainable growth since its inception, which might seem to disprove Bendroth's thesis. However, Newfrontiers is within the context of British Christianity where there had indeed been greater retrenchment.

As gender was not activated unprompted in my case study research interviewees, I sought to activate it in order to ascertain, even within complementarian leadership, what role women might have played in the succession. The finding is clear; there was in fact no involvement of women in the leadership discussions and decisions.[35] I would suggest this points to a "hard" complementarianism (my terminology).[36] When asked a similar question, Devenish, like Virgo, acknowledged that women did not participate, but added, "I'm not saying that was right. I'm just saying that's what happened. Whereas now, it's not quite how it works."[37] He gives examples of wives of leaders being at significant leadership events as well as women being members of "apostolic teams."[38] While stressing the continued belief in complementarity, such comments may be a recognition of past inadequacies; while complementarianism remains a *theologia ex mente*, these could be signs that it is weakening as a *theologia ex corde*. Alternatively, in metaphorical terms, this theology might be seen as palimpsestic, with complementarianism overwritten with attempts at greater gender inclusivity.

To conclude, founder succession within the theological framework of complementarianism preserved male hegemony in church affairs. For the leaders within the fifteen spheres, this was faithfulness to scriptural

---

33. Kay, *Apostolic Networks*, 330–31.

34. Bendroth, *Fundamentalism and Gender*, 116–17.

35. Virgo Interview II, 2.

36. A "softer" complementarianism is where apostolic leaders and those making the decisions are men, but their wives do nonetheless participate in leadership meetings and give input to the deliberations.

37. Devenish, Interview II, 16.

38. Devenish, Interview II, 15.

teaching; egalitarians would probably view such succession either as stemming from poor exegesis resulting in denying women their opportunity to be leaders or as female exclusion through backlash postfeminism. Greater reflexivity may have helped Newfrontiers acknowledge the role of women, even within a complementarian framework.

Having stated the above, it should be furthermore acknowledged that even additional layers of complexity exist surrounding gender and succession appointments and a lack of reflexivity on such matters. By this I specifically refer to the discourse that, in Newfrontiers, leaders not only had to be male but, in fact, they could only be a certain type of male which fit the network's construction of masculinity. Rather than explicate this further in this chapter on gender, I will return to this matter of masculinity construction in Newfrontiers and the lack of reflexivity thereon in chapter 26 when we reflect on the topic of successor identification methods.

Chapter Twenty-Two

Succession Ceremonies
Communicating and Enacting Organizational Beliefs

At first glance, the reader might seem surprised that a work on succession should devote considerable space to the matter of ceremonies that may be conducted in the transition of power and authority from one leader to another. We might be tempted to think that these are just a few brief moments that showcase the deliberations and processes of organizational succession. Yet, as I hope to reveal, succession ceremonies can be highly significant in communicating to all concerned what is taking place and what succession actually means to the organization. Indeed, this chapter will show that such ceremonies can communicate vast quantities of data concerning organizational beliefs, values, and theologies. To support this point, there will be an in-depth look into the transition ceremony enacted by International Aid Services. Through symbolic actions and the employment of physical symbols during the succession ceremony, IAS revealed much about its organizational theology and understanding of the meaning of succession for their organization. In Part VI, I will return to the matter of ceremonies to show that ceremonies may not just communicate organizational theologies but can make evident the inconsistences and lacunae in such theologies and how such lacunae may impair the succession itself.

SUCCESSION AS SYMBOLICALLY
ENACTED THEOLOGICAL TEXT

Having previously concentrated on succession within International Aid Services from the perspective of leadership style change and intrafamilial succession, in this chapter I turn to a third dimension of succession within IAS, namely that of the symbolic enactment of theology in the succession itself. Here I seek to analyze and interpret IAS's succession in a symbolic reading of the theological data observable during the succession ceremony held in South Sudan (March 2015). Eade advocates a similar approach to understand the "contrasting visions of the Roman Catholic Church" which are "acted out through the nuances of public ritual" at the pilgrimage shrine in Lourdes.[1] Such an approach provides rich theological data. This approach is supported by the growing field of ritual studies.[2] More specifically I draw upon the approach of Kaufman and Ideström and their call for a "sociomaterial understanding of the embodiment of the normative voices of tradition in ecclesial practices," such as liturgy.[3] The IAS ceremony was not a normative ritual from magisterial tradition, of course; rather it is a new sui generis ritual. Nonetheless, the analysis of artifacts is still helpful.[4] Kaufman and Ideström propose the study of "the relationality and interconnectedness of human and non-human actors in any social setting or situation and how this in a fundamental way shapes how knowledge and meaning is mediated and created."[5] Thus, following Kaufman and Ideström, I look at the use of place/space and artifacts such as a book and a key; such actors (human and non-human) work as "mediators of tradition rather than as vessels of transporting doctrinal information or theology that is left unchanged by the mediation process."[6] In this case, they are used for this first time not normatively but nonetheless mediate theology afresh.

In examining the symbols, particular attention will be paid to an analysis of the ceremony's celebratory style, latreutic dimension, contextualization, facilitation of liminality both to produce *communitas* and as symbolic didactic per se pertaining to missional goals and communication of *sacra*, and finally to the porrection of the physical symbols of a key and book. While evangelical, the faith of IAS was not aniconic.

---

1. Eade, "Introduction," xxiii.
2. Grimes, *Beginnings in Ritual Studies*; Bell, *Ritual Theory*.
3. Kaufman and Ideström, "Why Matter Matters," 84.
4. Lathrop, *Holy Things*.
5. Kaufman and Ideström, "Why Matter Matters," 98.
6. Kaufman and Ideström, "Why Matter Matters," 100.

Symbols

"A symbol is something that stands for or suggests something else; it conveys socially constructed means beyond its intrinsic or obvious functional use."[7] Symbols are used to convey meaning in the plastic arts,[8] literature, and in the field of religion.[9] Not only are symbols powerful didactic tools, they are a means of persuasive communication for leaders.[10]

Symbolic Enactments

CELEBRATION

The transition ceremony began with a celebratory communal walk or march around town.[11] This celebration included a marching band, singing, and ululation. It celebrated both the twenty-fifth anniversary of the founding of IAS as well as the leadership succession. It was symbolic of IAS's belief in divine guidance in their work, including the succession. A celebration may also be a didactic tool for leadership as celebrations provide opportunity for "arousal, heightened activity and emotional responsiveness."[12] Symbolically, succession, through celebration, is framed as a positive, God-ordained event.

CONTEXTUALIZED WORSHIP AS OUTWARD MOVEMENT YET INNER LATRIA

The IAS acts of worship enacted during the transition march include the physical; that is, the bodily processes of walking. This is a move toward God and one another. It involves the body yet is also God-focused praise. It is both physical and yet latreutic. A non-dichotomous view of body and spirit permits many cultures to use the body in significant ways in the worship of God. For example, in his study of Christian worship in Samoa, Kane states that movement and dance may "capture the nonverbal movements of the Holy Spirit."[13] The worship during the praise march at the IAS ceremony

7. Zott and Huy, "How Entrepreneurs Use Symbolic Management," 72.

8. Battistini, *Symbols and Allegories in Art*.

9. Dillistone, *Christianity and Symbolism*; Dilllistone, *Power of Symbols*.

10. Bolman and Deal, *Reframing Organizations*, 253.

11. A video report of the ceremony has now been archived. See chapter 14, note 1 for comments on accessing this material.

12. Turner, *Celebration*, 21.

13. Kane, "Celebrating Pentecost," 165.

is, furthermore, universal in that the participants in the praise march are of
all ages, men and women, as well as different races and nationalities. These
interracial and intercultural dimensions point to the eschatological worship
all of tribes and tongues foreseen in Rev 7:9; the worship is at the same
time, however, contextualized. The embodied yet inner spiritual dimension
shows IAS theology to be non-dualistic; succession thus is enacted in both a
natural and spiritual framework.

CONTEXTUALIZATION

The praise march displays a belief in contextual missiology, literally following the classic evangelical understanding of contextualization from the Lausanne movement's *The Willowbank Report on Gospel and Culture*, namely
that the church must be able to "celebrate, sing and dance" the gospel in
its own cultural medium.[14] The worship is not an imposition of European
modes and forms but something arising within the African context where
celebratory marching bands, singing, and ululation are common within
African churches of many types and nations.[15] Indeed, the paternal-filial
nature of the succession might also be viewed as contextual.[16]

Contextualization is furthermore evident in the emphasis on *epideixis*.[17] Elders, government representatives, and the founders were thanked.
In a culture of high "power distance," such honor is required.[18] Indeed, the

14. Stott, *Making Christ Known*, 102. The full text of *Willowbank* may found in Stott,
Making Christ Known, 73–113.

15. See Robert and Daneel, "Worship among Apostles and Zionists"; Gampiot,
Kimbanguism.

16. Ngomane, "Leadership Mentoring"; Tushima, "Leadership Succession Patterns."
While taking place in South Sudan, the ceremony was attended by workers from many
African nations. The works cited above refer to several African countries. For the pur-
poses of this chapter, I thus speak of a generalized "African" rather than specifically
South Sudanese context.

17. I have adopted the term from classical rhetoric. Aristotle describes the qualities
of epideictic speeches as, "The present is the most important; for all speakers praise
or blame in regard to existing qualities, but they often make use of other things, both
reminding [the audience] of the past and projecting the course of the future" (Aristotle,
On Rhetoric, 1358). *Epideixis* is used to refer to the kinds of subject that draw attention
to the speech, such as praise (Rüpke, "Epideixis"); it was both a specific genre but also
a more general term for speeches of praise present in other genres (Haskins, "Rhetoric,
Epideictic"). My adoption of the term refers both to the specific act of laudatory speech
and, by use of metonymy and more specifically synecdoche, to the broader celebratory
and laudatory event.

18. Hofstede, *Culture's Consequences: International Differences*; Hofstede, *Cultures
and Organizations*. The concept of "power distance" was introduced and defined in

place of those who have gone before, especially ancestors, is a central issue in African worldview, a matter with which the Christian church with its imported theology from Europe has had to engage in order for there to be a genuine African Christian theology.[19] The ceremony of March 2015 honors leaders, elders, and those who have gone before.

The *epideixis* not only honors in word but also with enactments. Despite the imposition of Western forms of government, in African tribal societies, community elders are often still the leaders in communal matters.[20] Daniel Zetterlund, in the speech below, is both ritually empowering elders and revealing that he understands the culture of his African colleagues and, furthermore, that he is willing to work under their guidance. Daniel Zetterlund articulated his contextual goal:

> And I didn't point to any Swedes. I pointed to the four African leaders sitting at the forefront. I said, "Elders, I come to you for counsel and advice." I didn't even look at my father. I looked at them. And I said, "Advise me when I've gone wrong. Counsel me when I need counsel." And I said something else. "Mentor me." And I said, "This key, I hold very dear. I think it will be a key not for opening most doors, but it will be a key where I will close doors."
>
> I think this is what I'm doing. I'm referring to those things. First, I think it's biblical. It's principled. But I think it's also contextually correct and how you address that to Africans.[21]

Such contextual submission to African conceptualizations of leadership went beyond intention. Daniel Zetterlund believes it was subsequently enacted in management processes within the movement.[22] The successor comments,

> So, from an organizational, hierarchical point of view, yeah, I have so much more authority, or hierarchically, than a director

---

chapter 4. For the reader's convenience, Hofstede's own definition of the term is repeated: "The power distance between a boss B and a subordinate S in a hierarchy is the difference between the extent to which B can determine the behavior of S and the extent to which S can determine the behavior of B" (Hofstede, *Culture's Consequences: Comparing Values*, 83).

19. Bediako, *Jesus and the Gospel in Africa*, 22–33; Pobee, *Towards an African Theology*, 94.

20. Donovan, *Christianity Rediscovered*; South Sudan Customary Authorities Project, *Now We Are Zero*.

21. Daniel Zetterlund Interview I, 50–51.

22. See Daniel Zetterlund Interview I, 51–52 for a narrative on the successor subsequently submitting to African elders in organizational problem-solving.

from a local implementation organization in [name of country].
But I subdued myself spiritually and said, "You are my counsel-
lor. You're my mentor."[23]

The succession theology is not one simply of power and authority transference but of submission and service.

LIMINALITY AND COMMUNITAS

A fourth symbolic enactment rich in data is that of liminality creation. The
praise march is a vibrant symbol that the workers of IAS are to be a liminal
people doing liminal things. Here I draw on classic understandings of liminality from van Gennep[24] and Victor Turner.[25] Turner has been called "the
most important cultural anthropologist of our time."[26] Enactments such as
ceremonies, celebrations, and rituals progress with a tripartite flow involving separation, margin (or liminality), and reintegration (or aggregation).
The liminal phase is outside normal structures and hierarchies, often invert-
ing them. The liminal state is a place of "optation."[27]

Five factors contributed to the liminality that was created through the
praise walk. First, the framing of the event as celebration, as celebrations are
liminal events that take place extraneous to the structuration of quotidian
activities.[28] Second, the physical setting of the march (spacial liminality).
Many epiphanies and theophanies happen in places outside routine space[29]
or in places on the margins.[30] Third, the activity of walking, which may be
emotionally and spiritually transformative,[31] as classically seen in pilgrimage.[32] While the Yei march was not a pilgrimage in the classic sense of leaving home, direction to a goal, and returning home on the same road,[33] it was
nonetheless a walk with a religious purpose, namely that of installing a new

23. Daniel Zetterlund Interview I, 51–52.

24. van Gennep, *Rites of Passage*.

25. Turner, *Dramas, Fields, and Metaphors*; Turner, *Celebration*; Turner, *From Ritual to Theatre*; Turner, *Ritual Process*; and others.

26. Moore, "Liminoid and Liminal Sacred Space," 38. See also Salamone and Snipes, *Intellectual Legacy of Victor and Edith Turner*.

27. Turner, *Dramas, Fields, and Metaphors*, 202.

28. Turner, *Celebration*.

29. Eliade, *Shamanism*; Giesen, "Performing the Sacred," 325–67.

30. Horvath and Szakolczai, *Walking into the Void*, 115, 128, 130.

31. Gros, *Philosophy of Walking*; Ingold and Vergunst, *Ways of Walking*.

32. Frey, "Stories of the Return," 89–109.

33. Dupront, *Du Sacré*; Horvath and Szakolczai, *Walking into the Void*, 152.

Christian leader. Fourth, Christian worship itself is often liminal activity.[34] Finally, rituals of status elevation in African societies are liminal events, where normal social norms are suspended.[35] This succession ceremony to install a new leader is one of status elevation.

Having shown the multiple ways in which the succession event induced and enacted liminality, I now turn to how these modes of liminality production reveal the theological nature of succession within IAS. Liminality leads to *communitas*,[36] a relatively undifferentiated society of equals where everyday social structures and relational hierarchies are suspended. Such movements from structurated society to *communitas* of equals may themselves be productive of new ways of being and seeing. In Turner's words, *communitas* has "an aspect of potentiality; it is often in the subjunctive mood."[37] To explain this further, Turner draws upon Martin Buber: In *communitas*, individuals "are not segmentalized into roles and statuses but confront one another rather in the manner of Martin Buber's 'I and Thou.'"[38] It is from Christians' walking together for spiritual purposes that *communitas* flows.[39]

The creation of *communitas*, moreover, creates the spiritual community from which the ministry of IAS must operate. It is a Christian community with spiritual goals. IAS's vision is a "godly transformed society," and its mission is articulated as "to save lives, promote self-reliance and dignity through human transformation, going beyond relief and development":[40] "Our biblical understanding of missions motivates everything we do. The unreached and under-privileged people's groups [*sic*] is our major focus in spreading the good news."[41] *Communitas* is, furthermore, a symbolic enactment of the values and theology of the organization, one of which states, "Equality: We believe in treating all people as we would like to be treated. We believe that people will feel valued and appreciated when we regard them with dignity and respect."[42] It is, moreover, a symbolic enactment of the very mission of the agency, for IAS is clear that it is called to serve

34. Alexander, *Victor Turner Revisited*.

35. Turner, *Ritual Process*, 167.

36. Turner, *Ritual Process*.

37. Turner, *Ritual Process*, 127.

38. Turner, *Ritual Process*, 132. See Buber, *I and Thou*.

39. Sallnow, "Communitas Reconsidered," 163–82; Eade and Sallnow, *Contesting the Sacred*.

40. International Aid Services, *2015 Annual Report*, 4.

41. International Aid Services archived material. See chapter 14, note 1.

42. International Aid Services archived material. See chapter 14, note 1.

those in liminality; that is, those marginalized by normal social structuration, such as those displaced through war or living with HIV/AIDS.[43] The enactment of liminality and *communitas* symbolically communicates that workers of IAS are to be a liminal people serving the marginalized peoples. It is an enactment of the mission.

This is further developed by conceptualizing the ceremony and worship as redressive rather than sublimational. To understand this requires a return to the classic structuralist understanding of liminality, *communitas*, and social states. Everyday social hierarchies and relationships are seen as "structure"; an individual or group who enters a transitional phase or ceremony is removed from the everyday flow of activities and enters a threshold or liminal state of "anti-structure."[44] Much of ritual and ceremony may be anti-structure but it enables people to pass through toward a new structure. Such an understanding has been applied to Pentecostal worship, for example. What has been called "ritual possession"[45] (that is, worship including *glossolalia*, prophetic utterances, and altar calls) is seen as inducing *communitas*, where anyone, regardless of status, may be used by God. Some see this in classic structuralist terms of sublimation, a kind of safety valve, which allows worshippers to express frustrations and their oppressed states but then facilitates their leaving the worship and returning, with acceptance, to the unjust structures of society. According to Hollenweger in his classic work on Pentecostalism, many Brazilian Pentecostals felt they had "no solutions to offer for the social and political problems of Latin America";[46] others found it helpful to express their disadvantages "liturgically" and found courage in meeting with those with similar disadvantages.[47] Alexander, however, in his study of ritual possession among black American Pentecostals, states that liminal *communitas* may also be redressive in that it "introduces into everyday life the alternative, communitarian relations."[48] He found that the Pentecostals of his study did not accept social conformity but were actively engaged in social and political actions to agitate for racial justice. Similarly, I suggest that the worship and praise of the IAS staff was redressive, for they had gathered not to accept the world as it is, but to move forward, under a new leader, to move toward IAS's vision of a "godly transformed society."[49]

43. International Aid Services archived material. See chapter 14, note 1.

44. Abrahams, "Foreword," v–xii.

45. Alexander, *Victor Turner Revisited*.

46. Hollenweger, *Pentecostals*, 105.

47. Hollenweger, *Pentecostals*, 459.

48. Alexander, *Victor Turner Revisited*, 84.

49. International Aid Services, *2015 Annual Report*, 4.

The appointment of a new leader was not a flow from anti-structure to structure; that is, to a maintenance of a new hierarchical status quo, but it should be seen rather as a move from "spontaneous" *communitas* to normative and ideological *communitas*.[50] While often there is a return to structure, there may instead be a continuation of *communitas*, either normative, where the spontaneous features are somewhat constrained (such as rules governing practice at pilgrimage sites), or ideological, where attributes of the *communitas* experience are formulated into a plan for societal reform.[51]

In summary, through the above analysis we see that the enactments of celebration, contextualization, and liminality creation symbolically reveal organizational theology; they are, moreover, enactments of the organizational mission of movement toward the margins with redressive motivation. Succession is part of the liminality creation and stirring of redressive vision—it is not to be seen as an institutional, hierarchical appointment.

Physical Symbols

In turning from symbolic enactments, attention will now be given to two physical symbols employed during the transition ceremony, namely the donation from founder to successor of a book and a key. The field of religion is replete with transition ceremonies, rituals, and commissions, often including symbolic artifacts (see, for example, 1 Kgs 1:39). In ecclesiastical practice today, churches hold services of installation, often ritually prescribed.[52] Such ceremonies and rites of leadership succession are symbolically rich. In the appointment of a new leader with the ordination of presbyter in the Anglican Communion, the Ordinal requires the bishop to donate a copy of the Bible to each ordinand.[53] This is in the long tradition of *porrectio instrumentorum* in the ceremonies of appointment to office in the early Western and medieval church.[54]

Should one be tempted to believe that it is largely the historical churches which enact symbolism (as traditions handed down from former pre-literate, pre-modernistic, and iconophilic eras), it is noteworthy that

50. Eade, "Introduction," x–xi.

51. Turner sees Pentecostalism as ideological *communitas* (Turner, *From Ritual to Theatre*).

52. See *Alternative Service Book*, 949–60, or https://www.churchofengland.org/prayer-and-worship/worship-texts-and-resources/common-worship/ministry/common-worship-ordination-services.

53. Buchanan, *Ordination Rites*.

54. Bradshaw, *Anglican Ordinal*, 2.

new evangelical churches and movements are not aniconic but do adopt symbolism in their transition rituals, even if they do less so in daily worship patterns than some older traditions. For example, Ulrich contains a photograph of a 2014 founder succession event at Ephrata Community Church in Pennsylvania, US.[55] In the center of the photograph stand the founder (right) and successor (left), either side of a shepherd's staff; the staff is the visual center. The symbol of the founder giving to the successor and the specific donation of a symbol representing care of the "flock" reveal the central message of the symbol; that is, one of transference of power and authority. Wheeler similarly relates donations of physical symbols within founder succession of megachurches; in one case the departing leader gave the successor a golden sprinkler head; "It represented that he [the successor] needed to be keeping his eye on everything going on on campus even down to the sprinklers."[56]

In the case of IAS, the use of physical symbols enhances the African contextualization: "And this is what appeals to African leaders as well, global leaders, the visual stuff, giving a key."[57] It also places the succession ceremony within the broader church tradition of the porrection of gifts to symbolize the appointment to office.[58]

BOOK

During the epideictic event in South Sudan, the founder gave the successor a book:

> We dreamt . . . about transformed communities and we would like you to continue dreaming. We want to give you a book, *Dare to Dream . . . Then Do It: What Successful People Know and Do.*[59] . . . Never forget that with a vision you can go very far.[60]

An analysis of this gift-symbol suggests that it is an enactment of blessing from a founder-patriarch, one which reveals to those gathered that he is supportive of the transition. It is also an act of counsel or guidance. A

---

55. Ulrich, *Celebrating 40 Years*, 142.

56. Wheeler, "Leadership Succession Process," 150.

57. Daniel Zetterlund Interview I, 50.

58. Bradshaw, *Anglican Ordinal*, 2.

59. Maxwell, *Dare to Dream*.

60. My transcription of the speech given by Leif Zetterlund at transition ceremony held in Yei, South Sudan, March 2015. Transcription is from video report from IAS, now archived. See chapter 14, note 1.

reading of the book shows that its theme is that of not accepting the status quo in life but envisioning a brighter and better future. This specific symbol is to encourage the new leader and those in attendance, to foster a forward-looking purpose, and to develop a resilience to achieve goals. It might also be a warning to maintain spiritual vision, a warning given to a successor who was (by consent of both founder and successor) more structured and bureaucratic in his style of leadership. The symbol could, therefore, be interpreted as not just encouraging guidance but a parting invocation to keep the organization progressing in the same direction.

In summary, the symbol of a book treating dream and vision reveals IAS's leadership theology and stresses that from succession should flow the envisioning of distal states as motivation to mission, which is to procure societal transformation. Succession is thus to further such vision.

Key

The second donation from founder to successor was a key:

> And today I would like to give this key to my successor, Daniel. A key . . . I am going to give you this key as a symbol from this event that this key will remind you about two things—not to be lost and not to be forgotten . . . but to open doors and also, maybe close doors. There are always situations in life where we have to be able to say "No." "No" to temptations. "No" to corruption. "No" to greed. Those doors will not be opened. They would be sealed. Closed. But the doors that will be open will continue leading people into prosperity, people into proper education, doors that will be opening the minds of people. Doors that will give people an opportunity to help themselves. So, I want you to receive this key as a symbol of what is ahead. I have not opened all the doors with it. There's still plenty of those in this wonderful country we are in now but also throughout the nations of the world that you will see being ready to receive you where you go.[61]

The donation of a key places this installation ceremony within the broader field of installation rituals in the church.[62] An analysis of this symbolic gift

61. Leif Zetterlund, speech at transition ceremony. Transcription is from video report from IAS, now archived. See chapter 14, note 1.

62. At the porrection of keys to a new incumbent in the Church of England, the churchwardens speak, "Receive these keys in token of the responsibility which we share" or a variant of these words. Examples of liturgies used in such services of institution and induction are numerous. See for example the following from 2020, accessed May

reveals the following matters. First, the act of giving is a symbol of passing on, literally and metaphorically giving to someone else. To those gathered to witness, it is thus a sign of voluntary relinquishment of power, of blessing and endorsement of the successor. Second, the use of a key ("to unlock") speaks of the role of a leader to release the potential within the organization and its workers—that leadership should not concern itself with a wrong form of control which uses people for its own ends but instead for their betterment, which will in turn accomplish the organization's goals. This symbol thus speaks to a foundational issue of transformational rather than transactional leadership.[63] According to Northouse's definitions, transactional leadership "focuses on the exchanges that occur between leaders and their followers,"[64] whereas transformational leadership is the "process whereby a person engages others and creates a connection that raises the level of motivation and morality in both the leader and the follower."[65] During the interviews, Leif Zetterlund explicated this aspect further:

> I think it should open relationships to donors, to new potential supporters and unlock the potential that people have within the organization. Unlock capacity that is built over a period of time. I mean many years. Those people who are still feeling that their capacity, their resources, their . . . it's like they are in a cage. If someone would help them to get out of the cage so that they could actually fly like a bird, but use them for the sake of the organization and their own future growth.
>
> To lock, when you are in top leadership, you need to be able to say "yes" and "no." If you are not willing to take that kind of role, I don't think you can stay as a leader. I wanted to remind him about the key could also close. And you have a mandate to close a door when it is necessary.[66]

The metaphor of unlocking speaks to both a third and fourth aspect of the symbol. The "locking/closing" speaks to the values and morality of the ministry, that matters such as "corruption" and "greed" will impede the organizational thrust and should thus be avoided. Symbolically, the founder is reinforcing the second organizational value, that of integrity. This, of course, needs to be a powerful guiding force in African contexts of rampant

12, 2023: https://fordhamchurch.org.uk/wp-content/uploads/2020/09/Institution-of-Francis-Blight-Order-of-Service.pdf.

63. Northouse, *Leadership*, 185–217; Burns, *Leadership*.

64. Northouse, *Leadership*, 186.

65. Northouse, *Leadership*, 186.

66. Leif Zetterlund Interview I, 28.

corruption.[67] The fourth aspect concerns the strategic choices that come with leadership.

To the above analysis, I wish to comment on a fifth nuance of the symbol, namely that a key is a powerful biblical symbol of authority, seen, for example, with the appointment of Eliakim to rule Jerusalem and the concomitant donation of the key to the house of David ("What he opens no one can shut, and what he shuts no one can open" [Isa 22:22]), and with the words of Christ to Peter upon his confession: "You are the Messiah, the Son of the living God." In Matt 16:19, Christ responds, "I will give you the keys of the kingdom of heaven; whatever you bind on earth will be bound in heaven, and whatever you loose on earth will be loosed in heaven." The giving of a key, therefore, is a symbol of the transference of authority, particularly God-appointed spiritual authority to lead others within the kingdom of God.

In theological terms, symbolic enactments of a donation and reception of a key reveal that ultimately and fundamentally the transference is one of spiritual authority. It symbolically and didactically frames, moreover, IAS's succession as a Christo-Petrine event, a framing of succession which Newfrontiers sought to avoid (see chapter 20).

SUMMARY AND ACHIEVEMENT OF TRANSITION CEREMONY

This intercultural act of worship fostered liminality (place, walking, and worship) which generated normative *communitas*. The theology was one of celebration, prophetic intercultural witness, and symbolically enacting of God's concern for those excluded from normal social structuration. Through such enactments a theological text was created, enhanced by the physical symbols of book and key. The theology of IAS as symbolically mediated is not one of sublimational withdrawal from the world but one that is redressive. Revealed through symbolism, succession was constructed as a Christo-Petrine event where the successor was to lead a people of *communitas* to redressive acts. Through the placing of the succession within an act of celebration, it conveyed that the transition should not be feared but was to be embraced; it communicated continuity of values and reassurance as the new leader had a confident sense of the future: "We know where we are heading as an

---

67. Transparency International, "Corruption Perceptions Index 2017." The index places South Sudan, the country of the ceremony, at number 179 out of 180 nations; that is, almost the most corrupt country on earth.

organization."[68] The ceremony, moreover, re-laid a foundation of the theo-
centric nature of the ministry—that the future would be prosperous if IAS
followed Christ, as articulated in the successor's closing remarks:

> May the Lord bless you and keep you. Don't ever leave His side.
> Abide in Him, as we will as an organization, and you will see
> that your life will be prosperous. And you will go places you
> never thought was possible.[69]

68. Daniel Zetterlund speech at transition ceremony.
69. Daniel Zetterlund speech at transition ceremony.

Chapter Twenty-Three ———————

Theology Matters!
Succession as Manifestation of
Leadership Theologies

IN PART VI, WE will look at the extent to which Christian organizations have a clear understanding and theology of leadership and how lack of such clarity may indeed affect several aspects of succession. In this chapter, through an analysis of the theologies of leadership within the case of Grace Network, we will begin to see the crucial nature of a common understanding of the nature and authority of leadership within an organization or movement. While a network of churches that lovingly served many, and had many years of fruitful ministry subsequent to the succession, different theological understandings as to the nature and meaning of succession and indeed leadership theology became problematic. Greater clarity at the point of succession might have helped obviate such problems. In this analysis, I suggest three features in the case of the succession in Grace Network which led to unsustainability. This is then followed by an exploration of theologies of leadership which produced these three problematic features.

The first feature is that there were different perspectives on the nature of the succession itself. For Blackwell, as one of the three founders, it changed little. Indeed, Groblewski was appointed so that there was little change. For Groblewski, however, he was assuming that his leadership had greater executive and individual authority post-succession. He felt the "weight" of leadership.[1] This began to lead to executive action: "But with the rise of the apostolic network churches, one of the first things I did when I acceded to the executive position [Executive Director] was insisted that the name change from Grace Presbytery to Grace Network."[2]

A second problematic feature was the minimization of the succession's significance, indeed a lack of acknowledgment that any change was taking place. This may, for example, be evidenced in the omission of any discussion of "terms" for the successor, such as expected hours of work and remuneration. Not to discuss these matters is to minimize the appointment and concomitant leadership changes; or, put differently, to discuss such terms would have per se acknowledged a positional change for Groblewski with a different measure of authority. It would have been an external practical and symbolic acknowledgment of leadership change.

This matter is related to, but is also distinguished from, the third point, namely that there was little discussion of authority in decision-making. This had already been the case prior to succession: "Uh—uh we never talked about co-equality. The words were never used and so forth, but essentially, I think we viewed ourselves, uh . . ."[3] The awkwardness of acknowledging the lack of clarity is confirmed by the repetitive paralinguistic utterances. This avoidance, however, became acute post-succession:

> But I think it might have set up some expectations that weren't realized, uh, in the sense that, uh, we never really, from my memory, we never really talked through extensively what a change to an executive director would mean.[4]

The succession was inadequate and confusing due to its being understood differently; its significance was minimized, and the avoidance of consideration of crucial succession features suggests that it was confusion over theology of leadership which contributed to the aforementioned insufficient enactments of succession. This may be seen both in examining the polity of the network and its member churches and in analyzing the different leadership theologies of the founders and the successor.

The first point may be seen in that the leadership modus operandi of member churches could be different from that of the network leadership: Church leaders and pastors had clear executive authority, and there was a clearly and duly appointed "senior pastor," or "the whole first among equals

1. Groblewski Interview I, 39.
2. Groblewski Interview I, 1.
3. Groblewski Interview I, 1.
4. Groblewski Interview I, 4.

thing . . . [yet] that model really never existed at the presbytery [Network] level."[5] Thus, confusion of polity and the theology from which it stemmed was not consistent at different levels within the movement.

This matter was compounded by the second matter, namely a confusion of theology within the network's senior leadership. More precisely stated, each of the network leaders espoused clear leadership theology, but it was not the same theology; this, moreover, was not fully acknowledged. Blackwell, as a founder, for example, held a strong theology of leadership based on distaste for legalism and control of people; this stemmed from a particular conceptualization of leadership as trait and character. The reaction to legalism is heard in his unprompted narrative which spoke in critical terms of other networks, which, he felt, were based on rules rather than Christian liberty.[6] That leadership is character (not skills) is heard in the following: "But we taught often on what we thought godly leaders should be like: not lording over, serving, being examples, leading like they were stewards of the . . . the . . . You know, biblically, stewards were managers of another's . . . someone else's";[7] "Grubby was clearly the type of leader that didn't lord over. He wasn't doing it for money. I mean like from First Peter, I mean he just . . . he didn't aspire to be the leader of our network. He was willing to do it."[8] It is not simply that character is the qualification but one character attribute in particular. The first character quality narrated by Blackwell (and on more than one occasion) is that of "not lording over," a reference to 1 Pet 5:3,[9] where Peter is reemphasizing the teaching of Christ (Matt 20:25 and Mark 10:42). Because we conceptualize linguistic form in spatial terms,[10] and because the metaphor "closeness" indicates strength of effect,[11] Blackwell's placement of "not lording over" nearest to "godly leaders" allows an interpretation that this is the most significant character quality in leadership. Thus, for Blackwell's understanding of leadership, we see, as with the citation of negative exempla of other legalistic networks, an aversion to leadership wielding power. Indeed, the Markan account's use of the same term employed in 1 Peter but succeeded by the grammatical construct of strong contrast, "Not so with you" (Mark 10:43), supports Blackwell's understanding. For Blackwell, therefore, an understanding of leadership

5. Groblewski Interview I, 16.
6. Blackwell Interview I, 24–25, 28.
7. Blackwell Interview II, 5–6.
8. Blackwell Interview I, 23.
9. Greek *katakyrieuontes*, at https://biblehub.com/interlinear/1_peter/5-3.htm.
10. Lakoff and Johnson, *Metaphors We Live By*, 126.
11. Lakoff and Johnson, *Metaphors We Live By*, 128–30.

is framed in terms of emphasizing the juxtaposition of "lording over" and the strong imperative to eschew such leadership methodology. For him, to restrain such tendencies toward wrong exercise of power, leadership must be seen in collegial terms: "Autonomous, uh, type leadership is not really Christian in my opinion."[12] When asked to explain further this understanding of church polity he explained:

> Blackwell: Well, I think plurality of elders. One person making all the decisions without anyone having input as well is dangerous. No one is fallible, or infallible rather. We're all fallible, I guess. And it's just meant, you know, a wise . . . I think church leadership is to be . . . have a number of elders with each . . . And I don't even think the senior leader should be able to veto them. It should be running on consensus. Now we . . . I don't think you can run—can operate a church on, what's the word? [long pause]
>
> Interviewer: Unanimity?
>
> Blackwell: . . . unanimity. Because that way, you could have six elders and one elder who controlled everything by saying "no." So, it's like . . . that gives the power to one person. Consensus, unanimity when you can have it. I mean, I think you should pray. And I think the network maybe can be the same way.[13]

Blackwell's principal understanding of leadership is to restrain the wrong exercise of power; this means (for him) that an episcopal approach would not be countenanced, but rather a Presbyterian model is necessitated.

In turning to the theology of leadership of the successor, we have already noted an internal phenomenological shift with appointment. He desired greater levels of empowerment to make decisions on behalf of the movement: "But I think I felt like my role was going to evolve into something more hierarchial [sic] as we began, and it didn't."[14] When this did not develop, Groblewski became frustrated.[15] His perspective with regard to leadership may best be explained by restating an earlier citation of

---

12. Blackwell Interview I, 6.

13. Blackwell Interview II, 4–5.

14. Groblewski Interview II, 13.

15. Groblewski Interview II, 12.

Wagner (chapter 17), that new forms and authority of leadership in new apostolic churches is the "most radical of the nine changes from traditional Christianity."[16] Wagner clarifies the difference as a greater amount of spiritual authority delegated by the Holy Spirit to individuals, designated by Wagner to be "charismatic leadership."[17] Such reformulation of leadership different from historic denominations is expressed in the following terms by Lawrence Khong, senior pastor of Faith Community Baptist Church in Singapore: "I will be a strong leader, one who believes what the Lord wants me to do and who pursues it with all my heart."[18] While agreeing with accountability, Khong believes that the church's focus on counterchecks to the leader has often led to "major roadblocks for God's appointed leaders to lead His people into victorious ministry."[19]

Considering the above, what may be seen within the Grace Network leadership team is two different conceptualizations of Christian leadership. One, particularly concerned with the harmful use of power, leads to the placement of checks and balances around the executive director enacted in the form of collegial leadership modes; the other aims to acknowledge that individuals may have a gift of leadership and seeks to empower such people to lead by articulating directional vision and strategy. In Groblewski's words, "There was a rift over the issue of leadership model, between collaborative team and directional . . ."[20] Yet even this description given by the successor, however, fails to provide a fuller understanding of the different leadership modes. To understand better the theological difference here, I turn to others in the "new apostolic churches," such as Kreider et al.[21] Kreider is the founder of DOVE International,[22] one of the eighteen cases of "new apostolic churches" described by Wagner.[23] Kreider et al. see in the Christian Scriptures three types of leadership or church government, whether at the congregational or broader network/denominational level, namely a "primary leader—episcopal government," "God calls a team to work together—presbyterian government," and "God speaks through His people in the local church—congregational government."[24] The authors argue for a

16. Wagner, *New Apostolic Churches*, 19.

17. Wagner, *New Apostolic Churches*, 20.

18. Khong, "Faith Community Baptist Church," 222.

19. Khong, "Faith Community Baptist Church," 222.

20. Groblewski Interview I, 5.

21. Kreider et al., *Biblical Role of Elders*.

22. https://dcfi.org/.

23. Wagner, *New Apostolic Churches*.

24. Kreider et al., *Biblical Role of Elders*, 78–88.

leadership model where all three principles are to be incorporated in order to make balanced decisions,[25] referring to this model as a "head, shoulders and body" model (taken from the simile for unity found in Ps 133).[26] At times, a whole congregation might need to be involved in decision-making. Mostly, however, a leadership team will seek to process matters and find unity. At other times the primary leader should be empowered to lead in a direction that he or she believes is from God (with input from others and with a process for appeal in place). I suggest that Groblewski's model may have more in common with Kreider et al.'s episcopal model, which is suggested by his emphasis on the term "hierarchical." Groblewski's theology of leadership was not the same as that of Blackwell.

Having suggested that different polity between churches and the network leadership level as well as divergent theologies within the network leadership were both problematic, there was a further contributory factor to the confusion of theology, namely the lack of acknowledgment of the differences: "There was this kind of a sense that everybody had the same understanding of . . ."[27] If a problem were suspected, it appears not to have been adequately resolved:

> I think Grubby, at times, felt like it made it harder for him to know how to relate to the other two guys and the other two networks. Like, he didn't know if he had full authority to just say absolutely [on behalf of Grace Network] in making a decision with those guys without coming back and talking to us. So, I think it probably was more difficult for him . . . we gave him a lot of freedom, but I think he felt tethered to us.[28]

Having stated an inadequate conceptualization of the nature of the appointment stemming from divergent theologies, the leadership team nonetheless functioned well in many ways with years of collaborative ministry. Both Blackwell as founder and Groblewski as successor believe this was due to mutual graciousness, love, and friendship. Such friendship can, however, obscure matters and enable avoidance of key "crucial conversations."[29] Avoid-

---

25. Kreider et al., *Biblical Role of Elders*, 89–90.

26. Kreider et al., *Biblical Role of Elders*, 89.

27. Blackwell Interview I, 10.

28. Blackwell Interview I, 4–5.

29. A phrase widely used in the business literature, popularized by Patterson et al., *Crucial Conversations*, with over five million sales (https://cruciallearning.com/books/). The term refers to "a discussion between two or more people where (1) stakes are high, (2) opinions vary, and (3) emotions run strong" (*Crucial Conversations*, 3). Literature indicates that much of management performance may not be driven by formal performance-management processes but the extent to which companies have

ance of potential problems may be possible in good times, but such matters may become overt during times of severe stress. When such times arose, which model of decision-making dominated? As Groblewski grappled with issues pertaining to the very integrity of the movement, he admits, "I think I was struggling with my own leadership."[30] This, according to Groblewski, drove the return to an even greater collegial style of leadership: "We kind of swung back to a three—three-headed deal," which reduced his acting in accord with apostolic leadership principles.[31] The network, having continued for years with unspoken leadership theology and two different operative models of polity, now exhibited corporate leadership stress, causing others in the movement to urge action because they viewed the existing Presbyterian leadership model as unsustainable. Under stress, the leadership model had indeed fully reverted to one that the executive director had hoped it would not be. This might be understood by reference to Girard's seminal work, *Violence and the Sacred*:

> The goal of religious thinking is the same as that of technological research—namely, practical action. Whenever man is truly concerned with obtaining concrete results, whenever he is hard pressed by reality, he abandons abstract speculation and reverts to a mode of response that becomes increasingly cautious and conservative as the forces he hopes to subdue, or at least to outrun, draw ever nearer.[32]

From the successor's narrative, we read that lack of clarity on leadership theology, polity, and leadership style eventually led to the leadership determining that their model was unsustainable; the network ceased to exist. This stemmed from an inadequate leadership succession years before: "In fact over the years there was a rift over the issue of leadership model, between collaborative team, and directional, between a 'conservative reformed group' and a 'little more charismatic group' . . . But it was the succession thing that was the fly in the ointment."[33] Indeed, Groblewski admits, "Our leadership model, the collaborative nature of the leadership model, was unsustainable. That was a key . . . In other words, it was a problem in

---

a clear ethos in which employees and managers engage in meaningful dialogue and crucial conversations to ensure achievement of standards (Patterson et al., *Crucial Conversations*, 11; Simon, *Hidden Champions*, 195).

30. Groblewski Interview I, 8.
31. Groblewski Interview I, 7.
32. Girard, *Violence and the Sacred*, 32.
33. Groblewski Interview I, 5.

succession that gave birth to a new network."[34] Succession, ill defined, differently understood, minimized in significance, all arising from confusion or collision of theologies of leadership, eventually led to the termination of Grace Network as an independent network. Theology matters—and matters in succession.

34. Groblewski Interview I, 5.

PART V

Succession Gestalt

Chapter Twenty-Four ──────────

Producing a Succession Gestalt

IN THIS CHAPTER, WE turn briefly to a concept I wish to introduce, namely that of "succession Gestalt." The German word "Gestalt" is used in various ways today in English. It is at its most literal level the German word for "form, shape, contour" but also means "figure, frame (of physique)" or more figuratively "kind, manner, way."[1] The term has been adopted, moreover, in some social sciences to refer to "an organized whole that is perceived as more than the sum of its parts."[2] It is in this latter vein that I introduce the term and apply it to the subject of this book, asking the question whether the various aspects in succession within organizations, particularly Christian agencies and movements, might together perform an enactment and structuration of succession which produces a cohesive whole model of succession. I show that this is possible by revisiting the three dimensions of succession already described in the founder succession of International Aid Services, namely the professionalization of leadership style, the dynamics of a father-son transition, and the succession ceremony as symbolically enacted text. These three motifs are not independent but interdependent:

---

1. "Gestalt," Cassell's German Dictionary, 263.

2. *Oxford Encyclopedic English Dictionary*, 591. It is often the case in English publications that the term is written with a lower case "g," "gestalt." I, however, maintain the German orthography which requires an upper case for nouns, thus "Gestalt."

1. The dynamic of professionalization is mediated and mitigated by the father-son relationship and by the *communitas* of the transition ceremony. This may be viewed in that, despite the markers of professionalization (financial restructuration, governance reformation, and written, not oral, strategy), the relationships of the key actors are humanized by the familial bonds: "And I just laid my hand around my brother and said, 'Yeah, he's my brother. You can't take that away from us. We're in the same organization'";[3] "[My father is] a great source of inspiration";[4] "I love him."[5] The second point may be seen with the father and son worshipping God and praying together and the Christo-Petrine framing of organizational succession: "And today I would like to give this key to my successor, Daniel."[6] Such enactments were not ones of professional bureaucratic management.

2. The paternal-filial succession navigates putative nepotism through professionalization and is universalized by the multicultural transition event. This may be seen in the new emphasis on written policies, the adoption of standards to meet governmental grant-making criteria, and particularly in the board of directors appointing the successor: "And today I'm glad it was on that level because it was not a father-son kind of issue. It was on a completely different level. And I was not actually involved in the decision-making process at all here."[7] The second part is seen by the various nationalities and races joining in worship, local African workers giving speeches, and the successor publicly submitting himself to African eldership.[8]

3. The celebration, *communitas* creation, symbolic enactments, and theologizing of the transition ceremony are mediated by the professionalization (written plans, formal evaluations, change from oral to written reporting, and decisions based on empirical data rather than intuition)[9] and by good bureaucratic governance through the involvement of the board of directors in the father-son successor appointment.[10]

3. Daniel Zetterlund Interview I, 45.
4. Daniel Zetterlund Interview II, 21.
5. Daniel Zetterlund Interview I, 30.
6. Leif Zetterlund, speech at transition ceremony.
7. Leif Zetterlund Interview I, 4.
8. Daniel Zetterlund Interview I, 50.
9. See Tashakori, *Managerial Succession*.
10. Daniel Zetterlund Interview I, 10.

All three motifs are thus each nuanced by the other two. Such matters could create tension as they relate to different exigencies and goals, such as complying with both Swedish good governance and African eldership, or the maintenance of Christian fraternity and devotion to God while complying with exacting auditing and accounting demands of European governments. If tension exists, it seems a productive one, where all three motifs cohere into a tripartite succession Gestalt, which made navigable the changing bureaucratic environment of donors yet maintained relationships of Christian fraternity, provided reassuring internal succession yet in an impartial manner, and enhanced a vibrant Christian spirituality which reemphasized the missional goals of the ministry and the theological nature of the succession itself.

In taking further my conclusion that such a Gestalt arises from an interdependency among the three motifs, I employ Thompson's theory of interdependencies to suggest that there is a specific type of interdependency present in this Gestalt production. Rather than "sequential" interdependency, where the enactment of each motif is contingent on a temporal enactment and completion by the others,[11] or "reciprocal" interdependency, where the outputs of each become inputs for the other parts,[12] the interdependency of the IAS Gestalt is rather one of "pooled" interdependency, where the temporal nature (sequence and contemporaneity) is less important, but each part "performs" adequately rendering "a discrete contribution to the whole and each is supported by the whole."[13] It is thus indeed possible for a number of aspects of succession to support each other and produce a cohesive enactment of succession. This was the case in the performance of succession within International Aid Services.

11. Thompson, *Organizations in Action*, 54.

12. Thompson, *Organizations in Action*, 55.

13. Thompson, *Organizations in Action*, 54.

PART VI

Succession and Organizational Self-Reflection

Successor Identification, Power, and Ceremony

Chapter Twenty-Five ————————

Succession and Reflexivity

HAVING PROVIDED CHAPTERS OF which the content touches upon on a number of important aspects of succession including leadership style change, successors' origins, theologies of apostleship, and gender, in this part of the book, I will endeavor to reflect on a number of other matters. This part will focus on organizational and theological reflexivity in the succession process and explore how crucial this is; indeed, how a lack of such reflection might impair succession. I intend to provide more data on three aspects of succession in each of the case studies, namely on methods of successor identification, on power in the appointment process of successors, and on succession ceremonies (providing additional reflection to chapter 22). Part VI aims to show that there are often theological inconsistences, indeed overlooked areas or lacunae, which can be revealed through such matters as successor identification methods, power, and ceremony. If overlooked, these matters affect succession.

INSTITUTIONAL AND THEOLOGICAL
REFLEXIVITY AND THE VOICES OF THEOLOGY

In chapter 10, I sought to explain reflexivity as it relates to empirical study of Christian founder succession. I wrote that a reflexive approach can be crucial to gaining a fuller description and that, moreover, in earlier studies of founder succession, a lack of reflexivity was detrimental to producing credible findings. While much of that chapter concerned epistemological and methodological reflexivity, elsewhere I have also made the case for reflexivity as a theological category.[1] In this chapter, I wish to examine not the researcher's theological reflexivity but that of the organizations which form the three case studies. To what extent was there appropriate and sufficient reflection on organizational theology (and theory) in the succession processes? More specifically, I wish to do this by seeking to identify the congruencies and incongruences within those theologies of succession; in other words, I seek to identify the interstices or lacunae in the theologies and reflections thereon, hence the term "lacunal reflexivity." Such an approach will point to the theories and theologies which informed succession and provide a tool for their critical evaluation.

I adopt this approach in light of the established benefits of institutional reflexivity in many fields. Reflexivity as an organizational-level construct is defined as "the extent to which group members overtly reflect upon, and communicate about the group's objectives, strategies (e.g., decision-making) and processes (e.g., communication), and adapt them to current or anticipated circumstances."[2] Organizational reflexivity has been shown to be beneficial in a number of ways, including increasing the agency of the institution's members;[3] facilitating greater team effectiveness;[4] enhancing institutional innovation;[5] building character among members and thus promoting better ethical responses.[6] To my knowledge, there have been no studies to date on institutional reflexivity (as a modern sociological concept) within Christian organizations, a surprising observation given the ubiquitous concern of mission drift (chapter 15).[7] While many of the above studies focus on performance, others position institutional reflexivity as a means of enabling reflection at the deeper level of values and worldview shaping decisions and performances.[8] It is at this level that I examine the lacunal

---

1. Bunton, "Reflexivity in Practical Theology," 83–84.

2. West et al., "Group Decision-Making," 296.

3. Swift and West, *Reflexivity and Group Processes*.

4. de Dreu, "Team Innovation," 285–98.

5. Farnese and Livi, "How Reflexivity Enhances Organizational Innovativeness," 525–36.

6. Antonacopoulou, "Sensuous Learning," 13–44. Further studies showing the organizational efficacy of institutional reflexivity include Mäkitalo and Säljö, "Invisible People," 160–78; Widmer et al., "Recent Developments," 2–11.

7. Of course, one could argue that much of ecclesiology is a reflection by the church on itself.

8. Antonacopoulou et al., "New Learning Organization."

reflexivity of organizational theology. In classic organizational learning, a distinction is made between "single-loop learning," where lessons are learned from actions framed within existing shared mental models and existing norms, and "double-loop learning," where the shared mental models and norms are themselves questioned.[9] I posit that an organizational theology can only be reflected upon with "double-loop learning," and it is this that requires theological reflexivity, to make known the prevailing theological (and theoretical) constructs which drive succession actions.

To develop this further, I propose a specific method of examining institutional reflexivity on succession theology. I do this partly following Baggett's approach in his ethnographic study of Habitat for Humanity,[10] an organization which presents itself today as follows:

> Habitat works together with families, local communities, volunteers and partners from around the world so that more people are able to live in affordable and safe homes. Our advocacy efforts focus on policy reform to remove systemic barriers preventing low-income and historically underserved families from accessing adequate, affordable shelter.[11]

While Baggett undertook a fuller, more multifaceted study of one organization than I could undertake in three cases, some of Baggett's ethnography describes and explains the ministry's theology, both at the official level, such as printed literature and mission statements, and the informal level, including the prevailing beliefs of volunteers, clients, and staff. One of Baggett's contributions is to give voice to many of the unheard participants' beliefs within Habitat for Humanity by bringing their theological understandings to bear on an understanding of corporate beliefs. Baggett shows incongruences between the official organizational theology and the theologies of the volunteers and staff. Such findings need not be a surprise if understood within the model of a "theology in four voices."[12] Applying this model, I argue that there can be degrees of congruity and incongruity between the voices which affect organizational belief and thus practice. It is such lacunae that I wish to explore as part of the book's analysis of successions.

9. Argyris and Schön, *Organizational Learning*.

10. Baggett, *Habitat for Humanity*.

11. https://www.habitat.org/our-work.

12. Cameron et al., *Talking about God in Practice*. The concept of "theology in four voices" was explained in chapter 10 as a theological model of the following: normative theology (scriptures, creeds etc.); formal theology (theology of theologians and dialogue with other disciplines); espoused theology (a group's articulation of its beliefs); and operant theology (the theology embedded within the actual practices of a group) (Cameron et al., *Talking about God in Practice*, 53–56).

In reflecting further on methodology, I am aware that theology in four voices was conceptualized within the context of theological action research (TAR),[13] a method which emphasizes "conversation, attentive to otherness" between the voices.[14] This raises questions as to whether or how the theology in four voices might be employed in methods other than TAR. Many have found the voices a useful analytic tool for other ethnographic approaches in ecclesiology,[15] something also acknowledged by Watkins, one of the developers of theology in four voices along with Cameron.[16] Theology in four voices has, for example, been used well by Loy in her PhD dissertation where she employs an ethnographic rather than TAR approach. There seems thus to be growing confidence in the voices being a helpful tool for a variety of approaches. My approach draws to some extent (but with differences) on the approach of Loy in her study of the theology of the development agency Christian Aid.[17] Loy draws from the four voices approach to examine the agency's beliefs but also combines this with a different model, that of explicit theology (official organizational theological statements), implicit theology (expressed through informal discourse) and null theologies (unspoken or only referred to obliquely).[18] My critique of Loy is that she ends up with a confused conflation of the systems, wrongly equating Christian Aid's "explicit" with Cameron's "formal" theology; Loy's "explicit" is not the same as "formal" academic theology according to Cameron's definition.[19] Loy concludes her study with "points of confluence and contradiction between the explicit, implicit and null theological voices" within Christian Aid.[20] Congruence was found on matters such as the belief widely held on the equality of all people and thus being non-discriminatory in who were chosen for assistance,[21] yet the official and explicit theology of the agency was an overt adoption of Barth's relational theology, something of which the staff were either unaware or understood differently.[22] The implicit theologies of the staff were largely contextual theologies, whereas the

13. Cameron et al., *Talking about God in Practice.*

14. Watkins, "Practising Ecclesiology," 36.

15. Kaufman and Ideström, "Why Matter Matters," 91.

16. Watkins, "Practising Ecclesiology," 24.

17. Loy, "Resurrection beyond the Secular."

18. Loy, "Resurrection beyond the Secular," 25–29.

19. Cameron et al., *Talking about God in Practice,* 54.

20. Loy, "Resurrection beyond the Secular," 94.

21. Loy, "Resurrection beyond the Secular," 98.

22. Loy, "Resurrection beyond the Secular," 97. In Cameron et al.'s terms, a gap between normative and espoused theologies.

explicit organizational theology was "from above." Many workers felt the organization was not acting according to its explicit theology.[23]

While there are matters in which Loy is to be critiqued, such as privileging the voices of the staff interviewees over others and, at times, methodological inconsistency by asserting quantitative claims despite not having a representative sample,[24] there is much in this work to inform my approach to the theologies of the three cases with regard to succession. Yet, my work stands in contradistinction to both Baggett and Loy in a number of ways: It is not an in-depth study of one organization but a focus on one aspect (succession) of three organizations. This leads to the most significant distinction, namely that both Baggett and Loy were able to show the lacunae between organizational espoused theologies and the operant theologies of the staff and volunteers. In my study, I have purposefully sought not to follow this approach but to obtain extensive interviews only with the founders and successors, in effect the organization's leadership who wield the most power, including in the construction of espoused theologies.[25] Yet, I believe a significant finding of this study is that the kinds of incongruities found by Baggett and Loy are still to be found even within the succession theologies of leadership. There are interstices between espoused theologies and operant theologies of the leaders and insufficient reflexivity thereon. Further theological reflexivity, indeed the lacunal reflexivity for which I call, would have assisted the successions in terms of clarity, congruity, and organizational focus.

To show the rationale for this assertion, I will examine three aspects of how the organizations in my case studies performed succession, namely successor identification methods, the use of power, and succession ceremonies. I will introduce relevant literature and examine espoused and operant theologies of succession through organizational text, interviews, symbols, and action. This will show the interstices in these voices of theologies and thus congruencies and incongruences between them, allowing reflection on the extent to which the cases confirm or differ from other research findings and on how reflexivity may have assisted succession.

---

23. Loy, "Resurrection beyond the Secular," 127.
24. Loy, "Resurrection beyond the Secular," 184.
25. This approach is explained more fully in chapter 11.

Chapter Twenty-Six ⸻

Successor Identification Methods

THE TWO FORMATIVE AND influential works on methods of successor identification are those of Vancil and Friedman and Olk,[1] both reviewed in chapter 2, where their well-used terminology of succession methods was explained ("relay succession," "heir apparent" or "crown heir," "horse race," "coup d'état," and "comprehensive search") and critical comments provided. To the comments in chapter 2, it is added that Friedman and Olk suggest that "outcome preference certainty" shortens the process of finding a successor and minimizes disruption.[2] If the criteria for selecting a successor are given, then it is more likely that "crown heir" succession will ensue. Uncertainty may lead to "horse race" or "comprehensive search." Legitimacy is ascribed to the succession by those affected if the successor is viewed as competent and the selection process fair. They suggest that "horse race" selection provides the greatest legitimacy. Their findings are also that perception of legitimacy is greater when incumbents lead the process. The issue of legitimacy is consequential as other leaders might depart the corporation should the processes be viewed as illegitimate.[3]

---

1. Vancil, *Passing the Baton.* Friedman and Olk, "Four Ways to Choose a CEO," 141–64.

2. Friedman and Olk, "Four Ways to Choose a CEO," 147.

3. Friedman and Saul, "Leader's Wake," 619–42.

INTERNATIONAL AID SERVICES

The succession method with IAS was at the initiation of the international board/executive team with a concomitant search being enacted to find a successor, leading to the international board's making the decision. This approach was a "comprehensive search" as "numerous qualified candidates for the position of CEO were evaluated."[4] The employment of the "comprehensive search" method alerts us to a possible lacuna; a "comprehensive search" usually takes place when there is little outcome preference certainty. I argue that, in contradistinction, there was indeed outcome preference certainty in the succession process, seen in the need for the successor to have an unwavering commitment to the missiological aims of IAS[5] as well as to possess the requisite skills for addressing the challenges of a changing donor environment. If such outcome certainty was indeed the case, then a "comprehensive search" (according to Friedman and Olk) becomes unnecessary, as the organization knows exactly the kind of successor they desire and may already have strong inclinations even to the successor's identity. Indeed, such certainty usually leads to the "heir apparent" succession method. Given this, it is possible to find a lacuna between the espoused method of comprehensive search (which would normally accompany outcome uncertainty) and an operant method of crown heir, knowing exactly the kind of person needed; despite a wider search, the board had already discussed a preference for an internal candidate.[6]

I suggest, furthermore, that this relates also to insufficient reflexivity on matters of leadership theory. IAS undertook no reflection on formal theory but placed emphasis on the changing donor environment.[7] This makes manifest operant theory, namely that of contingency leadership.[8] Contingency leadership theory is a "leader-match" theory: "Effective leadership is *contingent* on matching a leader's style to the right setting."[9] In focusing on styles and situations, this theory distances itself from person-based leadership theory.

This view of the importance of leader/situation match was confirmed by the founder:

4. International Aid Services, "Press Release," June 23, 2014 (attached as Appendix B); Leif Zetterlund Interview I, 12.

5. Leif Zetterlund Interview I, 19.

6. Daniel Zetterlund Interview I, 9.

7. Daniel Zetterlund Interview I, 31–32.

8. Fiedler, *Theory of Leadership Effectiveness*; Fiedler and Chemers, *Leadership and Effective Management*, and *Improving Leadership Effectiveness*.

9. Northouse, *Leadership*, 123 (italics in original).

> [Speaking of successor] He's not practical the way that I am, but he's much more academic and more structured than I am. So, I could see that bringing in somebody from that point of view, now when bureaucracy is becoming a number one thing for donors and partners and systems must be in place, it might be a very healthy thing for the organization in order to grow forward, grow both in depth and also be able to actually spread out to other countries as well.[10]

This interpretation of IAS's actions as an application of contingency theory may, furthermore, be supported by evidence suggesting that IAS aimed for favorableness on the three scales of contingency theory (position power, task structure, and leader-member relations):[11] The successor position power was made clearer through the changes to international governance and the CEO's role with regard to the board; task structure was improved with, for example, greater definition of vision and strategy;[12] and leader-member relations were enhanced by the consultation process with staff.[13]

A conscious reflection on theory may have facilitated other self-understandings of the organization and led to further helpful steps forward for the organization. For example, after being severely disappointed with the Swedish government funding changes, organizational inspiration may have been needed; reflection on charismatic understandings of leadership may have made this more visible, which may, in turn, have led to different or additional leadership actions to bring inspiration after such disappointment. Of course, IAS may well have been wise to adopt a contingency approach given the exigencies of public funding, but this approach's privileging over other understandings may have obscured alternative or additional leadership strategies which could have benefited the organization at that time.

NEWFRONTIERS

The espoused theology of succession for Newfrontiers has earlier been described (chapters 17, 20, and 21). Significant aspects of such espoused theology are that Newfrontiers' succession was to be "kinesisoclastic" and an enactment of apostolic multiplication. The former manifests in Virgo's understanding of New Testament succession from the day of Pentecost's

---

10. Leif Zetterlund Interview I, 8–9.

11. Fiedler and Chemers, *Improving Leadership Effectiveness*, 46.

12. International Aid Services, *Fit for Purpose*.

13. Leif Zetterlund Interview I, 9. For criticism of contingency theory, see Northhouse, *Leadership*, 128–30.

being "Peter's moment, not Peter's movement." I give particular significance to this theological position due to its repetition in the interviews (see Virgo Interview I, 28–29, for example, and elsewhere), as well as to its emphasis achieved by Virgo's use of alliteration and homeoteleuton. Commitment to apostleship is indeed a strong defining characteristic of Newfrontiers' adherents.[14] It is an espoused theology that apostles are "master builders" (1 Cor 3:10).[15] The succession method chosen was a form of "horse race," observing which leaders oversaw growing congregations, thus a sign that others were following them. This resulted in fifteen becoming "heirs apparent" at a later stage.

Despite such espoused theologies, there was, moreover, operant theology manifest through the succession, seen in metaphoric privileging and gendered conceptualizations of leadership type. The first matter is the privileging of the conceptualization of apostles as architects. While apostleship as architect is espoused, *it is its privileging over other conceptualizations which is not espoused but operant.* A multi-modal analysis of the special edition of the *Newfrontiers Magazine*[16] as the official explanation of succession reveals the privileging of architectural images from around the world on both front and back covers; virtually every picture is of a building. Greater reflexivity may have been helpful at this point, because the operant theology contained therein may be interpreted as showing the crucial understanding of succession is that of organizational, structural change rather than an emphasis on people and ethnic diversity. A privileging of the architecture (in a metaphorical sense) of church government and structural change means that without due reflection the organization may look for structural leaders rather than leaders with greater pastoral gifts.[17] There is, thus, a theological lacuna between espoused theology of apostles as architects and operant theology concerning the *privileging* of apostles as architects over other understandings of apostleship within Newfrontiers (for example, of apostles as fathers); this impinges on apostolic selection criteria. Furthermore, as Kay has indicated, emphasizing the metaphor of apostles as builders might also mean that they might need to destroy what exists before they can begin to build.[18] This potential aspect of ministry was also not part of the reflection

14. Kay, *Apostolic Networks*, 319.

15. Devenish, *Fathering Leaders*, 87.

16. *Newfrontiers Magazine, Forward Together.*

17. I am aware that in the New Testament, building images are at times used to refer to people (for example, 1 Pet 2:5), but many of the images in the Newfrontiers magazine are not of a "spiritual house" (to use the Petrine language) but of parliaments, bridges, and palaces.

18. Kay, "Apostolic Networks in Britain Revisited," 11.

and could be problematic for the organization; closing existing churches produces pain and dissent.

The second lacuna concerns theologies and typologies of leadership gender. By that, I do not mean that the movement was complementarian, for that is an espoused, indeed a normative theology, which explicitly precludes women from apostolic succession (chapter 21). What I suggest, however, is that there is an operant theology concerning the *types* of masculinity to which apostleship can be ascribed or the ways in which masculinity is constructed—and that there is little reflexivity on this in the succession process. I am aware that such comments touch upon issues of gender construction and theology, a vast and complex field encompassing many disciplines.[19] Despite the debates within this field, the correlation between gender construction and religion/theology has been increasingly made obvious.[20] Studies have explicated the religious construction of gender among modern-day Wesleyans[21] and among evangelicals,[22] while others even describe the construction of fatherhood within Newfrontiers[23] and masculinity in general within this network.[24]

Through a reading of Newfrontiers texts and ethnographic observations of Newfrontiers churches,[25] a picture emerges not just of leadership as male but as a certain type of male. Studying sermons of Newfrontiers leaders, Aune shows how masculinity is constructed against the perceived background of men being absent from family life and not taking leadership both in the family and church.[26] While this is espoused, at the operant level, masculinity is constructed through the movement in various ways. Wignall shows, for example, the importance of physicality in Newfrontiers discourse, suggesting that the movement draws on the "Muscular Christianity" movement[27] which correlates physicality, strength, and morality.[28] Wignall shows how men in Newfrontiers, including leaders, make people aware of

19. See for example Sage's journal *Men and Masculinities*, https://us.sagepub.com/en-us/nam/journal/men-and-masculinities#description.

20. Satlow, "'Try to be a Man,'" 19–40; Castelli, "Gender, Theory, and the Rise of Christianity," 227–57; Thatcher, *Oxford Handbook of Theology, Sexuality, and Gender*.

21. Weaver Swartz, "Wesleyan (Anti)Feminism," 1–11.

22. Sheldon, "Wild at Heart," 977–98.

23. Aune, "Fatherhood in British Evangelical Christianity," 168–89.

24. Wignall, "'Man after God's Own Heart,'" 389–411.

25. Aune, "Postfeminist Evangelicals"; Wignall, "'Man after God's Own Heart,'" 389–411.

26. Aune, "Postfeminist Evangelicals," 195, 203.

27. Putney, *Muscular Christianity*, 14–16.

28. Coleman, "Of Metaphors and Muscles," 39–53.

their physical fitness,[29] while Aune notes that discussions on masculinity encompass sport.[30] The discourse on manhood, moreover, lauds aggression and risk-taking, as seen when a leader of the student and youth work at a large Newfrontiers church states that manhood is "not about being nice and being a peacemaker. It's about being aggressive and taking risks."[31] Furthermore, the catalyst for Newfrontiers' succession came from Mark Driscoll, a man at the time highly regarded as a significant leader, yet who in 2014 was removed from leadership of his church due to a bullying leadership style.[32] Wignall comments that those masculinities are shaped in dialogue with an "imaginary outside world that is perceived as having lost its ability to shape young men appropriately."[33] While leadership and apostleship are male at the normative and espoused level, at the operant level leadership is understood within a certain construction of manhood. Thus, when leaders were seeking to recognize those men who had apostolic gifts, were they also seeking a certain perception of man and potentially excluding those who did not fit their operant understanding of masculinity? It is possible that such non-conforming men might nonetheless be strategic "architects." This points to insufficient reflexivity on this lacuna between espoused and operant theologies of leadership gender type. This matter can be problematic, furthermore, due to the attributional notion of espoused theology, that the people are to recognize the gifts of apostles and follow them. As Wignall states, adherents "consume and self-create identities within the permissible cosmologies set down by leadership teams."[34] Lack of full reflexivity on such matters may in this case mean that organizational leaders perceived to have constructed a certain masculinity were chosen, while others were excluded. Recognition by the people may be an enactment of operant conceptualizations of manhood where people ascribe apostleship to those who fit the operant model. Leadership selection and follower attribution thus manifest a theological circularity which could not be seen within the network without greater lacunal reflexivity (although perhaps more readily observable by others outside the network).

29. Wignall, "'Man after God's Own Heart,'" 399, 400.

30. Aune, "Postfeminist Evangelicals," 196.

31. Cited in Wignall, "'Man after God's Own Heart,'" 397.

32. Glenza, "Controversial Seattle Pastor."

33. Wignall, "'Man after God's Own Heart,'" 397.

34. Wignall, "'Man after God's Own Heart,'" 408.

GRACE NETWORK

The espoused method of successor selection for Grace Network was for the board of directors to appoint an executive director. This is consistent with a theology of Presbyterian leadership. The operant theology, however, was also congregational, manifest by members voting to appoint Groblewski at the network conference. The very method of appointment, therefore, showed incongruity and exposes ambiguity concerning the locus of power; is it with the board, the voting church leaders, or, indeed, with international partners who insisted on such an appointment?[35] Such ambiguity was compounded by this succession being a coercive isomorphic response. Such a response to exogenous pressure mitigated against due reflexivity on polity and led to "decoupling" which "enables organizations to maintain standardized, legitimating, formal structures while their activities vary in response to practical considerations,"[36] something which churches and Christian ministries have been shown to do.[37] The lack of lacunal reflexivity on such "decoupling" was further reinforced by "outcome preference certainty."[38] From the outset, the directors had a certainty of purpose in any appointment, namely organizational culture preservation and a desire for as little change as possible,[39] both of which favored an internal candidate. These matters point to a further aspect of inadequate reflection, namely of the dominant metaphor of Grace Network as an organism with DNA. This was an espoused conceptualization within the network, an understanding leading to a fear of "mutation."[40] Lack of due reflexivity on such matters was problematic in that the dominant metaphor obscured other understandings of the situation by insisting on the truth of the metaphoric entailment.[41] I suggest that greater reflexivity might have made available further theoretical and helpful ways of considering succession, such as the need also to take into account contextual and contingent matters.

To explain further this last point requires some attempt to differentiate between theology and theory, as outlined in chapter 7. Theory is a way

---

35. Of course, such ambiguities may exist in other denominations. Power within the Anglican Church, for example, may lie with a bishop, clergy, or a lay synod.

36. Meyer and Rowan, "Institutional Organizations," 58.

37. Chaves, *Ordaining Women*; Prichard, "*Grandes Dames*," 39–57.

38. Friedman and Olk, "Four Ways to Choose a CEO," 147.

39. Blackwell Interview I, 4.

40. Blackwell Interview II, 15.

41. Boréus and Bergström, "Metaphor Analysis and Critical Linguistics," 149; Lakoff and Johnson, *Metaphors We Live By*, 159–84.

of "conceptualizing" leadership,[42] or an "approach to leadership,"[43] a way of perceiving it, which emphasizes matters other than the numinous or authoritative religious scriptures (matters such as behaviors, traits, or situational factors). Blackwell, for example, in talking of the servant nature of a leader, and citing the Bible in so doing, is, of course, engaged in a theological reflection on the nature of leadership and its qualifying character, as many others do.[44] There is, however, a widely held leadership theory of servant leadership; it is my contention that reflection on theory and not solely theology may also have helped Grace Network for the following reasons. The leadership theory of servant leadership was articulated in Greenleaf's foundational works[45] and was primarily inspired not by Christian Scriptures but Herman Hesse's novel *Die Morgenlandfahrt*, itself inspired by eastern philosophy.[46] This was first translated into English in 1956[47] and soon read by Greenleaf.[48] This is not to say that servant leadership theory does not, in places, concur with Christian perspectives; indeed, Blanchard openly synthesizes Greenleaf's concepts with the scriptural teachings of Christ.[49]

For Greenleaf, servant leadership concerns

> the care taken by the servant—first to make sure that other people's highest priority needs are being served. The best test, and difficult to administer, is: do those served grow as persons; do they, *while being served*, become healthier, wiser, freer, more autonomous, more likely themselves to become servants?[50]

Servant leadership theory thus focuses on placing the needs of others above oneself, on moral behavior to others, including followers and organizations. It implies shifting one's organizational power to those being led.[51]

---

42. Northouse, *Leadership*, 4.

43. Northouse, *Leadership*, 2.

44. Agosto, *Servant Leadership*; Kelley, *Servant Leadership*; Roach, *Servant-Leadership Style of Jesus*; Whitehead, *Servant Leadership*; and others.

45. Greenleaf, *Servant as Leader; Institution as Servant*; and *Servant Leadership*.

46. See Banks and Ledbetter, *Reviewing Leadership*, 108.

47. Hesse, *Journey to the East*.

48. Greenleaf , *Servant as Leader*, 9–10.

49. Blanchard, "Heart of Servant-Leadership," xi.

50. Greenleaf, *Servant as Leader*, 15 (italics in original).

51. Spears enumerates the characteristics of a servant leader (Spears, "Tracing the Past," 4–8). Liden et al., "Servant Leadership: Development of a Multidimensional Measure," 161–77, and Liden et al., "Servant Leadership: Antecedents, Processes and Outcomes," 357–79, offer a more sophisticated model of servant leadership combining antecedent conditions, servant leader behaviors, and outcomes.

In Blackwell's narratives, it is possible to discern that his concept of leadership is similar to this theory of servant leadership:

> But we taught often on what we thought godly leaders should be like: not lording over, serving, being examples, leading like they were stewards . . . You know, biblically, stewards were managers of another's, someone else's. And we wanted to see leaders leading like it wasn't theirs. It was God's.[52]

Indeed, Blackwell's view accords with Northouse's summation of servant leadership: "Rather than using their power to dominate others, leaders should make every attempt to share their power and enable others to grow and become autonomous. Leadership framed from this perspective downplays competition in the organization and promotes egalitarianism."[53]

It is maintained that due reflexivity on this matter of leadership theory could have helped Grace Network see some of the weaknesses in their position. For example, servant leadership theory has been criticized for being utopian and minimizing the importance of leadership behaviors such as directing and goal-setting.[54] It may, furthermore, be a moralistic philosophy rather than a pragmatic theory.[55] Such criticisms are noteworthy in light of the criticism Grace Network received from within its network, that their leadership model was unable to handle crises and produce directive leadership on agreed collaborative matters,[56] a criticism with which the executive director agreed. Thus, Grace Network's perceived leadership weakness may also be reflected in the weakness of this theory, giving further credence to the assertion that servant leadership theory was operant for this network.

If the leaders of Grace Network had shown reflexivity on such theoretical matters, they may have been aware of the balancing benefits of theories other than servant leadership. Contingency theory, for example, suggests that they look not just at the character of the successor but whether there was contingent match; that is, whether the successor had the appropriate skill to lead given the contextual challenges the organization faced.[57] Furthermore, understandings of transformational leadership theory may have helped the network address how its participants could, through synergism, accomplish greater effectiveness and might have offered a different way forward in their

---

52. Blackwell Interview II, 5–6.
53. Northouse, *Leadership*, 233.
54. Gergen, "Bad News for Bullies," 54.
55. Northouse, *Leadership*, 235.
56. Groblewski Interview I, 5.
57. Fiedler and Chemers, *Improving Leadership Effectiveness*.

difficulties.[58] The unreflective adherence to the paradigm of "organization as organism with DNA" and the outcome certainty of "no change" obscured the need for lacunal reflexivity concerning leadership theory and succession methods and selection which may have helped bring clarity to the type of leadership actions needed.

SUMMARY

While it may be possible to discern elements of the "heir apparent" selection method in Grace Network, the method, however, fits none of the categories in the succession literature, as Grace Network's succession was a reaction to isomorphic pressures, which led to an unreflexive decision of little meaning to many in the organization. This appears to identify a gap in the research literature, as there have been no studies on correlation between succession and isomorphism. IAS's succession differs from the expected succession patterns as outlined both by Vancil[59] and Friedman and Olk,[60] in that outcome certainty and comprehensive search are rarely associated, indicating incongruities between espoused method (search) and operant method (heir apparent). Newfrontiers does not conform to existing research models, particularly in that the succession ratio of one to fifteen seems sui generis and thus benefits understanding of succession as an "extreme" or unique case.[61] Nonetheless, lacunal reflexivity on method does show incongruity between espoused and operant theology of apostleship and gender type. This was not accounted for in the succession. The three cases furthermore seem to confirm, in varying degrees, the literature that is conclusive on the significance of the predecessor leader in many succession matters, including timing, selection, and successor socialization.[62] In the case of IAS, this was true in that the founder's involvement provided practical assistance to the process and his blessing provided legitimacy. With Newfrontiers, the founder's involvement was crucial; Virgo had the final authority to approve the fifteen; he wrote about the process; he introduced and commended the successors at the 2011 conference.

58. Burns, *Leadership*; Bass, *Leadership and Performance*; Antonakis, "Transformational and Charismatic Leadership," 256–88.

59. Vancil, *Passing the Baton*.

60. Friedman and Olk, "Four Ways to Choose a CEO," 141–64.

61. See Abramson, *Case for Case Studies*, on unique cases.

62. Vancil, *Passing the Baton*, 257; Friedman and Olk, "Four Ways to Choose a CEO," 141–64.

Chapter Twenty-Seven ———————

Who Really Makes the Decisions?
Succession and Power

"POWER" IS THE SECOND aspect of succession to be examined for congruities and incongruities between espoused and operant theology and theory of succession. Leadership transition is about the "passage of power."[1] Tashakori in her study of founder succession gives considerable place to the examination of power.[2] Few took up that matter until Block and Rosenberg conducted comparative empirical research on founder and non-founder director power (see chapter 2).[3] Tashakori found that in successful transitions, the successor had "substantial" power. There is the potential power of the successor and realized power (actual power gained while in office). The successor can derive power from four sources: coalition with the board; coalition with the founder; coalition with investors; and through his or her personal characteristics such as skill, competence, and personality. Even if potential power is high, the successor must still convert it into realized power.

Power realization most crucially depends on the founder/successor relationship.[4] The founder may assist the successor by providing legitimacy and ensuring opportunities to lead. This is determined, however, by

1. McDonald, "Foreword," xii.

2. Tashakori, *Managerial Succession*.

3. Block and Rosenberg, "Toward an Understanding of Founder's Syndrome," 353–68.

4. See also Vancil, *Passing the Baton*.

the extent to which the founder is dependent on the successor, as well as by the founder's own attributes and management style. Founders are more likely to build a coalition with the successor if the founder perceives that the successor has abilities lacking in the founder but needed at that time. Furthermore, founders need the personal attributes that enable them to relinquish control. The entrepreneurial style, with its involvement in so many aspects of the enterprise, means that founders can find it difficult to allow a successor to lead with a different style.[5] For successors to flourish, Tashakori stresses the importance of "competence," which can be dependent on knowledge of the "industry" and administrative ability, and of the ability to build positive interpersonal relationships.

The problem with this conceptualization is that much still depends on the successor, whereas others (founder or board) exercise power and may be unwilling to release enough power to the successor. The matter is thus more dynamic and relationally contingent than Tashakori allows.

Block and Rosenberg studied power in founder succession, finding that founders tend to exercise greater power than successors. Their findings should, however, be treated with caution as they do not take into account organizational size or longevity. In new and small organizations, the founder will hold great power as fewer matters are delegated. Both Tashakori and Block and Rosenberg, furthermore, pay insufficient attention to other environmental factors which may influence power relations.[6]

INTERNATIONAL AID SERVICES

Power in the succession process lay with the international executive board. It was the board chairperson who initiated discussion on succession; the board considered candidates and the board appointed the successor.

For IAS, power and decision-making seemed less a matter for theological reflection but one of pragmatism and good governance. As suggested earlier, succession decisions were made less within a theological framework but more within the framework of contingency leadership theory, although the organization would not have been aware of such theory. There was little reflection on theology or theory, but a concern for the successor to suit the exigencies of the exogenous environment. This itself points to potential areas requiring greater reflexivity, namely the evidence pointing to contingency theory shaping decisions, as previously stated, and indeed the lack of theological reflexivity, apart from requiring the successor to be an

5. Tashakori, *Managerial Succession*, 87.
6. Pfeffer and Salancik, *External Control of Organizations*.

evangelical Christian. For example, reflection on biblical models of leadership may have helped guide the process further by emphasizing qualifying characteristics other than leader-situation fit.

A further lack of reflexivity concerning power of decision concerns the role of the founder. The details of any communications between him and the board were not explored empirically in my study for this book; while all are clear that he played no role, however, it is, of course, likely that the international board wished to honor him, taking seriously his views gleaned from any informal conversation or passing comments. The official narrative of the founder not being part of the decision-making process needed to be constructed to counter potential charges of nepotism, but it is difficult to imagine that the board did not listen to the founder at all, after his twenty-five years of service and leadership. This is, of course, suggestive and would need to be investigated further.

NEWFRONTIERS

Power in the succession processes of Newfrontiers officially lay with the International Apostolic Team. This team determined the succession method, timing, and selection of apostolic sphere leaders. Successor decisions were not taken to congregations or to the international conference for approval; that is, by voting. At the operant level, however, there was deference to Virgo on appointments.[7] This gave him power of veto. A greater lacuna, however, concerns the espoused theology of decision-making (founder and team) and the power that was given to Newfrontiers congregations around the world, not in terms of voting power but in terms of "attributional theory." To understand this more fully, comment will be made on Newfrontiers' theology of succession as well as charismatic leadership theory.

The Newfrontiers espoused theology of leadership at the level of the international network of churches is that of apostolic. In theological terms, a person is an apostle by virtue of a God-given gift.[8] Newfrontiers' succession theology was that Virgo and others could not create apostles but could commend men they believed were exercising apostolic ministry. The appointee could only function as apostle if followed by people; that is, by recognition of his gift.[9] This theology, in fact, places considerable power with the people to attribute apostleship, hence "attributional theory."

7. Devenish Interview I, 78.

8. Virgo Interview I, 30–31.

9. Virgo Interview I, 33.

There are similarities between the Newfrontiers theology of apostolic recognition and attribution of charisma within charismatic leadership theory (although the qualities sought in Christian apostolic leadership may vary from those sought in business organizational settings). House's well-known work on charismatic leadership posits that charismatic leaders demonstrate a number of behaviors: being a role model for the beliefs and values they desire followers to adopt;[10] appearing competent to followers;[11] articulating "transcendent" goals which become the basis of a cause;[12] communicating high expectations for, and confidence in, followers' abilities to meet those expectations;[13] and arousal of motives relevant to the accomplishment of the mission.[14] To these behaviors, Shamir et al. also add the ability to link followers' self-concepts to organizational identity and to work for intrinsic rewards.[15]

In deliberating the succession, the Newfrontiers leaders did not consider theory.[16] Perhaps the emphasis on "hearing God" and the weight given to prophecy obscured the need for consideration of theory.[17] Nonetheless, it is possible to discern adherence to beliefs in accord with theory, in this case the theory of charismatic leadership deriving from Weber's account of authority.[18] In theoretical terms, such a conceptualization is "charismatic" leadership, for, like Weber's definition, there is, or is seen to be, a divine presence with that person. Certainly, according to Virgo, apostles cannot be produced by other people: "No man can make an apostle."[19] Furthermore, similar to Weberian and Durkheimian theory, a theology of charismatic leadership emphasizes the need for recognition of that gift by others. Speaking of Paul's visit to Jerusalem, Virgo explains,

> Well, actually, Paul says I went down to Jerusalem. I submitted my gospel. And those who were before him, as he put it, gave us the right hand of fellowship. In other words, we interpreted that, they acknowledged their authentic apostolic gift. They didn't make Paul an apostle, God did, but they observed it, recognized

10. House, "1976 Theory of Charismatic Leadership," 194–96.

11. House, "1976 Theory of Charismatic Leadership," 197.

12. House, "1976 Theory of Charismatic Leadership," 197.

13. House, "1976 Theory of Charismatic Leadership," 198–200.

14. House, "1976 Theory of Charismatic Leadership," 201–3.

15. Shamir et al., "Motivational Effects of Charismatic Leadership," 577–94.

16. Devenish Interview I, 43.

17. Virgo Interview II, 24, 30 is an example.

18. Weber, *Theory of Social and Economic Organization*, 358–59.

19. Virgo Interview I, 32.

it. Now that was the philosophy we brought to bear. So, we are saying, "Where do we see?" We're not making somebody, uh, an apostle. We're saying, "Look, there's—the proof. There's the evidence. That's what we recognize. That's what other people already are drawing from them."[20]

Newfrontiers, in its founder and successors, saw apostles as having a divine gift, which could not be produced or multiplied by people; furthermore, this gift was confirmed when others recognized it by following the gifted apostle. While Virgo was thinking in theological terms, it is possible also to interpret this in terms of charismatic leadership theory.

I take lengths to explain the charismatic theory of leadership because I posit that due reflexivity thereon could have helped bring clarity to the succession processes. Despite espoused theology of apostolic team leadership and the role of the people as "recognizers," there was little theological reflexivity on this dual aspect of multiplication. Newfrontiers' dependence on the people to recognize the apostolic gift is an "attributional theory of charisma."[21] This conceptualization of apostleship, however, fails to take into account adequately exactly how and why people respond or acknowledge that people respond to a leader from their own normative models of leadership. The GLOBE Project, for example, studied leadership conceptualization in many nations.[22] It found that high levels of "humane-oriented" leadership produces effective results in almost every nation, with the exception of Russia, where the people actually perform better under authoritarian leadership. Thus, people's understanding of normative leadership is culturally and contextually dependent.

In the case of Newfrontiers, attribution and endorsement from the people may further be complicated by the likely distribution of personality types among its leaders[23] and among committed adherents.[24] Using the Francis Psychological Type Scales, these studies suggest that Newfrontiers church leaders are likely to adopt a structured and organized approach: "There is a toughness about this style of leadership that is unlikely to be distracted by opposition."[25] Concerning the wider core membership of Newfrontiers, the 2012 study found an "overall preference for STJ"[26] which

---

20. Virgo Interview I, 33.

21. House, "Leadership in the Twenty-First Century," 414.

22. House et al., *Strategic Leadership across Cultures.*

23. Francis et al., "Psychological Type Profile," 61–69.

24. Francis et al., "Called for Leadership," 220–28.

25. Francis et al., "Psychological Type Profile," 67.

26. Sensing, Thinking, Judging types according to the Francis Psychological Type Scales.

may indicate congregations are less "suited for shaping new visions and for inspiring new congregations in complex and changing environments."[27] Given this, the wider Newfrontiers membership might find it difficult to recognize those gifts and preferences, such as intuition, which might be needed to develop new forms of church and apostolic ministry, for they are not the broader preferences of the majority of Newfrontiers adherents.

In matters of power in succession, therefore, the espoused theology places the locus on the founder and the international apostolic team, whereas operant beliefs empower the people to a greater extent than reflected upon by the leadership. Insufficient reflexivity is seen in that Virgo and team did not consult with wider membership as did Grace Network and IAS, something which may have helped them avoid the situation in the first two years post-succession in which there was considerable uncertainty where churches fit, with some congregations joining an apostolic sphere only quickly to change their minds. Furthermore, there was little reflexivity on any contextual factors that affect how people recognize leadership. Roberts and Bradley state that in times of crisis people are more likely to ascribe charisma to leaders.[28] Thus, environmental stability/instability affects enactments of succession. The period of such uncertainty might have been avoided if greater reflexivity on this matter had been undertaken pre-succession. The lacuna between espoused power (founder and team) and operant power is thus partly responsible for a period of uncertainty post-succession.

GRACE NETWORK

According to article V of their constitution, the decision with regard to appointment of the executive director within Grace Network lay with the board of directors.[29] The decision was taken, however, to the broader membership of the network at a conference, not just for consultation but also for approval (voting). Thus, the normative and espoused position with regard to decision-making power was mediated through an operant theology of members' power. Furthermore, the effectual power given to the network's overseas partners who urged the appointment was also operant. The matter of power is further complicated by the dissonance between the espoused theology of Blackwell (chapter 23) which conceived of the successor's operating within the constraints of Presbyterian co-equality and the

27. Francis et al., "Called for Leadership," 227.
28. Roberts and Bradley, "Limits of Charisma," 253–75.
29. Grace Network, *Constitution*, art. V.

preferred theology of the successor who desired greater apostolic authority and executive capacity. Power and authority were contested matters within the movement. It was unclear whether they resided in the executive team, executive director, overseas partners, or network members or indeed some unstated combination of these categories. Sufficient reflexivity may have assisted the team and may have avoided the eventual inability of the leaders to function in times of stress. Indeed, it was the results of a lack of such reflexivity which eventually caused the cessation of the network.[30]

SUMMARY

In turning again to the scarce literature on power in transitions, in many ways, my cases confirm Tashakori's findings on power;[31] for example, the finding of the significance of the post-succession dyadic relationship between founder and successor is applicable. Tashakori found that succession was far more likely to proceed well, with the successor turning potential power into realized power, if there was a coalition between founder and successor. This aspect had different nuances in each of the three case studies. With Newfrontiers, Virgo divested himself of all formal authority at succession. He remained available for advice, for personal counsel, and for preaching. In this case, the post-succession dyadic relation was not a hindrance to realized power among the fifteen apostles; indeed, if invited, he preached to congregations in support of the new leadership. In this sense, the successors did have a "coalition" with the founder which increased their authority. With IAS, both protagonists speak of an open and clear post-succession relationship. The founder took many steps to communicate that he was no longer the leader (for example, his speech and the symbolic gifts at the transition ceremony). He acknowledged that the successor had the requisite skills to lead this ministry in this season[32] and communicated his availability to advise and support.[33] Thus, this also confirms Tashakori's findings.

Similarly, her findings are supported by examining the post-succession relationship between the executive director of Grace Network and the founders, but in a different way from the first two cases. There was a lacuna between the theology of leadership of Blackwell and that of Groblewski, which the successor experienced as a restraint upon his leadership. In Tashakorian terms, his potential power was not fully realized due to theological

---

30. Groblewski Interview I, 5.

31. Tashakori, *Managerial Succession.*

32. Leif Zetterlund Interview I, 9.

33. Leif Zetterlund Interview II, 5–6.

differences. Though negative, this, however, also supports Tashakori's findings on the importance of founder/successor relations as one of the critical factors in organizational success.

Chapter Twenty-Eight ————

How Ceremony Reveals Espoused and Operant Theologies

WHILE THERE IS OFTEN reference to transition ceremonies within organizational development literature, I have found no empirical studies. This is surprising in light of the considerable study of transition ceremonies in the field of anthropology (see chapter 22). Bolman and Deal, in their classic work on organizational leadership, reference the importance of ceremonies in organizational transitions, believing them to "create order, clarity, and predictability,"[1] or to have a quadripartite functionality: stabilization, socialization, reassurance, and communication to external constituencies.[2] Transition may consist of meetings, interviews, training, and contracts, yet humans also need drama and symbol to comprehend and adjust to change: "Without ritual and ceremony, transition remains incomplete, a clutter of comings and goings."[3] In their work on organizational cultures, Deal and Kennedy introduce the concept of "strong culture," where strong culture organizations consistently perform better than others.[4] This is because a strong culture has a system of informal rules that indicate how to behave

1. Bolman and Deal, *Reframing Organizations*, 265.
2. Bolman and Deal, *Reframing Organizations*, 266.
3. Bolman and Deal, *Reframing Organizations*, 408.
4. Deal and Kennedy, *Corporate Cultures*, 7.

and what is expected, thus leading to greater efficiency.[5] Workplace ceremonies are one mechanism of building and communicating such strong cultures: Ceremonies place the culture on display and provide experiences that are remembered by employees.

While the literature is helpful, the above comments are practitioner observations and not derived from empirical study. The observations may nonetheless be of assistance when applied to practical theology. As ceremonies in the organizational world are planned by leadership, and given the comments on the provision of strong culture, socialization, and reduction of ambiguity, it seems likely that such ceremonies manifest the espoused doctrine and values of the organization. This perception is helpful when it comes to the ceremonies of the three case studies, which also were planned by the senior leadership and have the function of expressing the espoused view of the transitions. This is supported both by Hammarberg and Baggett.[6] Hammarberg describes the ceremonial processes of transition after the death of the president of the Church of Jesus Christ of Latter-Day Saints. The church employs ceremony and symbolism to reinforce its theology that the church is a "house of order" under the Melchizedek priesthood, and the president is "prophet, seer, and revelator."[7] The body of the departed president is placed for viewing in the Hall of the Prophets, thus symbolically communicating that presidents are prophets. Various groups make decisions concerning who should succeed him, and then this is brought to a vote at the General Conference at which members raise hands in "a collective gesture of affirmation."[8] Such a symbolic display of unity reinforces the espoused theology that they are a "house of order" with good governance.

A further example that succession ceremonies are enactments of espoused theologies may be seen in Baggett.[9] After a lengthy description of the operant theologies of the staff and volunteers of Habitat for Humanity, much of which differs from the espoused theology of Fuller, Habitat for Humanity's founder, Baggett describes a housing dedication ceremony in the US (when a home for those on low incomes is completed and the homeowner is ceremonially invested of the construction). A standard format for the ceremony includes the reading of scriptures, a testimony from an existing homeowner about how their life has changed because of Habitat's ministry, and a short sermon on the importance of faith, but faith

---

5. Deal and Kennedy, *Corporate Cultures*, 15.

6. Hammarberg, "Ritual Drama," 42–43; Baggett, *Habitat for Humanity*.

7. Hammarberg, "Ritual Drama," 42.

8. Hammarberg, "Ritual Drama," 42.

9. Baggett, *Habitat for Humanity*.

which results in practical actions. The ceremony culminates in the donation of keys and a Bible to the new owner of the house: "Our hope is that this house will keep your family safe and warm and this Bible will nourish your spirits throughout your lives."[10] The ceremony communicates the goals of the organization, its founding evangelical Christian spirituality, and its values and focus on meeting people's needs. It sacralizes housebuilding and weaves the individual volunteers participating into "webs of significance."[11] In other ways, however, the ceremony exposes the incongruences of the ministry's espoused theologies with those theologies operant in many of the committees, offices, and lives of its workers and volunteers. The ceremony emphasized the role of the Bible and is shaped by the founder's evangelicalism: For example, for Fuller, volunteers building a house are "part of the movement of the Spirit."[12] Baggett shows throughout his study that the beliefs and spiritual practices of the staff and volunteers are often incongruent with the espoused theology, exemplified by the following staff member: "For me, what motivates my work is just a general commitment to humanity. It has nothing to do with God or religion."[13]

What can be learned about the espoused and operant theologies of Newfrontiers, IAS, and Grace Network from their succession ceremonies?

INTERNATIONAL AID SERVICES

I have already written (chapter 22) that the ceremony may be read as a theological text—and, in light of the comments above on the nature of ceremonies, as a text particularly of espoused theology. I will not repeat the details of my earlier analysis, but, in focusing only on succession theology, I propose that the espoused theology of succession within IAS is that succession should be contextualized, that succession is best enacted as a form of patriarchal blessing, as seen with the blessing and *porrectio instrumentorum* initiated by the founder, and that a crucial aspect of succession is authority transference, symbolized by the key.[14] The theology of succession is fundamentally a Christo-Petrine transference of authority. Having been appointed as CEO of IAS, Daniel Zetterlund culminates his remarks with a blessing, which frames his role in priestly terms: "May the Lord bless you

10. Baggett, *Habitat for Humanity*, 188.

11. Geertz, "Thick Description," 5, cited in Baggett, *Habitat for Humanity*, 189.

12. Baggett, *Habitat for Humanity*, 199.

13. Matthew Carletti, staff member, cited in Baggett, *Habitat for Humanity*, 201.

14. See Kaufman and Ideström, "Why Matter Matters," 84–102, on artifacts in theology.

and keep you,"[15] a truncated version of the priestly blessing found in Num 6:24–26.

While much is planned and orchestrated by the leaders, thus suggesting espoused theology guiding the enactments, actions may, of course, spontaneously occur or be symbolically enacted of a less conscious theology. I suggest two things that manifest IAS's organizational operant theology. First, due to the multiple references to "key" in the speeches of the founder and successor, I interpret the dominant symbol in the ceremony as the donation of the key (as previously explained in chapter 22). This suggests at the operant level that the dominant understanding of succession theology is that of transference of authority together with the centrality of decision-making; at an operant level, this aspect is privileged over others. Secondly, and relatedly, I posit that the identity transformation of the successor is not espoused but is nonetheless to be understood at the operant level; it is a transcendental transformation. Indeed, this reflection is supported by Kapferer in his work on the transformative nature of ritual: "Rites of transition often seem to end on a transcendental note and this enables them, I consider, to carry the transformation effected in the process of the rites to externally located contexts of meaning and action."[16]

From the transition ceremony, therefore, I discern espoused theology yet also operant theologies, which stress the importance of the authority of the leader and point to the Petrine nature of his position; IAS did not reflect on these theological aspects. In this case, the insufficient reflexivity did not produce significant incongruity; it may nonetheless lead to potential problems with regard to understanding the precise nature of successor decision-making authority and the extent to which leadership is to be collegial or individual. This matter could have been addressed through lacunal reflexivity, for my interpretation is only made manifest by examining the lacunae between espoused and operant theologies. A reason for insufficient theological reflexivity concerning succession was the emphasis being placed on the changing environment in which IAS as a grant-recipient organization operated, and the concomitant realization that the successor must be able to adjust the organization to focus on the new environment.[17] Succession for IAS was a pragmatic response to a problem.

15. Transcription of speech given at transition ceremony held in Yei, South Sudan, March 2015.

16. Kapferer, "Power of Ritual," 14.

17. Leif Zetterlund Interview I, 9; Daniel Zetterlund Interview I, 33–35.

NEWFRONTIERS

Through Virgo's many books, conferences, online sermons, and articles, Newfrontiers sought to establish not just an espoused theology (that is, the group's articulation of its beliefs) but also a normative theology.[18] Specifically with regard to succession, an espoused theology was also developed. In the case of Newfrontiers, however, the transition ceremony seems to provide less manifestation of it. The ceremony took place during a conference with some five thousand attendees. There had been multiple communications throughout the preceding period explaining how Newfrontiers would navigate succession. Indeed, a special issue magazine was produced. Thus, before the occasion of the ceremony, the theology and mode of succession had been extensively communicated. At the conference, Virgo introduced the fifteen men who were to be appointed. He commended them and asked people to gather around them to pray for them.

A reading of these enactments shows three aspects of espoused succession theology. First, succession is to take place with the blessing and agreement of the founder. The provision of his blessing affirms the new leaders and communicates to the people that they are expected to follow the new leadership. Secondly, the ceremony enacts the belief that apostles are not created and that Virgo himself has no special power to create the apostles. This is a ceremonial enactment of the theology diffused in the special edition magazine: "We have no permission from God to create apostles."[19] Virgo is not appointing but commending, believing this to be the biblical model: "Paul did not nominate Timothy as an apostle but was happy to commend him and encourage the saints to receive him as they would Paul himself."[20] This leads to the third point, namely, that in the commendation for those to be received as apostles, a theology of apostleship by recognition is made manifest, which is an "attributional theory of charisma."[21] Yet, this aspect is not enacted in the ceremony in the sense of all the people voicing agreement. This voicing of agreement, as in the Latter-Day Saints' "collective gesture of affirmation,"[22] did not take place. For Newfrontiers the voicing of agreement, or the contrary, was to come in the acts of the people by following the new leadership and by placing their churches under their apostolic authority.

18. See Cameron et al., *Talking about God in Practice*, 53–56.
19. Virgo, "Firstline," 5.
20. Virgo, "Firstline," 5.
21. House, "Leadership in the Twenty-First Century," 414.
22. Hammarberg, "Ritual Drama," 42.

In the case of Newfrontiers, there was little additional operant theology to be deduced from the succession ceremony itself. Operant theology with regard to succession does exist, but it concerns gender and conceptualization of apostleship (addressed earlier).

GRACE NETWORK

Grace Network had no written theology of succession. The ceremony to install Groblewski as executive director took place as part of a regular network conference during which a unanimous vote supported his appointment. He was installed at the same conference. The installation ceremony included prayer for Groblewski, *cheirotonia*, and anointing with oil, all framed by the reading of God's words to Moses to appoint Joshua and commission him for leadership through the laying on of hands (Num 27:18–23).

This brief ceremony indicates the espoused theology of succession was that their modern network succession enactment was in the biblical tradition of leadership appointments, with the Old Testament text, especially that of succession from Moses to Joshua, as the privileged model. However, I conclude that there were high levels of ambivalence regarding the succession, seen in not just a lacuna between espoused and operant theologies but that the operant belief actually contradicted the espoused. Operant beliefs indicate that the event was not a significant occasion in the ministry's development. This was due to the event being a response to isomorphic pressures. The successor's wife was not present, despite a spouse usually being present at the installation of church elders. The ceremony occurred within the context of no agreement of job description or terms of employment; the triumvirate's leading of the movement continued much as before the installation. Such enactments speak of the operant theology which in this case undermined the espoused theology of Moses-Joshua succession. A strong operant theology was framing the succession, despite the overt ceremonial acts. This operant theology is manifest in a number of ways, including: "loose coupling";[23] the minimizing of the succession by the successor—"it wasn't a big deal";[24] and the awkwardness for Blackwell, one of the founders, fully to acknowledge the appointment: "We called him 'executive director' [laughs]."[25] Thus, there existed a large interstice between espoused and operant theology of ceremony. Furthermore, I suggest that even seeking to ground the ceremony within the biblical text of Num 27 was

23. Scott and Meyer, "Preface," 2.
24. Groblewski Interview I, 36.
25. Blackwell Interview I, 12.

problematic, manifesting further an operant understanding of succession theology. Although Joshua is commissioned in this text, Moses continues in leadership, including decisions concerning going to war (chapter 31), the division of spoils and the allocation of land. Thus, the Num 27 text, while a commissioning text, is not a text of leadership authority transference. Its use in the ceremony, probably unintentionally and without reflection, does ironically encapsulate the operant theology well! In the case of Grace Network, insufficient attention to the considerable incongruences between its espoused and operant theologies was severely problematic, causing later confusion in decision-making and an inability for the network leadership to lead through turbulent events. Lack of theological reflexivity was detrimental to the longevity of the ministry.

In returning to the literature and in line with Hammarberg,[26] enactments have symbolic meaning. Ceremonies are texts which reveal espoused theology yet may well have operant characteristics. For IAS that operant theology pertained to leadership authority; for Grace Network it undermined the significance of the Moses-Joshua portrayal of succession.

26. Hammarberg, "Ritual Drama," 42.

PART VII

Fears, Failings, and Findings

Chapter Twenty-Nine ——————

What Are We Afraid of When Considering Succession?

IN INVESTIGATING THE THREE main cases of succession presented in this book, but also in reading of other succession examples as well as correspondence with those part of succession processes, it became clear that there were some concerns widely shared when Christian organizations considered how to proceed with their succession goals and processes. In this chapter, I will return to a few such concerns which have either previously been adumbrated in this book or mentioned elsewhere in the literature on succession. In so doing, I hope to acknowledge such common concerns, trusting that foregrounding them might assist others as they consider organizational succession. I will focus on three concerns which seem to be among the most common, if not the most common, namely the fear of the loss of distinctive vision and values (particularly uniquely Christian vision and values), the loss of organizational vibrancy due to the routinization of charisma, and the concern that founders might remain in post too long and thereby impede the organization's optimal opportunities for succession.

LOSS OF DISTINCTIVE VISION AND VALUES

As we saw (chapter 15), there appears to be a common concern in evangelical organizations of what has been called "mission drift." This applies particularly to the feared dynamic of a Christian ministry experiencing greater secularization, something succinctly described with the following explanation: "Functional atheism is the path of least resistance."[1] This analysis was also echoed by Crane: "It's the exception that an organization stays true to its mission. The natural course—the unfortunate natural evolution of many originally Christ-centered missions—is to drift."[2] This fear tends to bring continuance of values and ethos to the foreground when considering whom to appoint as a successor, as exemplified in the succession of Life Impact Ministries, where the successor noted that the founders had a "strong desire that the core values of the mission be carried on. Those values are often not seen in mission agencies and one of the reasons Life Impact Ministries exists in the first place."[3] This same concern was evident in the deliberations of Grace Network and their desire not to "eviscerate the culture of Grace Network."[4] This was also articulated by one of the founders, who recommended the following: "Turn it over to somebody with similar DNA who has similar values and mode of operation,"[5] because if an organization tried to change the DNA, "you mutate into something."[6] As shown in chapter 15, such fears very commonly lead to selecting internal rather than external successors.

ROUTINIZATION OF CHARISMA

A second concern, whether this specific nomenclature is employed or not, is that of charisma routinization, at term made famous by Weber and introduced in chapter 3. To restate here in Weber's words,

> The term "charisma" will be applied to a certain quality of an individual personality by virtue of which he is set apart from ordinary men and treated as endowed with supernatural, super-human, or at least specifically exceptional powers or qualities. These are such as are not accessible to the ordinary person but

1. Greer and Horst, *Mission Drift*, 42–43.
2. Interview with Greer, February 2013, in Greer and Horst, *Mission Drift*, 19.
3. Correspondence from Knauss, Oct 29, 2018 (cited with permission).
4. Groblewski Interview I, 13.
5. Blackwell Interview II, 14.
6. Blackwell Interview II, 15.

are regarded as of divine origin or as exemplary, and on the basis
of them the individual concerned is treated as a leader.[7]

In Weber's understanding, routinization is the establishment of rules,
constitution, eligibility tests, and economic structures of a new (religious)
group or community. Thus, according to this theory, a pioneering leader
with charismatic authority is often succeeded by others who formalize and
bureaucratize. This fear, of course, is related to the first fear mentioned
above, namely, to conserve distinctive values and to obviate any loss of such
distinctive vision and values and concomitant mission drift. This fear relates
to the belief that a pioneering organization or ministry might move into a
phase of greater bureaucratization where decisions are made according to
policies, written procedures, and the like, rather than through the following of a spiritual vision and leadership stemming from the charismatic gift
of the leader. Of course, such greater documentation and decision-making
according to written polices can be anathema to a visionary pioneer and
founder of a new movement who emphasizes obtaining directional guidance from God and collaboration on the basis of similar vision and relationships rather than hierarchical structures. Such strong antipathy to such a
phenomenon was seen in the case of Newfrontiers, who did not use the term
"routinization," but spoke of the fear of "institutionalization." There was, for
example, a negative view of hierarchal structures. Referring to new apostolic
networks, Devenish writes, "The last thing that the founding fathers of these
movements would want is to see their living, relational leadership structures being institutionalized into something more rigid and hierarchical by
a second generation of leaders."[8] The prevention of such institutionalization
would be by means of maintaining "the biblical emphasis on family relationship, particularly the continuing need for fathers."[9] In choosing a successor, or, in the case of Newfrontiers, successors, Christian organizations
tend to seek a person of charismatic authority who might continue and even
enhance the vision and spiritual nature of the organizational raison d'être
and who will not lead the ministry to over bureaucratization.

---

7. Weber, *Theory of Social and Economic Organization*, 358–59.

8. Devenish, *Fathering Leaders*, 12.

9. Devenish, *Fathering Leaders*, 12–13.

FOUNDERS/LONG-TERM LEADERS
REMAIN IN POST TOO LONG

In this book, I have not thus far written of the interesting case of leadership succession within First Baptist Church, Dallas, Texas. This was not a case of founder succession, but one of (intended) pastoral succession in what was at that time (early 1990s) the largest congregation in the United States. For some who know of this case and indeed have read published work on this case,[10] reflection thereon seems to produce fear that a founder or long-term leader may not want to leave office, even if that leader has clearly and publicly indicated that they do so desire to leave the post. Criswell had been the senior pastor for some forty-six years. A new pastor, Gregory, was appointed in January 1991 with the understanding that, after some months of transition, Criswell would resign. The latter remained involved in many church issues and continually decided to remain in office, making various delays to his departure. Gregory felt he was in a difficult position, believing that Criswell's presence and actions, such as Criswell publicly criticizing his named successor, were undermining him. In mid-1992, Criswell stated that he would now remain for a further two years. In September 1992, Gregory announced, from the pulpit, his resignation, subsequently publishing a candid account from the successor's perspective of his experiences and frustrations as a designated successor who found that the predecessor would not actually relinquish authority. In this case, after the named successor's resignation, Criswell resumed responsibilities and remained in office for a further ten years. This case, more widely known due to the publication of Gregory's account, became a negative exemplum of succession for others who were motivated not to find themselves in a similar position.[11] Indeed, it was the reading of Gregory's account of the disastrous succession that motivated one senior leader to begin succession planning with the intention of not becoming another Criswell. This leader was "really convicted" upon reading of Criswell and determined not be like him.[12]

Given common concerns over the matters raised in this chapter, it would seem advisable for those considering succession to do the following: to adopt a plan to remind and reinforce values; to ensure continuation of dynamic spirituality rather than over-bureaucracy; and to have a stated timeline for succession that does not change, or one that is determined by

---

10. Described in Gregory, *Too Great a Temptation*.

11. See Wheeler, "Leadership Succession Process," 123.

12. Wheeler, "Leadership Succession Process," 174.

an independent body, not merely the predecessor leader (similar to that advocated by Eisold).[13]

13. Eisold, "Succeeding at Succession," 619–32.

Chapter Thirty ———————————————

What Impairs Succession?

HAVING IDENTIFIED SEVERAL COMMON concerns for Christian organizations when approaching succession, especially founder succession, we now turn to reflect on several other matters which have been problematic in succession processes.

EQUIVOCAL POWER TRANSFERENCE

Leadership is about power. This is just as true in a Christian ministry. Someone, or some group of people, will have to make decisions concerning vision, strategy, personnel, and finances; this is power. Succession, therefore, is about transference of power, or, as McDonald more poetically describes it, leadership transition is about the "passage of power."[1] The complexities of power transference were made evident in several studies. Dyck et al. is a longitudinal study of a failed succession, where the successor resigned within six months of appointment. One of their key findings was that title, power, control, and responsibility must transfer simultaneously for succession to transpire smoothly and clearly for all those concerned.[2] This power transference had not transpired in the succession studied by Dyck et al., with sad results for many of the key people involved in the succession planning and transaction.

1. McDonald, "Foreword," xii.
2. Dyck et al., "Passing the Baton," 149.

FOUNDER INTERFERENCE

Tashakori's research finds that founders can be reluctant to relinquish leadership.[3] Founders remaining in post too long is also the negative observation of Barnes and Kaftan and of Daily and Dollinger.[4] Indeed, this phenomenon was seen in the case of First Baptist Church, Dallas, where even a non-founding leader can be reluctant to relinquish power, in this case causing the publicly named successor to resign.[5] Other leaders may step down but then quickly resume leadership when they disagree with post-succession actions of successors, as was the case in the founder succession at the Crystal Cathedral.

Such matters speak to the vital role of the founder or departing leader in creating the optimal environment for successful succession. Rubenson and Gupta offer a contingency model suggesting that succession is unlikely in the following three scenarios: no great change in organizational needs; change in needs with an adaptable founder; change in needs with a lack of adaptability in the founder but where the founder is able to impede succession.[6] Where there is a change in needs, lack of adaptability, and where the founder is able to impede succession, it is impeded. Impairment, moreover, may also happen when the founder, post-succession, takes on an unhelpful role. Literature has suggested six possible roles, namely "monarch," "general," "ambassador," and "governor,"[7] as well as "inventor" and "transition czar."[8] Literature concurs that the monarch and general role do not provide for good succession (that is, not releasing responsibility or even regaining power subsequent to succession).[9]

FOUNDER-SUCCESSOR DYADIC RELATIONSHIP

The dyadic relationship between founder/predecessor and successor is a subset of the aforementioned role of the founder; it also relates to the matter of power. This nature of this relationship was deemed to be significant by Tashakori who found that succession was far more likely to proceed well,

3. Tashakori, *Managerial Succession*, 35–40.

4. Barnes and Kaftan, *Organizational Transitions*, 153; Daily and Dollinger, "Empirical Examination," 117–36.

5. Gregory, *Too Great a Temptation*.

6. Rubenson and Gupta, "Initial Succession," 21–35.

7. Sonnenfeld and Spence, "Parting Patriarch of a Family Firm," 355–75.

8. Poza, *Family Business*, 27–33.

9. Daily and Dollinger, "Empirical Examination," 117–36; Poza, *Family Business*.

with the successor turning potential power into realized power, if there was a coalition between founder and successor.[10] The founder may assist the successor by providing legitimacy and ensuring opportunities to lead. This may be determined, however, by the extent to which the founder is dependent on the successor as well as by the founder's own attributes and management style. Founders are more likely to build a coalition with the successor if the founder perceives that the successor has abilities lacking in the founder but needed at that time. Furthermore, founders need the personal attributes that enable them to relinquish control. The entrepreneurial style, with its involvement in so many aspects of the enterprise, means that founders can find it difficult to allow a successor to lead with a different style.[11] For successors to flourish, Tashakori stresses the importance of "competence," which can be dependent on knowledge of the "industry" and administrative ability, and of the ability to build positive interpersonal relationships.

ORGANIZATIONAL IDENTITY THREAT

That organizational identity threat can impair succession was shown by Balser and Carmin.[12] As stated in chapter 3, "Organizational identity is the set of features that members understand to be central, distinctive, and enduring within their organization,"[13] while the identity threat is "when organizational members interpret events or situations as challenges to or violations of or danger to that which they believe are central and distinctive features. Such threats can be external, for example a reduced donorship, or internal, such as prioritising one value over another."[14] The researchers found that staff had been recruited to this international nonprofit organization because of its vision and values; they reacted adversely to what they saw as a change of ethos under the leadership of the successor. Balser and Carmin showed how founder succession may "bring to the surface latent differences in understandings of identity and be interpreted as internal identity threats if individuals believe modifications will devalue features they regard as central and distinctive to their organizations."[15]

---

10. Tashakori, *Managerial Succession*. This is also confirmed by Vancil, *Passing the Baton*.

11. Tashakori, *Managerial Succession*, 87.

12. Balser and Carmin, "Leadership Succession," 185–201.

13. Balser and Carmin, "Leadership Succession," 186.

14. Adapted from Balser and Carmin, "Leadership Succession," 187.

15. Balser and Carmin, "Leadership Succession," 198.

LACK OF THEOLOGICAL REFLEXIVITY

The topic of theological reflexivity has been given considerable space in this book. At this point, it will merely be reiterated that lack of reflexivity on the organizational theology, most specifically its theology of leadership, can impair a succession. This book has shown this in the case of Newfrontiers, where a certain theology of apostleship and the confirmation of appointment by people's decision to follow the putative apostle yielded considerable power to people in congregations around the world, a people likely to be less astute in such decisions according to the psychological profiles of Newfrontiers leaders[16] and adherents in the congregations.[17] There was a lack of reflexivity on such matters and indeed on the types of masculinities required to be designated as apostles. In the case of Grace Network we saw how a lack of reflexivity on the nature and theology of leadership was problematic, causing confusion about the role of the executive director. In this case, the nature of leadership and succession appointment was contested between theologies of succession as Moses-Joshua transference and succession as "no big deal." Espoused and operant theologies in this movement created a lacuna which proved to be problematic in succession.

LACK OF SUCCESSOR SOCIALIZATION

Once a successor has been designated, it is likely that the successor is not yet prepared to take on the responsibilities, yet successors may be engaged to do so without adequate preparation. This is a lack of socialization; that is, gaining the correct organizational knowledge and also knowledge of how to leverage the organization's various relationships, both internal and external. Even in the case of a succession that in many ways went well (International Aid Services), we saw that the (internal) successor felt that there was insufficient socialization to the new role and the issues that he would face. This was a perspective which the founder also later acknowledged.

Furthermore, a particular factor in the lack of socialization may be a lack of making manifest and addressing the many matters that can remain tacit within an organization. This was shown clearly by Kikoski and Kikoski who found that high functioning organizations are influenced by the tacit knowledge of their leaders.[18] This raises questions of which knowledge is to be transmitted during leadership succession and how the transmission is

---

16. Francis et al., "Psychological Type Profile," 61–69.
17. Francis et al., "Called for Leadership," 220–28.
18. Kikoski and Kikoski, *Inquiring Organization*.

to be affected. As was seen in chapter 2, Peet conducted a study to test the efficacy of Generative Knowledge Interviewing (GKI) as a method of tacit knowledge transmission, by introducing "generative listening" to discern the tacit "core capacities" embedded in the patterns of the stories.[19] This test was successful: Staff grew in understanding their roles and core capabilities as well as in taking less time to make decisions. The GKI process helped them understand why the outgoing leader's results were achieved and assisted performance replication. It seems likely that without attempts to retrieve and store the founder's tacit knowledge, much data and wisdom may be lost to the enterprise once the founder moves on.

19. Peet, "Leadership Transitions," 45–60.

Chapter Thirty-One ——————

How to Succeed at Succession
Findings

In this final chapter, it may be helpful to reflect on the ground that has been covered in the previous chapters. Succession has been named as an important factor in the life of any organization, whether business, educational establishment, church, or Christian ministry. We have stated, furthermore, that succession can be a complex matter, requiring thought, planning, and skillful execution for an organization to move forward under new leadership so that it can grasp the opportunities and face the challenges of the day. Since the 1960s, organizational scholars have developed insight into the multiple facets of succession such as origins, rates, power dynamics, socialization, and the like. Many of these findings are useful for an understanding of matters that even Christian movements face. A few have attempted empirical study of such movements, but such attempts lack methodological rigor and may even obfuscate the topic rather than bring understanding. With this in mind, I have suggested some other ways to reflect on the subject, particularly that of narrative research. This was applied to three examples of founder succession within international Christian movements.

I posit that this study was original in methodology as well as in the data presented. One original aspect was seeking to bring together both a more social scientific understanding of organizations with reflection on the organizations' theologies. As stated in chapter 13, "The secrets of both the sacred and the secular are often revealed more in their adumbrations and interpenetrations than in their separation."[1] Studying religion is not a question of materialism *or* theology, for "institutions are symbolic systems which have nonobservable, absolute, transrational referents and observable social relations which concretize them."[2]

This study has shown, moreover, many facets of succession within Christian organizations and movements. It has shown the significance of successor origins, examined matters such as changes in leadership style due to succession, intrafamilial succession, gender implications, and succession as apostolic multiplication or even of "kinesisoclasm." We have reflected on the importance of selection methods, power, and the theologies, whether espoused or operant, revealed in succession ceremonies. Despite these multifaceted dynamics in succession, I have furthermore suggested that such matters may nonetheless cohere and produce what I have termed a succession Gestalt, where the parts are interdependent in a synergistic way and produce a holistic model of succession.

This work has, furthermore, examined the theologies of such organizations, pointing at times to gaps or lacunae between the official, espoused theologies and the operant theologies discerned through the symbols and actions of those involved in implementing succession. I have stressed the crucial nature of reflexivity on such matters so that problems may be avoided.

PRACTICAL FINDINGS AND GUIDANCE

It is natural, and indeed commendable, to look to other examples not only to inform our own understanding, but also to shape our actions. Learning is made practical through application of knowledge and wisdom to other situations. While seeking to avoid generalization from this small *n* study, it is nonetheless hoped that some of the findings and observations might prove transferable to other cases, which in turn might help others plan and enact succession. What might such guidance be in practical terms? A few matters will briefly be presented.

The Founder or Departing Leader Is to Initiate Discussion on Succession

This can be helpful to those in the organization who realize that a change should occur, often due to the age and length of time in office of the founder.

1. Demerath et al., *Sacred Companies*, vi.
2. Friedland and Alford, "Bringing Society Back in," 249.

Initiation by the current leader facilitates conversation on the topic without others feeling they are seeking to remove unduly a respected leader. This dynamic was mentioned by participants in Wheeler's study.[3]

The Departing Leader Is to Execute Strategic Change While Still in Position

If the outgoing leader has continually embraced changes and optimized organizational positioning, the incoming leader will not be required to make immediate strategic change upon appointment. This gives time to build trust. This has been stated clearly as Hutzschenreuter et al. reflect on the relationship between leadership succession and strategic change:

> Long tenure may reflect leaders' ability and willingness to continuously initiate appropriate strategic change. As a result, new leaders following long-tenured predecessors may find their firm better aligned to the environment than new leaders following short termed predecessors, reducing the need for post-succession strategic change.[4]

The Use of External Advisors or People Other Than an Existing Leader to Speak into the Situation

This can be the kind of dispassionate organ suggested by Eisold.[5] Such an organ assisted the succession in the case of International Aid Services. It can also be others directly making the organization aware of the issues. While not invited to do so as such, the external input of Driscoll served as a catalyst for Newfrontiers to think further about succession, even though the movement rejected some of Driscoll's specific guidance.

Clarity Regarding the Characteristics and Skills Needed in the Successor

Christian groups may be confused on this point. Theological literature seems to indicate that a successor should be just like the founder or previous

---

3. Wheeler, "Leadership Succession Process."

4. Hutzschenreuter et al., "How New Leaders Affect Strategic Change," 741.

5. Eisold, "Succeeding at Succession," 619–32.

leader[6] and indeed that there is a normative theology of succession.[7] Yet in the case of IAS, a contingency theory of leadership shaped their desire to appoint a successor with different skills from the outgoing leader, someone whose gifts and skills might better suit the current and anticipated environment, which was one markedly different from the environment in which the movement had been founded twenty-five years earlier. An organization must agree on its theology and theory in order to know whom to appoint.

The Need for Successor Socialization

As previously mentioned, the need for training and preparation is crucial so that organizational knowledge and values do not dissipate during the succession processes.[8] The importance of socialization was furthermore seen in the interview data from both Daniel Zetterlund and Leif Zetterlund.

Clarity of Power Transference

Title, power, and responsibility must transfer simultaneously, and this must be clearly communicated to all concerned.[9] Such matters are enhanced when there is a "coalition" between the departing leader and successor, showing, as stated earlier, the crucial nature of the ongoing dyadic relationship between the departing leader and the successor.[10] Cases such as International Aid Services and Newfrontiers show a positive and ongoing relationship or "coalition" between the founder and successor; this does much to ensure successful succession. Gregory, in stark contrast, shows the destructive dynamics of a succession where a mutually honoring and supportive relationship between an outgoing leader and successor did not exist.[11]

Continuation of Founding Charisma

Whatever the difference in style and emphasis between founder and successor (and such difference may be beneficial, certainly if one applies

---

6. Fountain, "Investigation," 187–204.

7. Pugh, "Succession Plans," 117–30.

8. Kikoski and Kikoski, *Inquiring Organization*; Peet, "Leadership Transitions," 45–60.

9. Dyck et al., "Passing the Baton," 143–62.

10. Tashakori, *Managerial Succession*.

11. Gregory, *Too Great a Temptation*.

contingency leadership theory), there nonetheless needs still to be a continuation of founding charisma and vision. Indeed, the appointment of a new leader can be an opportunity for "recharismaticization."

MATTERS FOR FURTHER STUDY

Having stated the above findings, even guidance, there is clearly still much to do to obtain a better understanding of how Christian agencies transfer power. At some point, there will indeed be a greater number of cases of founder succession from a man to a woman (and vice versa), as there indeed already are in the business world.[12] This would provide opportunities to study cross-gender succession to ascertain how gender dynamics affect this subject. Moreover, while international, the three main cases in this study had been founded by men from the Western world (United Kingdom, United States, and Sweden). How might organizations begun in other nations and cultures approach the crucial matter of succession, especially those in cultures of high power distance? What local cultural and contextual factors might shape the theologies and processes? Furthermore, this research into Christian movements has taken place within evangelicalism. What of groups and churches in different theological traditions? How might they articulate theology and theory to enact succession? There is clearly a rich field to be studied.

It is hoped that this work on succession will enhance our understanding of this topic and indeed help Christian leaders looking to navigate succession. It might play a role in ensuring that some ministries are not simply a one-generation phenomenon but rather have longevity for the benefit of others in the future.

---

12. Halkias et al., *Father-Daughter Succession*.

Appendix A —————————————

International Aid Services
Statement of Values

Missions: Our biblical understanding of missions motivates everything we do. The unreached and under-privileged people's groups [*sic*] is our major focus in spreading the good news.

Integrity: We believe that integrity is the foundation of our Christian character. Character is not inherited but is built daily by the way one thinks and acts, thought by thought, action by action.

Relational Leadership and Team Work: We believe in a team-based approach to leadership. We invest in leaders and train them to realize their full potential as well as giving them tools and opportunities to be effective leaders. We believe healthy leaders produce healthy communities.

Empathy (Compassion): We show compassion to a hurting and broken world—feeling the feelings and emotions of others and being motivated to act.

Equality: We believe in treating all people as we would like to be treated. We believe that people will feel valued and appreciated when we regard them with dignity and respect.

Appendix B

International Aid Services
Press Release of June 23, 2014

In 2012, the Executive Board of International Aid Services (IAS) began the undertaking of a leadership search and transition plan for the position of Chief Executive Officer (CEO) within the organizational structure of IAS. In February of 2014, after having evaluated numerous qualified candidates for the position of CEO, the Executive Board of IAS unanimously agreed that Daniel Zetterlund was to be offered the role of CEO for International Aid Services beginning January 1, 2015. The recommendation by the Executive Board was approved by the IAS General Assembly held in May of 2014.

As of May 24, 2014, Daniel Zetterlund has assumed the transitional duties of IAS Deputy CEO until the end of the year when he will accept the position of CEO for IAS beginning January 1, 2015. Daniel's international management credentials and proven leadership skills have made him the perfect candidate for this position, and IAS is fortunate that Daniel has agreed to take on this new challenge of moving IAS forward in its organizational mission and vision.

The current CEO of IAS, Leif Zetterlund, after January 1, 2015, will transition into other leadership roles within IAS. IAS is excited to announce these new changes, and the organization wishes to extend our utmost appreciation and gratitude for the stewardship and leadership exercised by Leif Zetterlund during the twenty-five years of the organization's existence. A solid foundation has been laid, and we look forward to continuing to build on that groundwork and expand our organizational capacity under the new leadership of Daniel Zetterlund.

Sincerely,

Douglas Mann
Chairman, IAS Executive Board
President, IAS America

Appendix C ——————————————————

Sources for Documentary Analysis of Newfrontiers

WEBSITE FOR NEWFRONTIERS TOGETHER

https://newfrontierstogether.org/

VIRGO'S ARTICLES AND SERMONS

1. "Together on a Mission 2009. Newfrontiers—Past, Present and Future: Part 3. Our Future"[1]

2. "The End of the Beginning"[2]

3. "Honouring the Future"[3]

4. "Newfrontiers Redefined"[4]

---

1. Virgo, "Together on a Mission 2009."
2. Virgo, "End of the Beginning."
3. Virgo, "Honouring the Future."
4. Virgo, "Newfrontiers Redefined."

MAGAZINE—SUCCESSION EDITION

Forward Together: No Well-Worn Paths. Newfrontiers Magazine, Volume 4, Issue 3 (2011).

Appendix D ───────────────

Grace Network By-Laws
Section III-B

CHARISMATIC

By "Charismatic," we mean that we are committed to the present day demonstration of the gifts of the Holy Spirit, as outlined in the first epistle to the Corinthians and in the Book of Acts. Our posture is to encourage the exercise of such expressions in our public gatherings as the Spirit inspires and directs their use.

APOSTOLIC

By "Apostolic," we understand that we are committed to following the Apostles' doctrine and practice as described in the New Testament. The objective of the apostles was to see churches planted. This "apostolic" gift is functional today. In expression of this, we will promote high quality ministry to provide support and resources to equip the leadership of member churches. We will also extend the gospel with power, compassion and relevance through church planting and mission projects which engage in church planting or pastoral training.

REFORMED

By "Reformed," we understand that we share a common commitment to the truths that were reclaimed by the Reformation. While we do not wish to perpetuate animosities aroused by the disputes of the Reformation, we are convinced of the primacy of the "Doctrines of Grace." These include: the need for God's grace to draw us and convince us of the truth of the Gospel, that justification is received by faith and that good works will follow our reception of the Gospel, and that because of the sufficiency of God's grace we will be kept and enabled to endure to the end. Moreover, we hold to the sole, absolute authority of the Bible. These concepts will also be expressed by earnest, loyal and accountable relationships with each other in the context of grace, spiritual authority and spiritual unity. Spiritual authority is given by God, but is solely dependant [*sic*] on the recognition and voluntary submission of those governed. The local autonomy of each congregation is fully recognized and heartily supported.

We embrace each local church as self-governing and led by Elders. These men have the responsibility and final say in matters regarding the spiritual and governmental oversight of each church.

We value the opportunity to relate to the leadership of one another's churches. We value earnest, loyal, and accountable relationships and the unity that the Holy Spirit brings.

We recognize the spiritual leadership of the Directors of the Network to give oversight and direction to the Presbytery and to counsel churches and their leaders. Their spiritual authority is given by God, but is solely dependant [*sic*] on voluntary submission.

EVANGELICAL

By "Evangelical," we understand that we are committed to the historic truths of the faith, including the inspiration and infallibility of Scripture, the deity of Christ, His virgin birth and miracles, His penal death for our sins and His physical resurrection and personal return. We also include the proclamation of the Gospel as the means that God has chosen to use to win those who are separated from Himself. This term also describes the attitudes we have as churches in terms of taking assertive steps to ensure that we are actually winning souls, i.e. leading others to the Savior.

Appendix E

Grace Network
Statement on History and Succession

IN THE LATE 1970s, the move of the Holy Spirit which came to be known as "The Charismatic Renewal" swept much of the Christian world. Many new expressions of the Body of Christ emerged in the form of new churches and ministries, embracing a new found emphasis on the gifts and the work of the Holy Spirit.

Three pastors, John Manzano, Dick Blackwell, and Jimmy Hollandsworth, who were impacted by the renewal recognized the need for authentic relationship and mutual accountability beyond their local churches and began to meet together for fellowship. In the 1980s, as their churches grew, planted other churches and added more leaders, they formed an apostolic network of churches called Grace Presbytery International.

As the network grew, the constituent churches began to share ministry and to cross pollinate. Churches were planted collaboratively in the U.S.A., as well as, in Haiti, Uruguay and Cameroon. When Jimmy Hollandsworth retired, Jack Groblewski was appointed a network director and later became the senior director.[1]

---

1. From https://onefocus.global/about/.

Bibliography

Abelman, Robert, and Gary Pettey. "How Political Is Religious Television?" *Journalism Quarterly* 65:2/3 (1988) 313–59.

Abrahams, Roger D. Foreword to *The Ritual Process: Structure and Anti-Structure*, by Victor Turner, v–xii. Hawthorne, NY: Aldine de Gruyter, 1995.

Abramson, Paul R. *A Case for Case Studies: An Immigrant's Journal*. Newbury Park, CA: Sage, 1992.

Adams, John C. "Linguistic Values and Religious Experience: An Analysis of the Clothing Metaphors in Alexander Richardson's Ramist-Puritan Lecture on Speech." *Quarterly Journal of Speech* 9 (Feb 1990) 58–68.

Adams, Tom. *Founder Transitions: Creating Good Endings and New Beginnings*. Executive Transitions Monograph Series 3. Baltimore: Annie E. Casey Foundation, 2005.

Adizes, Ichak. *Corporate Lifecycles: How and Why Organizations Grow and Die and What to Do about It*. Paramus, NJ: Prentice Hall, 1988.

Adler, Nancy J., and Susan Bartholomew. "Managing Globally Competent People." *Academy of Management Executive* 6 (1992) 52–65.

Aeschylus. *The Eumenides*. In *The Oresteia*, translated by Douglas Young, 97–134. Norman, OK: University of Oklahoma Press, 1974.

Agosto, Efrain. *Servant Leadership: Jesus and Paul*. St. Louis: Chalice, 2005.

Aldridge, Alan. "Negotiating Status: Social Scientists and Anglican Clergy." In *Studying Elites Using Qualitative Methods*, edited by Rosanna Hertz and Jonathan B. Imber, 111–23. Thousand Oaks, CA: Sage, 1995.

Alexander, Bobby C. *Victor Turner Revisited: Ritual as Social Change*. Atlanta: Scholars, 1991.

Allgood, Susan, and Kathleen A. Farrell. "The Match between CEO and Firm." *Journal of Business* 6:2 (2003) 317–41.

The Alternative Service Book: Series Authorized for Use in the Church of England in Conjunction with The Book of Common Prayer, Together with The Liturgical Psalter. Cambridge: Cambridge University Press, 1980.

Andelson, Jonathan G. "Postcharismatic Authority in the Amana Society: The Legacy of Christian Metz." In *When Prophets Die: The Postcharismatic Fate of New Religious Movements*, edited by Timothy Miller, 29–45. Albany: State University of New York Press, 1991.

Antal, James M. *Considering a New Call: Ethical and Spiritual Challenges for Clergy.* Bethesda, MD: Alban Institute, 2000.

Anthony, Michael J., and Mick Boersma. *Moving On, Moving Forward: A Guide for Pastors in Transition.* Grand Rapids: Zondervan, 2007.

Antonacopoulou, Elena P. "Sensuous Learning: What Is It and Why It Matters in Addressing the Ineptitude in Professional Practice." In *Sensuous Learning for Practical Judgment in Professional Practice.* Vol 1, *Arts-Based Methods,* edited by Elena P. Antonacopoulou and Steven S. Taylor, 13–44. London: Palgrave Macmillan, 2007.

Antonacopoulou, Elena P., et al. "The New Learning Organization: PART I— Institutional Reflexivity, High Agility Organising and Learning Leadership." *Learning Organization* 26:3 (Jan 2019) 304–18.

Antonakis, John. "Transformational and Charismatic Leadership." In *The Nature of Leadership,* edited by David V. Day and John Antonakis, 256–88. 2nd ed. Thousand Oaks, CA: Sage, 2012.

Argyris, Chris, and Donald A. Schön. *Organizational Learning: A Theory of Action Perspective.* Reading, MA: Addison-Wesley, 1978.

Aristotle. *On Rhetoric.* Translated by George A. Kennedy. Oxford: Oxford University Press, 1991.

Aronoff, Craig, and John L. Ward. *Preparing Successors for Leadership: Another Kind of Hero.* New York: Palgrave Macmillan, 2011.

Associated Press. "'Hour of Power' Preacher Removed by Father." Jan 13, 2015. https://www.foxnews.com/story/hour-of-power-preacher-removed-by-father.

Aune, Kristin J. "Fatherhood in British Evangelical Christianity: Negotiating with Mainstream Culture." *Men and Masculinities* 13:2 (2010) 168–89.

———. "Postfeminist Evangelicals: The Construction of Gender in the New Frontiers International Churches." PhD diss., King's College, University of London, 2004.

Avery, William O. *Revitalizing Congregations.* Bethesda, MD: Alban Institute, 2002.

Baggett, Jerome, P. *Habitat for Humanity: Building Private Homes, Building Public Religion.* Philadelphia: Temple University Press, 2001.

Balser, Deborah B., and JoAnn Carmin. "Leadership Succession and the Emergence of an Organizational Identity Threat." *Nonprofit Management and Leadership* 20:2 (2009) 185–201.

Banks, Markus. *Using Visual Data in Qualitative Research.* London: Sage, 2007.

Banks, Robert J., and Bernice M. Ledbetter. *Reviewing Leadership: A Christian Evaluation of Current Approaches.* Grand Rapids: Baker Academic, 2004.

Barnes, Louis, B. "Incongruent Hierarchies: Daughters and Younger Sons as Company CEOs." In *Organizational Transitions for Individuals, Families and Work Groups,* edited by Louis B. Barnes and Colleen Kaftan, 212–21. Englewood Cliffs, NJ: Prentice-Hall, 1991.

Barnes, Louis B., and Simon A. Hershon. "Transferring Power in the Family Business." In *Organizational Transitions for Individuals, Families and Work Groups,* edited by Louis B. Barnes and Colleen Kaftan, 222–35. Englewood Cliffs, NJ: Prentice-Hall, 1991.

Barnes, Louis B., and Colleen Kaftan, eds. *Organizational Transitions for Individuals, Families and Work Groups.* Englewood Cliffs, NJ: Prentice-Hall, 1991.

Barthes, Roland. "Introduction à l'analyse structurale des récits." In *L'Analyse structurale du récit—Communications 8,* 7–33. Paris: Editions du Seuil, 1981.

———. "Introduction to the Structural Analysis of Narrative." In *Image-Music-Text*, 79–124. London: Fontana, 1977.

Bass, Bernard M. *Bass and Stogdill's Handbook of Leadership: A Survey of Theory and Research*. New York: Free, 1990.

———. *Leadership and Performance Beyond Expectations*. New York: Free, 1985.

Battistini, Matilde. *Symbols and Allegories in Art: A Guide to Imagery*. Los Angeles: Getty, 2005.

BBC. "Turkey's Erdogan Son-in-Law Made Finance Minister amid Nepotism Fears." July 10, 2018. https://www.bbc.com/news/world-europe-44774316.

Bebbington, David W. "The Evangelical Quadrilateral: A Response." *Fides et Historia* 47:1 (2015) 87–96.

———. *Evangelicalism in Modern Britain: A History from the 1730s to the 1980s*. London: Unwin Hyman, 1989.

———. *Evangelicalism in Modern Britain: A History from the 1730s to the 1980s*. Taylor and Francis e-Library, 2004. https://doi.org/10.4324/9780203359907.

Beckmann, Matthew N., and Richard L. Hall. "Elite Interviewing in Washington, DC." In *Interview Research in Political Science*, edited by Layna Mosley, 196–208. Ithaca, NY: Cornell University Press, 2013.

Bediako, Kwame. *Jesus and the Gospel in Africa: History and Experience*. Maryknoll, NY: Orbis, 2004.

Bell, Catherine. *Ritual Theory, Ritual Practice*. Oxford: Oxford University Press, 2009.

Bendroth, Margaret L. *Fundamentalism and Gender: 1875 to the Present*. New Haven: Yale University Press, 1993.

Bennis, Warren G., and Burt Nanus. *Leaders: The Strategies for Taking Charge*. New York: Harper & Row, 1985.

Bergström, Göran, and Kristina Boréus. "Analyzing Text and Discourse in the Social Sciences." In *Analyzing Text and Discourse: Eight Approaches for the Social Sciences*, edited by Kristina Boréus and Göran Bergström, 1–22. London: Sage, 2017.

Bergström, Göran, et al. "Discourse Analysis." In *Analyzing Text and Discourse: Eight Approaches for the Social Sciences*, edited by Kristina Boréus and Göran Bergström, 208–41. London: Sage, 2017.

Björkvall, Anders. "Multimodal Discourse Analysis." In *Analyzing Text and Discourse: Eight Approaches for the Social Sciences*, edited by Kristina Boréus and Göran Bergström, 174–207. London: Sage, 2017.

Blake, John. "Two Preaching Giants and the 'Betrayal' That Tore Them apart." *CNN*, Sep 19, 2012. http://www.cnn.com/2012/11/17/us/andy-stanley/index.html.

Blanchard, Ken. "The Heart of Servant-Leadership." In *Focus on Leadership: Servant-Leadership for the Twenty-First Century*, edited by Larry C. Spears and Michele Lawrence, ix–xii. New York: John Wiley & Sons, 2002.

Block, Stephen R., and Steven A. Rosenberg. "Toward an Understanding of Founder's Syndrome: An Assessment of Power and Privilege among Founders of Nonprofit Organizations." *Nonprofit Management and Leadership* (Summer 2002) 353–68.

Bogner, Alexander, and Wolfgang Menz. "The Theory-Generating Expert Interview: Epistemological Interests, Forms of Knowledge, Interaction." In *Interviewing Experts*, edited by Alexander Bogner et al., 43–80. Basingstoke: Palgrave Macmillan, 2009.

Bolman, Lee G., and Terrence E. Deal. *Reframing Organizations: Artistry, Choice, and Leadership*. 4th ed. San Francisco: Jossey-Bass, 2008.

Bommer, William H., and Alan E. Ellstrand. "CEO Successor Choice, Its Antecedents and Influence on Subsequent Firm Performance: An Empirical Analysis." *Group and Organization Management* 21:1 (1996) 105–23.

Boréus, Kristina, and Göran Bergström. "Content Analysis." In *Analyzing Text and Discourse: Eight Approaches for the Social Sciences*, 23–52. London: Sage, 2017.

———. "Metaphor Analysis and Critical Linguistics." In *Analyzing Text and Discourse: Eight Approaches for the Social Sciences*, 146–73. London: Sage, 2017.

Boréus, Kristina, and Göran Bergström, eds. *Analyzing Text and Discourse: Eight Approaches for the Social Sciences*. London: Sage, 2017.

Boroditsky, Lera. "Metaphoric Structuring: Understanding Time through Spatial Metaphors." *Cognition* 75 (2000) 1–28.

Bradshaw, Paul F. *The Anglican Ordinal: Its History and Development from the Reformation to the Present Day*. London: SPCK, 1971.

Bratcher, Ed, et al., eds. *Mastering Transitions*. Portland, OR: Multnomah, 1991.

Brauch, Manfred T. *Hard Sayings of Paul*. Sevenoaks, UK: Hodder and Stoughton, 1990.

Briggs, Charles L. *Learning How to Ask: A Sociolinguistic Appraisal of the Role of the Interview in Social Science Research*. New York: Cambridge University Press, 1986.

Brinkmann, Svend, and Steinar Kvale. *InterViews: Learning the Craft of Qualitative Research Interviewing*. 3rd ed. Thousand Oaks, CA: Sage, 2015.

Buber, Martin. *I and Thou*. Translated by Walter Kaufmann. New York: Touchstone, 1996.

Buchanan, Colin. *Ordination Rites in Common Worship*. Cambridge, UK: Grove, 2006.

Bunton, Peter. "Founder Succession in International Christian Networks and Organizations: A Narrative Case-Study Approach." PhD diss., University of Manchester, 2020. https://www.research.manchester.ac.uk/portal/files/164141071/FULL_TEXT.PDF.

———. "Reflexivity in Practical Theology: Reflections from Studies of Founders' Succession in Christian Organizations." *Practical Theology*, 12:1 (2019) 81–96.

Burns, James M. *Leadership*. New York: Harper Perennial, 2010.

Burris, Christopher T., and Geoffrey S. Navara. "Morality Play—or Playing Morality? Intrinsic Religious Orientation and Socially Desirable Responding." *Self and Identity* 1 (2002) 67–76.

Cabrera-Suarez, Katiuska, et al. "The Succession Process from a Resource-and-Knowledge-Based View of the Firm." *Family Business Review* 14:1 (2001) 37–47.

Cameron, Helen, et al. *Talking about God in Practice: Theological Action Research and Practical Theology*. London: SCM, 2010.

Canadian Religious Conference. *The Spirit of the Founders and Our Religious Renewal*. Ottawa: Canadian Religious Conference, 1977.

Cannella, Albert, A., and Michael Lubatkin. "Succession as a Sociopolitical Process: Internal Impediments to Outsider Selection." *Academy of Management Journal* 36 (1993) 763–93.

Carlson, Mim, and Margaret Donohoe. *The Executive Director's Guide to Thriving as a Nonprofit Leader*. San Francisco: Jossey-Bass, 2010.

Carman, Joanne G., and Rebecca Nesbit. "Founding New Nonprofit Organizations: Syndrome or Symptom?" *Nonprofit and Voluntary Sector Quarterly* 42:3 (2013) 603–21.

Carroll, Glenn R. "Dynamics of Publisher Succession in Newspaper Organizations." *Administrative Science Quarterly* 29 (1984) 93–113.

Cassells' German Dictionary. London: Cassell & Co., 1978.

Castelli, Elizabeth A. "Gender, Theory, and the Rise of Christianity: A Response to Rodney Stark." *Journal of Early Christian Studies* 6:2 (1998) 227–57.

Cawkwell, George L. "ΝΟΜΟΦΥΛΑΚΙΑ and the Areopagus." *Journal of Hellenic Studies* 108 (1988) 1–12.

Chamberlayne, Prue, et al. "Introduction: The Biographical Turn." In *The Turn to Biographical Methods in Social Science*, edited by Prue Chamberlayne et al., 1–30. London: Routledge, 2000.

Chatman, Seymour. *Story and Discourse: Narrative Structure in Fiction and Film.* Ithaca, NY: Cornell University Press, 1978.

Chaves, Mark. *Ordaining Women: Culture and Conflict in Religious Organizations.* Cambridge, MA: Harvard University Press, 1997.

———. "Ordaining Women: The Diffusion of an Organizational Innovation." *American Journal of Sociology* 101:4 (1996) 840–73.

Cherrington, Ruth. "Generational Issues in China: A Case Study of the 1980's Generation of Young Intellectuals." *British Journal of Sociology* 48:2 (1997) 302–20.

Cionca, John R. *Discerning the Time for a Change in Ministry.* Grand Rapids: Baker, 1994.

Clandinin, D. Jean, and F. Michael Connelly. *Narrative Inquiry: Experience and Story in Qualitative Research.* San Francisco: Jossey-Bass, 2000.

Clifford, Anne M. *Introducing Feminist Theology.* Maryknoll, NY: Orbis, 2002.

Clinton, J. Robert. *The Making of a Leader: Recognizing the Lessons and Stages of Leadership Development.* Colorado Springs: NavPress, 1988.

Clutterbuck, David. "Handing Over the Reins: Should the CEO's Successor Be an Insider or an Outsider?" *Corporate Governance* 6 (1998) 78–85.

Coleman, Simon. "Of Metaphors and Muscles: Protestant 'Play' in the Disciplining of the Self." In *The Discipline of Leisure: Embodying Cultures of "Recreation,"* edited by Simon Coleman and Tamara Kohn, 39–53. New York: Berghahn, 2007.

Collins, Jim, and Jerry I. Porras. *Built to Last: Successful Habits of Visionary Companies.* 3rd ed. New York: Harper Business, 2002.

Conger, Jay A. "Max Weber's Conceptualization of Charismatic Authority: Its Influence on Organizational Research." *Leadership Quarterly* 4:3 (1993) 277–88.

Conger, Jay A., and Rabindra N. Kanungo. *Charismatic Leadership in Organizations.* Thousand Oaks, CA: Sage, 1988.

Cormode, D. Scott. "Does Institutional Isomorphism Imply Secularization? Churches and Secular Voluntary Associations in the Turn-of-the-Century City." In *Sacred Companies: Organizational Aspects of Religion and Religious Aspects of Organizations*, edited by N. J. Demerath et al., 116–31. New York: Oxford University Press, 1998.

Cornelius, Lucille J. *The Pioneer: History of the Church of God in Christ.* Memphis: Church of God in Christ, 1975.

Cox, James L. *An Introduction to the Phenomenology of Religion.* London: Continuum, 2010.

Coxon, Anthony P. M., et al. *Images of Social Stratification.* London: Sage, 1986.

Cunningham, Loren, and David J. Hamilton. *Why Not Women? A Fresh Look at Scripture on Women in Missions, Ministry, and Leadership.* Seattle: YWAM, 2000.

Daily, Catherine M., and Marc J. Dollinger. "An Empirical Examination of Ownership Structure in Family and Professionally Managed Firms." *Family Business Review* 5:2 (1992) 117–36.

Davidoff, Leonore, and Catherine Hall. *Family Fortunes: Men and Women of the English Middle Class, 1780–1850*. London: Hutchinson Education, 1987.

Davidsson Bremborg, Anna. "Interviewing." In *The Routledge Handbook of Research Methods in the Study of Religion*, edited by Michael Stausberg and Steven Engler, 310–22. London: Routledge, 2014.

Davie, Grace, and David Wyatt. "Document Analysis." In *The Routledge Handbook of Research Methods in the Study of Religion*, edited by Michael Stausberg and Steven Engler, 151–60. London: Routledge, 2014.

Davis, John A., and Renato Tagiuri. "The Influence of Life-Stage on Father-Son Work Relationships in Family Companies." *Family Business Review* 2:1 (1989) 47–76.

de Dreu, Carsten K. W. "Team Innovation and Team Effectiveness: The Importance of Minority Dissent and Reflexivity." *European Journal of Work and Organizational Psychology* 11:3 (2002) 285–98.

De Pree, Max. *Leadership Is an Art*. New York: Currency Doubleday, 1989.

———. *Leadership Jazz*. New York: Currency Doubleday, 1992.

———. *Leading without Power: Finding Hope in Serving Community*. San Francisco: Jossey-Bass, 1997.

Deal, Terrence E., and Allan A. Kennedy. *Corporate Cultures: The Rites and Rituals of Corporate Life*. Reading, MA: Addison-Wesley, 1982.

Deal, Terrence E., and M. K. Key. *Corporate Celebration: Play, Purpose, and Profit at Work*. San Francisco: Berrett-Koehler, 1998.

Della Porta, Donatella, and Mario Diani. *Social Movements: An Introduction*. 2nd ed. Oxford: Blackwell, 2009.

Demerath, N. J., and Terry Schmitt. "Transcending Sacred and Secular: Mutual Benefits in Analyzing Religious and Nonreligious Organizations." In *Sacred Companies: Organizational Aspects of Religion and Religious Aspects of Organizations*, edited by N. J. Demerath et al., 381–400. New York: Oxford University Press, 1998.

Demerath, N. J., et al. *Sacred Companies: Organizational Aspects of Religion and Religious Aspects of Organizations*. New York: Oxford University Press, 1998.

Denzin, Norman K. *Interpretative Biography*. Newbury, Park, CA: Sage, 1989.

Denzin, Norman K., and Yvonna S. Lincoln, eds. *Handbook of Qualitative Research*. Thousand Oaks, CA: Sage, 1994.

———. *Handbook of Qualitative Research*. 2nd ed. Thousand Oaks, CA: Sage, 2000.

———. *The Qualitative Inquiry Reader*. Thousand Oaks, CA: Sage, 2002.

Deutche Welle. "Erdogan's Son-in-Law Resigns as Turkey's Finance Minister." August 11, 2020. https://www.dw.com/en/turkey-erdogans-son-in-law-resigns-as-finance-minister/a-55537624

Devenish, David. *Demolishing Strongholds: Effective Strategies for Spiritual Warfare*. Bletchley: Authentic, 2000.

———. *Fathering Leaders—Motivating Mission: Restoring the Role of the Apostle in Today's Church*. Bletchley, UK: Authentic, 2011.

———. *Succession or Multiplication? Transitioning a Movement to Next Generation Leadership*. Milton Keynes: Authentic, 2020.

———. *What on Earth Is the Church for? A Blueprint for the Future for Church Based Mission and Social Action*. Bletchley, UK: Authentic, 2006.

Diani, Mario. "The Concept of Social Movement." *The Sociological Review* 40:1 (1992) 1–25.

Dillistone, Frederick W. *Christianity and Symbolism*. London: Collins, 1955.

————. *The Power of Symbols*. London: SCM, 1986.

DiMaggio, Paul J., and Walter W. Powell. "The Iron Cage Revisited: Institutional Isomorphism and Collective Rationality in Organizational Fields." *American Sociological Review* 48:2 (1983) 147–60.

Dollhopf, Erica J., and Christopher P. Scheitle. "Decline and Conflict: Causes and Consequences of Leadership Transitions in Religious Congregations." *Journal for the Scientific Study of Religion* 52:4 (2013) 675–97.

————. "Explaining Variations in the Non-profit Founding Process: Founder and Organizational Factors." *Nonprofit Management and Leadership* 27:2 (2016) 261–72.

Donovan, Vincent J. *Christianity Rediscovered*. 2nd ed. Maryknoll, NY: Orbis, 2003.

Driel, Barend van, and James T. Richardson. "Categorization of New Religious Movements in American Print Media." *Sociological Analysis* 49 (1988) 171–83.

Dupront, Alphonse. *Du Sacré: Croisades et Pèlerinages–Images et Langages*. Paris: Gallimard, 1987.

Durkheim, Emile. *The Elementary Forms of the Religious Life*. Translated by Joseph W. Swain. New York: Free Press, 1965.

Dyck, Bruno, et al. "Passing the Baton: The Importance of Sequence, Timing, Technique and Communication in Executive Succession." *Journal of Business Venturing* 17 (2002) 143–62.

Dyer, Kevin. "Leadership Transition: Painful but Necessary." *Evangelical Missions Quarterly* 25:2 (1989) 172–73.

Eade, John. "Introduction to the Illinois Paperback." In *Contesting the Sacred: The Anthropology of Christian Pilgrimage*, edited by John Eade and Michael J. Sallnow, ix–xxviii. Urbana: University of Illinois Press, 2000.

Eade, John, and Michael J. Sallnow, eds. *Contesting the Sacred: The Anthropology of Christian Pilgrimage*. Urbana: University of Illinois Press, 2000.

Early, Gene. "A Second Generation Leadership Succeeds the Founder: What Is the Process?" *Transformation*, 18:1 (2001) 1–8, 55.

Edwards, Aaron. "The Violence of Bureaucracy and the Gospel of Peace: A Theological Response to an Academic Problem." *International Journal of Public Theology* 12 (2018) 195–217.

Eisner, Elliot W. *The Enlightened Eye: Qualitative Inquiry and the Enhancement of Educational Practice*. Old Tappan, NJ: Macmillan, 1991.

Eisold, Kenneth. "Succeeding at Succession: The Myth of Orestes." *Journal of Analytical Psychology* 53 (2008) 619–32.

Eitzen, D. Stanley, and Norman R. Yetman. "Managerial Change, Longevity, and Organizational Effectiveness." *Administrative Science Quarterly* 17 (1972) 110–16.

Eliade, Mircea. *Shamanism: Archaic Techniques of Ecstasy*. London: Penguin, 1989.

Evangelica Testificatio—On the Renewal of the Religious Life According to the Teaching of the Second Vatican Council. Apostolic Exhortation of His Holiness Paul VI. June 29, 1971. http://www.vatican.va/holy_father/paul_vi/apost_exhortations/documents/hf_p-vi_exh_19710629_evangelica-testificatio_en.html.

Family Owned Business Institute. "Family Firm Facts." April 26, 2023. https://www.gvsu.edu/fobi/family-firm-facts-5.htm.

Farnese, Maria L., and Stefano Livi. "How Reflexivity Enhances Organizational Innovativeness: The Mediation Role of Team Support for Innovation and Individual Commitment." *Knowledge Management Research and Practice* 14:4 (2016) 525–36.

Feldman, Martha S., and Julka Almquist. "Analyzing the Implicit in Stories." In *Varieties of Narrative Analysis*, edited by James A. Holstein and Jaber F. Gubrium, 207–28. Thousand Oaks, CA: Sage, 2012.

Fiedler, Fred E. *A Theory of Leadership Effectiveness*. New York: McGraw-Hill, 1967.

Fiedler, Fred E., and Martin M. Chemers. *Improving Leadership Effectiveness: The Leader Match Concept*. 2nd ed. New York: Wiley, 1984.

———. *Leadership and Effective Management*. Glenview, IL: Scott, Foresman, 1974.

Finkelstein, Sydney. "Power in the Top Management Teams: Dimensions, Measurement, and Validation." *Academy of Management Journal* 35 (1992) 505–38.

Flick, Uwe. *An Introduction to Qualitative Research*. 5th ed. London: Sage, 2014.

Foss, Sonja, K. *Rhetorical Criticism: Exploration and Practice*. 3rd ed. Long Grove, IL: Waveland, 2004.

Foucault, Michel. *The Archaeology of Knowledge*. London: Tavistock, 1972.

———. "Politics and the Study of Discourse." In *The Foucault Effect: Studies in Governmentality*, edited by Graham Burchell et al., 53–72. London: Harvester Wheatsheaf, 1991.

Fountain, A. Kay. "An Investigation into Successful Leadership Transitions in the Old Testament." *Asian Journal of Pentecostal Studies*, 7:2 (2004) 187–204.

Francis, Leslie J., et al. "Called for Leadership: Psychological Type Profile of Leaders within the Newfrontiers Network of Churches in the United Kingdom." *Journal of Psychology and Theology* 40:3 (2012) 220–28.

———. "Psychological Type Profile of Lead Elders within the Newfrontiers Network of Churches in the United Kingdom." *Journal of Beliefs and Values* 30:1 (2009) 61–69.

Frey, Nancy L. "Stories of the Return: Pilgrimage and Its Aftermaths." In *Intersecting Journeys: The Anthropology of Pilgrimage and Tourism*, edited by Ellen Badone and Sharon R. Roseman, 89–109. Chicago: University of Illinois Press, 2004.

Friedland, Roger, and Robert R. Alford. "Bringing Society Back in: Symbols, Practices, and Institutional Contradictions." In *The New Institutionalism in Organizational Analysis*, edited by Walter W. Powell and Paul J. DiMaggio, 232–63. Chicago: University of Chicago Press, 1991.

Friedman, Stewart D., and Paul Olk. "Four Ways to Choose a CEO: Crown Heir, Horse Race, Coup d'Etat, and Comprehensive Search." *Human Resource Management* 34:1 (1995) 141–64.

Friedman, Stewart D., and Kathleen Saul. "A Leader's Wake: Organizational Member Reaction to CEO Succession." *Journal of Management* 17:3 (1991) 619–42.

Frost, Michael, and Alan Hirsch. *The Shaping of Things to Come: Innovation and Mission for the 21st-Century Church*. Peabody, MA: Hendrickson, 2004.

Gampiot, Aurélien M. *Kimbanguism: An African Understanding of the Bible*. Translated by Cécile Coquet-Mokoko. University Park, PA: Pennsylvania State University Press, 2017.

Gamson, William A., and Norman A. Scotch. "Scapegoating in Baseball." *American Journal of Sociology* 70:1 (1964) 69–72.

Garman, Andrew N., and J. Larry Tyler. "What Kind of CEO Will Your Hospital Need Next? A Model for Succession Planning." In *Better CEO-Board Relations: Practical Advice for a Successful Partnership*, edited by Karen Gardner, 3–8. Chicago: Health Forum Inc., 2007.

Geertz, Clifford. "Thick Description: Toward an Interpretive Theory of Culture." In *The Interpretation of Cultures*, 3–30. New York: Basic Books, 1973.

Gennep, Arnold van. *The Rites of Passage*. Translated by Monika B. Vizedom and Gabrielle L. Caffee. 2nd ed. Chicago: University of Chicago Press, 2019.

Gergen, David. "Bad News for Bullies." *U.S. News and World Report* 140:23 (Jun 19, 2006) 54.

Giambatista, Robert C., et al. "Nothing Succeeds Like Succession: A Critical Review of Leader Succession Literature Since 1994." *The Leadership Quarterly* 16 (2005) 963–91.

Gibbs, Eddie. *Leadership Next: Changing Leaders in a Changing Culture*. Leicester: InterVarsity, 2005.

Giesen, Bernhard. "Performing the Sacred: A Durkheimian Perspective on the Formative Turn in the Social Sciences." In *Social Performance: Symbolic Action, Cultural Pragmatics and Ritual*, edited by Jeffrey C. Alexander et al., 325–67. Cambridge, UK: Cambridge University Press, 2006.

Gilham, Bill. *The Research Interview*. London: Continuum, 2000.

Girard, René. *Violence and the Sacred*. Baltimore: Johns Hopkins University Press, 1977.

Glassman, Ronald M., and William H. Swatos. *Charisma, History, and Social Structure*. New York: Greenwood, 1986.

Glenza, Jessica. "Controversial Seattle Pastor Steps Down amid Bullying and Plagiarism Claims." *The Guardian*, Oct 15, 2014, US ed. https://www.theguardian.com/us-news/2014/oct/15/controversial-seattle-pastor-steps-down-amid-bullying-and-plagiarism-claims.

Global Advance. "Global Advance President and Founder." https://www.globaladvance.org/about.

Gomez-Mejía, Luis R., et al. "The Role of Family Ties in Agency Contracts." *Academy of Management Journal* 44 (2001) 81–96.

Gordon, Gil E., and Ned Rosen. "Critical Factors in Leadership Succession." *Organizational Behavior and Human Performance* 27:2 (1981) 227–54.

Grace Network. *By-Laws*. Unpublished document, 2008.

———. *Constitution*. Unpublished document, n.d.

Graves, Michael P. "Functions of Key Metaphors in Early Quaker Sermons, 1671–1700." *Quarterly Journal of Speech* 69 (Nov 1983) 364–78.

Greenleaf, Robert K. *The Institution as Servant*. Westfield, IN: Greenleaf Center for Servant Leadership, 1972.

———. *The Servant as Leader*. Westfield, IN: Greenleaf Center for Servant Leadership, 2008.

———. *Servant Leadership: A Journey into the Nature of Legitimate Power and Greatness*. New York: Paulist, 1977.

Greer, Peter, and Chris Horst. *Mission Drift: The Unspoken Crisis Facing Leaders, Charities, and Churches*. Minneapolis: Bethany House, 2014.

Gregory, Joel. *Too Great a Temptation: The Seductive Power of America's Super Church*. Fort Worth: Summit Group, 1994.

Greiner, Larry E. "Evolution and Revolution as Organizations Grow." In *Organizational Transitions for Individuals, Families and Work Groups*, edited by Louis. B. Barnes and Colleen Kaftan, 345–57. Englewood Cliffs, NJ: Prentice-Hall, 1991.

Grimes, Ronald L. *Beginnings in Ritual Studies*. 3rd ed. Scotts Valley, CA: CreateSpace Independent, 2013.

Groblewski, Jack. "Designer People!" Unpublished letter, 2012.

————. "Supply Side Theology: The Five Fold Ministry! Ephesians 4:11." Unpublished paper, 2012.

Gros, Frédéric. *A Philosophy of Walking*. Translated by John Howe. London: Verso, 2014.

Grusky, Oscar. "Corporate Size, Bureaucratization, and Managerial Succession." *American Journal of Sociology* 67:3 (1961) 261–69.

————. "The Effects of Succession: A Comparative Study of Military and Business Organization." In *The New Military: Changing Patterns of Organization*, edited by Morris Janowitz, 83–111. New York: Russell Sage, 1964.

Gubrium, Jaber F., et al., eds. *The Sage Handbook of Interview Research: The Complexity of the Craft*. 2nd ed. Thousand Oaks, CA: Sage, 2012.

Guest, Robert H. "Managerial Succession in Complex Organizations." *American Journal of Sociology* 68 (1962) 47–54.

Habbershon, Timothy G., and Joseph H. Astrachan. "Perceptions Are Reality: How Family Meetings Lead to Collective Action." *Family Business Review* 10:1 (1997) 37–52.

Habib, Usman. "A New Paradigm in Leadership Development: Church of God Mission International." PhD diss., University of Manchester, 2014.

Hadden, Jeffrey K. "Religion and the Construction of Social Problems." *Sociological Analysis* 41 (1980) 99–108.

————. "Religious Movements." *Encyclopaedia of Sociology*, 2001. https://www.encyclopedia.com/social-sciences/encyclopedias-almanacs-transcripts-and-maps/religious-movements.

Halkias, Daphne, et al., eds. *Father-Daughter Succession in Family Business: A Cross-Cultural Perspective*. Farnham, UK: Gower, 2011.

Hammarberg, Melvyn. "Ritual Drama of Leadership Transition among Latter-Day Saints." *Expedition Magazine* 50:2 (2008) 42–43. http://www.penn.museum/sites/expedition/?p=8993.

Hanks, Geoffrey. *60 Great Founders*. Fearn, UK: Christian Focus, 1995.

Haskins, Ekaterina. "Rhetoric, Epideictic." In *The International Encyclopedia of Communication*, edited by Wolfgang Donsbach. 2008. https://doi.org/10.1002/9781405186407.wbiecro46.

Haveman, Heather A., and Mukti V. Khaire. "Survival Beyond Succession? The Contingent Impact of Founder Succession on Organizational Failure." Presented at Proceedings of the Conference on Evolutionary Approaches to Entrepreneurship in Honour of Howard Aldrich. College Park, MD, University of Maryland, October 3, 2002.

Haworth, M. "Tips for Better Succession Planning." *The Journal for Quality and Participation* (Fall 2005) 3–15.

Hermanns, Harry. "Narrative Interview." In *Handbuch Qualitative Sozialforschung*, 2nd ed. Edited by Uwe Flick et al., 182–85. Munich: Psychologie Verlags Union, 1995.

Hesse, Hermann. *The Journey to the East*. Translated by Hilda Rosner. New York: Picador, 1956.

Hijmans, Ellen. "The Logic of Qualitative Media Content Analysis: A Typology." *Communications* 21 (1996) 93–109.

Hofstede, Geert. *Culture's Consequences: Comparing Values, Behaviors, Institutions, and Organizations across Nations*. Thousand Oaks, CA: Sage, 2001.

————. *Culture's Consequences: International Differences in Work-Related Values*. Beverly Hills: Sage, 1980.

———. *Cultures and Organizations: Software of the Mind.* New York: McGraw-Hill, 1991.

Hollenweger, Walter J. *The Pentecostals: The Charismatic Movement in the Churches.* Translated by Richard A. Wilson. Minneapolis: Augsburg, 1972.

Holstein, James A., and Jaber F. Gubrium. *The Active Interview.* Thousand Oaks, CA: Sage, 1995.

Holstein, James A., and Jaber F. Gubrium, eds. *Inside Interviewing: New Lenses, New Concerns.* Sage: Thousand Oaks, CA, 2003.

———. *Varieties of Narrative Analysis.* Thousand Oaks, CA: Sage, 2012.

Horvath, Agnes, and Arpad Szakolczai. *Walking into the Void: A Historical Sociology and Political Anthropology of Walking.* London & New York: Routledge, 2018.

House, Robert J. "A 1976 Theory of Charismatic Leadership." In *Leadership: The Cutting Edge,* edited by James G. Hunt and Lars L. Larson, 189–207. Carbondale, IL: Southern Illinois University Press, 1976.

———. "Leadership in the Twenty-First Century: A Speculative Inquiry." In *The Changing Nature of Work,* edited by Ann Howard, 411–50. San Francisco: Jossey-Bass, 1995.

House, Robert J., et al., eds. *Culture, Leadership, and Organizations: The GLOBE Study of 62 Societies.* Thousand Oaks, CA: Sage, 2004.

———. *Strategic Leadership across Cultures: The GLOBE Study of CEO Leadership Behavior and Effectiveness in 24 Countries.* Los Angeles: Sage, 2014.

Howarth, David. *Discourse.* Buckingham, UK: Open University Press, 2000.

Hufford, David J. "The Scholarly Voice and the Personal Voice." *Western Folklore* 54:1 (1995) 57–76.

Hunter, Mark. "Bethany Church Grows from House to Multiple Campuses in 50 Years." *The Advocate,* Nov 15, 2013. https://www.theadvocate.com/baton_rouge/entertainment_life/faith/article_5ed617ed-324b-5foe-8b1b-1bed7c614bfe.html.

Huson, Mark R., et al. "Internal Monitoring Mechanisms and CEO Turnover: A Long-term Perspective." *The Journal of Finance* 56:6 (2001) 2265–97.

Hutzschenreuter, Thomas, et al. "How New Leaders Affect Strategic Change Following a Succession Event: A Critical Review of the Literature." *The Leadership Quarterly* 23:5 (2012) 729–55.

Ingold, Tim, and Jo L. Vergunst, eds. *Ways of Walking: Ethnography and Practice on Foot.* Farnham: Ashgate, 2008.

International Aid Services. *2015 Annual Report.* http://www.ias-intl.org/wp-content/uploads/2017/01/AR_2015_MASTER_v2_Res_Low.pdf.

International Aid Services. *Fit for Purpose: A Strategy for Sustained Growth 2016–2020,* 2016. http://www.ias-intl.org/wp-content/uploads/2016/05/Fit-for-purpose_a-strategy-for-sustained-growth_2016–2020_FINAL.pdf.

International Aid Services. "Press Release." Jun 23, 2014. http://www.ias-intl.org/se/?author=1&paged=3.

Jago, Aruther G. "Leadership: Perspectives in Theory and Research." *Management Science* 28:3 (1982) 315–36.

Jung, Dongil, and John J. Sosik. "Who Are the Spellbinders? Identifying Personal Attributes of Charismatic Leaders." *Journal of Leadership and Organizational Studies* 12 (2006) 12–27.

Kane, Thomas A. "Celebrating Pentecost in Leauva'a: Worship, Symbols, and Dance in Samoa." In *Christian Worship Worldwide: Expanding Horizons, Deepening Practices,* edited by Charles E. Farhadian, 156–70. Grand Rapids: Eerdmans, 2007.

Kapferer, Bruce. "The Power of Ritual: Transition, Transformation and Transcendence in Ritual Practice." *The International Journal of Social and Cultural Practice* 1 (1979) 3–19.

Kaufman, Tone S., and Jonas Ideström. "Why Matter Matters in Theological Action Research: Attending to the Voices of Tradition." *International Journal of Practical Theology* 22:1 (2018) 84–102.

Kay, William K. *Apostolic Networks in Britain: New Ways of Being Church.* Milton Keynes: Paternoster, 2007.

———. "Apostolic Networks in Britain Revisited." *Pneuma* 38 (2016) 5–22.

Kelly, James N. "Management Transitions for Newly Appointed CEO's." *Sloan Management Review* 22 (1980) 37–45.

Kelley, Rhonda H. *Servant Leadership: A Biblical Study for Becoming a Christlike Leader (A Woman's Guide).* Birmingham, AL: New Hope, 2011.

Kesner, Idalene F., and Terrence C. Sebora. "Executive Succession: Past, Present and Future." *Journal of Management* 20:2 (1994) 327–72.

Kets de Vries, Manfred F. R. "The Dynamics of Family Controlled Firms: The Good and the Bad News." *Organizational Dynamics* 21:3 (1993) 58–71.

Khong, Lawrence. "Faith Community Baptist Church." In *The New Apostolic Churches: Rediscovering the New Testament Model of Leadership and Why It Is God's Desire for the Church Today,* edited by C. Peter Wagner, 213–26. Ventura, CA: Regal Books, 1998.

Kikoski, Catherine K., and John F. Kikoski. *The Inquiring Organization: Tacit Knowledge, Conversation, and Knowledge Creation: Skills for 21st-Century Organizations.* Thousand Oaks, CA: Sage, 2004.

King, Ursula. *Women and Spirituality: Voices of Protest and Promise.* Basingstoke: Macmillan, 1989.

Kirkpatrick, Shelley A., and Edwin A. Locke. "Leadership: Do Traits Matter?" *The Executive* 5 (1991) 48–60.

Kondra, Alex Z., and Deborah C. Hurst. "Institutional Processes of Organizational Culture." *Culture and Organizations* 15:1 (2009) 39–58.

Kondrath, William M. "Transitioning from Charismatic Founder to the Next Generation." *Journal of Religious Leadership* 9:2 (2010) 83–115.

Kreider, Larry, et al. *The Biblical Role of Elders for Today's Church: New Testament Leadership Principles for Equipping Elders.* Lititz, PA: House to House, 2019.

Krippendorff, Klaus. *Content Analysis: An Introduction to its Methodology.* London: Sage, 2013.

Kvale, Steinar. *InterViews: An Introduction to Qualitative Research Interviewing.* Thousand Oaks, CA: Sage, 1996.

Kvale, Steinar, and Svend Brinkmann. *InterViews: Learning the Craft of Qualitative Research Interviews.* 2nd ed. London: Sage, 2009.

Laclau, Ernesto, and Chantal Mouffe. *Hegemony and Socialist Strategy: Towards a Radical Democratic Politics.* London: Verso, 1985.

Lakewood Church. "Our History." https://www.lakewoodchurch.com/about/history.

Lakoff, George, and Mark Johnson. *Metaphors We Live By.* 2nd ed. Chicago: University of Chicago Press, 2003.

Lathrop, Gordon W. *Holy Things: A Liturgical Theology.* Minneapolis: Fortress, 1998.

Lausanne Covenant. https://lausanne.org/content/covenant/lausanne-covenant.

Lavietes, Stuart. "Rev. Robert Schuller, 88, Dies; Built an Empire Preaching Self-Belief." *New York Times*, Apr 2, 2015. http://www.nytimes.com/2015/04/03/us/rev-robert-h-schuller-hour-of-power-evangelist-dies-at-88.html.

Letham, Robert W. A. "Reformed Theology." In *New Dictionary of Theology*, edited by Sinclair B. Ferguson et al., 569–72. Leicester: InterVarsity, 1988.

Liberty Journal. https://www.liberty.edu/journal/.

Liberty University. "Statement of Mission and Purpose." http://www.liberty.edu/index.cfm?PID=6899.

Liddell, Henry G., and Robert Scott, eds. *A Greek-English Lexicon*. New York: American Book, 1901.

Liden, Robert C., et al. "Servant Leadership: Antecedents, Processes and Outcomes." In *The Oxford Handbook of Leadership and Organizations*, edited by David V. Day, 357–79. Oxford: Oxford University Press, 2014.

———. "Servant Leadership: Development of a Multidimensional Measure and Multi-level Assessment." *Leadership Quarterly* 19 (2008) 161–77.

Lightfoot, J. B. *St. Paul's Epistle to the Galatians*. London: Macmillan, 1981. Orig. 1865.

Lijphart, Arend. "The Comparable-Case Strategy in Comparative Research." *Comparative Political Studies* 8:2 (1971) 158–77.

Lindberg, Mary C. *The Graceful Exit: A Pastor's Journey from Good-Bye to Hello*. Herndon, VA: Alban Institute, 2013.

Linde, Charlotte. "Narrative and Social Tacit Knowledge." *Journal of Knowledge Management* 5:2 (2001) 160–70.

Lindsay, D. Michael. "Elite Power: Social Networks within American Evangelicalism." *Sociology of Religion* 67:3 (2006) 207–27.

Lobdell, William, and Mitchell Landsberg. "Rev. Robert H. Schuller, Who Built Crystal Cathedral, Dies at 88." *Los Angeles Times*, Apr 2, 2015. http://www.latimes.com/local/obituaries/la-me-robert-schuller-20150403-story.html.

Lord, Robert G., et al. "A Meta-Analysis of the Relation Between Personality Traits and Leadership Perceptions: An Application of Validity Generalization Procedures." *Journal of Applied Psychology* 71 (1986) 402–10.

Loy, Catherine M. "Resurrection beyond the Secular: Pursuing a Theological Paradigm of International Development." PhD diss., King's College London, 2015.

Lozano, John M. *Foundresses, Founders, and Their Religious Families*. Translated by Joseph Daries. Chicago: Claret Center for Resources in Spirituality, 1983.

Second Vatican Council. "Dogmatic Constitution on the Church, *Lumen gentium*, November 21, 1964." Vatican website. http://www.vatican.va/archive/hist_councils/ii_vatican_council/documents/vat-ii_const_19641121_lumen-gentium_en.html.

Lummis, Adair T. "What Do Lay People Want in Pastors? Answers from Lay Search Committee Chairs and Regional Judicatory Leaders." *Pulpit and Pew Research Reports*, Spring 2003. Durham, NC: Duke Divinity School.

Mäkitalo, Åsa, and Roger Säljö. "Invisible People: Institutional Reasoning and Reflexivity in the Production of Services and 'Social Facts' in Public Employment Agencies." *Mind, Culture, and Activity* 9:3 (2002) 160–78.

Marger, Martin N. *Elites and Masses: An Introduction to Political Sociology*. Belmont, CA: Wadsworth, 1986.

Martin, Alice. "How Do We Say Goodbye?" In *Saying Goodbye: A Time of Growth for Congregations and Pastors*, edited by Edward A. White, 62–63. Bethesda, MD: Alban Institute, 1990.

Martin Taylor, Ann. *Reciprocal Duties of Parents and Children*. London: Taylor and Hessey, 1818.

———. *Reciprocal Duties of Parents and Children*. Modern ed. Charleston, SC: BiblioBazaar, 2009.

Mason, C. H. *The History and Life Work of Elder C. H. Mason*. Memphis: Church of God in Christ, 1987.

Maxwell, John C. *Dare to Dream . . . Then Do It: What Successful People Know and Do*. Nashville: Thomas Nelson, 2006.

———. *Developing the Leaders around You: How to Help Others Reach Their Full Potential*. Nashville: Thomas Nelson, 1995.

———. *Developing the Leader within You*. Nashville: Thomas Nelson, 1993.

———. *The Twenty-One Irrefutable Laws of Leadership: Follow Them and People Will Follow You*. Nashville: Thomas Nelson, 1998.

Mayring, Philipp. "Qualitative Content Analysis." In *A Companion to Qualitative Research*, edited by Uwe Flick et al., 266–69. London: Sage, 2004.

———. "Qualitative Inhaltsanalyse." In *Qualitative Forschung: Ein Handbuch*, edited by Uwe Flick et al., 468–75. Hamburg: Rowohlts Enzyklopädie, 2005.

McCauley, Robert N., and E. Thomas Lawson. *Bringing Ritual to Mind: Psychological Foundations of Cultural Forms*. Cambridge: Cambridge University Press, 2002.

McDonald, Alonzo L. Foreword to *Passing the Baton: Managing the Process of CEO Succession*, by Richard F. Vancil, xi–xiv. Boston: Harvard Business School Press, 1987.

McDuff, Elaine M., and Charles W. Mueller. "Gender Differences in the Professional Orientations of Protestant Clergy." *Sociological Forum* 17:3 (2002) 465–91.

McEachern, William A. *Managerial Control and Performance*. Lexington, MA: Heath, 1975.

McKenna, David L. *The Leader's Legacy: Preparing for Greater Things*. Newburg, OR: Barclay, 2006.

McKim, Donald K. "Reformed Theology." In *Westminster Dictionary of Theological Terms*, 234. Louisville, KY: Westminster John Knox, 1996.

McLaughlin, Thomas A. *Moving beyond Founder's Syndrome to Nonprofit Success*. Washington, DC: BoardSource, 2008.

McNair Scott, Benjamin G. *Apostles Today. Making Sense of Contemporary Charismatic Apostolates: A Historical and Theological Appraisal*. Eugene, OR: Pickwick, 2014.

McTeer, William, et al. "Manager/Coach Mid-Season Replacement and Team Performance in Professional Team Sport." *Journal of Sport Behavior* 18:1 (1995) 58–68.

Mead, Loren B. *A Change of Pastors—and How It Affects Change in the Congregation*. Herndon, VA: Alban Institute, 2005.

———. *Critical Moment of Ministry: A Change of Pastors*. New York: Alban Institute, 1986.

Means, J. "Negro Bishops Take Feud over Leadership to Court." *Commercial Appeal* (Nov 16, 1966), 23.

Melton, J. Gordon. "When Prophets Die: The Succession Crisis in New Religions." In *When Prophets Die: The Postcharismatic Fate of New Religious Movements*, edited by Timothy Miller, 1–12. Albany: State University of New York Press, 1991.

Mentzer, Marc S. "The Leader's Succession-Performance Relationship in a Non-Profit Organization." *Canadian Review of Sociology* 30:2 (1993) 191–204.

Merrill, Barbara, and Linden West. *Using Biographical Methods in Social Research.* London: Sage, 2009.

Merriam, Sharan B. *Qualitative Research: A Guide to Design and Implementation.* San Francisco: Jossey-Bass, 2009.

Meuser, Michael, and Ulrike Nagel. "The Expert Interview and Changes in Knowledge Production." In *Interviewing Experts*, edited by Alexander Bogner et al., 17–42. Basingstoke: Palgrave Macmillan, 2009.

Meyer, John W., and Brian Rowan. "Institutional Organizations: Formal Structure as Myth and Ceremony." In *The New Institutionalism in Organizational Analysis*, edited by Walter W. Powell and Paul J. DiMaggio, 41–62. Chicago: University of Chicago Press, 1991.

Miller, Timothy, ed. *When Prophets Die: The Postcharismatic Fate of New Religious Movements.* Albany: State University of New York Press, 1991.

Moore, Robert L. "Liminoid and Liminal Sacred Space." In *The Archetype of Initiation: Sacred Space, Ritual Process, and Personal Transformation. Lectures and Essays by Robert L. Moore*, edited by Max J. Havlick, 37–56. Bloomington, IN: Xlibris Corporation, 2001.

Morck, Randall, et al. "Management Ownership and Market Valuation: An Empirical Analysis." *Journal of Financial Economics* 18 (1988) 293–315.

Morgan, Gareth. *Images of Organization.* 2nd ed. Thousand Oaks, CA: Sage, 1997.

Moses, Jonathon W., and Torbjørn L. Knutsen. *Ways of Knowing: Competing Methodologies in Social and Political Research.* 2nd ed. Basingstoke: Palgrave Macmillan, 2012.

Moustakas, Clark. *Phenomenological Research Methods.* Thousand Oaks, CA: Sage, 1994.

Mullins, Tom. *Passing the Leadership Baton: A Winning Transition Plan for Your Ministry.* Nashville: Thomas Nelson, 2015.

Murray-Williams, Stuart. *Church after Christendom.* Milton Keynes: Paternoster, 2004.

Mutuae Relationes: Directives for the Mutual Relations between Bishops and Religious in the Church, May 14, 1978. Vatican website. http://www.vatican.va/roman_curia/congregations/ccscrlife/documents/rc_con_ccscrlife_doc_14051978_mutuae-relationes_en.html.

Nelson, Chad, and Robert H. Woods. "Content Analysis." In *The Routledge Handbook of Research Methods in the Study of Religion*, edited by Michael Stausberg and Steven Engler, 109–21. London: Routledge, 2014.

Neuendorf, Kimberley A. *The Content Analysis Guidebook.* London: Sage, 2002.

Neuner, Peter. "Apostolic Succession." In *Religion Past and Present: Encyclopedia of Theology and Religion*, edited by Hans Dieter Betz et al., 1:335–39. Leiden/Boston: Brill, 2007.

Newfrontiers. *Newfrontiers Magazine.* Special issue, *Forward Together: No Well-Worn Paths*, July–September 2011.

Newfrontiers Together. "About Newfrontiers." https://newfrontierstogether.org/about-us/our-history/.

Ngomane, Richard M. "Leadership Mentoring and Succession in the Charismatic Churches in Bushbuckridge: A Critical Assessment in the Light of 2 Timothy 2:1–3." PhD diss., University of Pretoria, 2013.

Nicholson, Roger S. "The Challenge of the Interim Time." In *Temporary Shepherds: A Congregational Handbook for Interim Ministry*, edited by Roger S. Nicholson, 3–13. Bethesda, MD: Alban Institute, 1998.

Northouse, Peter G. *Leadership: Theory and Practice*. 6th ed. Los Angeles: Sage, 2013.

Ocasio, William. "Institutionalized Action and Corporate Governance: The Reliance on Rules of CEO Succession." *Administrative Science Quarterly* 44 (1999) 384–416.

Owens, Robert R. "The Dark Years (1961–1968): Leadership Styles and Organizational Types in the Transition from the Founder to the Successors in the Church of God in Christ." PhD diss., Regent University, 2000.

————. *Never Forget! The Dark Years of COGIC History: Leadership, Routinization, and Transformation in a Charismatic Organization—From the Founder to the Successors in the Church of God in Christ 1961–1968*. Fairfax, VA: Xulon, 2002.

Oxford Encyclopedic English Dictionary. Edited by Joyce M. Hawkins and Robert Allen. Oxford: Oxford University Press, 1991.

Packard, Joshua R. "Resisting Institutionalization: Religious Professionals in the Emerging Church." *Sociological Inquiry* 81:1 (2011) 3–33.

Paris, Peter J. *Black Religious Leaders: Conflict in Unity*. Louisville, KY: Westminster John Knox, 1991.

Patterson, Kerry, et al. *Crucial Conversations: Tools of Talking When Stakes Are High*. 2nd ed. New York: McGraw-Hill Education, 2002.

Patton, Michael Q. *Qualitative Research and Evaluation Methods*. Thousand Oaks, CA: Sage, 2002.

Paul VI. *Apostolicam actuositatem*. Papal decree. Vatican website. November 18, 1965. http://www.vatican.va/archive/hist_councils/ii_vatican_council/documents/vat-ii_decree_19651118_apostolicam-actuositatem_en.html.

Pedersen, Jesper S., and Frank Dobbin. "In Search of Identity and Legitimation: Bridging Organizational Culture and Neoinstitutionalism." *American Behavioral Scientist* 49 (2006) 897–907.

Peet, Melissa. "Leadership Transitions, Tacit Knowledge Sharing and Organization Generativity." *Journal of Knowledge Management* 16:1 (2012) 45–60.

Perry, John T., and Xin Yao. "To Get the Best New CEO, Must the Old CEO Go? Power Distribution in External CEO Successions." *Managerial and Decision Economics* 32:8 (2011) 505–25.

Peterson, Steven D. "Case Study of Liberty University's Succession Plan from Founder to Second-Generation Leader." DEd diss., Liberty University, 2014.

Pew Research Center. "Members of the Church of God in Christ." https://www.pewresearch.org/religion/religious-landscape-study/religious-denomination/church-of-god-in-christ/.

Pfeffer, Jeffrey, and Gerald R. Salancik. *The External Control of Organizations*. New York: Harper & Row, 1978.

Phillips, William B. *Pastoral Transitions: From Endings to New Beginnings*. Bethesda, MD: Alban Institute, 1994.

Plathe, Anthony H. "The Pastor Says Goodbye: How to Move Through Good Friday to Easter." In *Saying Goodbye: A Time of Growth for Congregations and Pastors*. Edited by Edward A. White, 49–56. Bethesda, MD: Alban Institute, 1990.

Pobee, John. *Towards an African Theology*. Nashville: Abingdon Press, 1979.

Poggenpoel, Marie, and Chris Myburgh. "The Researcher as Research Instrument in Education Research: A Possible Threat to Trustworthiness?" *Education* 124:2 (2003) 418–21.

Potter, Jonathan, and Alexa Hepburn. "Eight Challenges for Interview Researchers." In *The Sage Handbook of Interview Research: The Complexity of the Craft.* 2nd ed. Jaber F. Gubrium et al., 555–70. Thousand Oaks, CA: Sage, 2012.

Powell, Walter W., and Paul J. DiMaggio, eds. *The New Institutionalism in Organizational Analysis.* Chicago: University of Chicago Press, 1991.

Poza, Ernesto J. *Family Business.* Mason, OH: South-Western, 2004.

Poza, Ernesto, et al. "Changing the Family Business through Action Research." *Family Business Review* 11:4 (1998) 311–23.

———. "Does the Family-Business Interaction Represent a Resource or a Cost?" *Family Business Review* 17:2 (2004) 99–118.

Prichard, Rebecca B. "*Grandes Dames, Femmes Fortes,* and *Matrones*: Reformed Women Ministering." In *Religious Institutions and Women's Leadership: New Roles inside the Mainstream*, edited by Catherine Wessinger, 39–57. Columbia, SC: University of South Carolina Press, 1996.

Pring, Julian T. *The Oxford Dictionary of Modern Greek.* Oxford: Oxford University Press, 1965.

Prior, Lindsay. *Using Documents in Social Research.* London: Sage, 2003.

Puchta, Claudia, and Jonathan Potter. *Focus Group Practice.* London: Sage, 2004.

———. "Manufacturing Individual Opinions: Market Research Focus Groups and the Discursive Psychology of Attitudes." *British Journal of Social Psychology* 41 (2002) 345–63.

Pugh, Ben. "Succession Plans: Is There a Biblical Template?" *Journal of the European Pentecostal Theological Association* 36:2 (2016) 117–30.

Punch, Keith F. *Introduction to Social Research: Quantitative and Qualitative Approaches.* London: Sage, 2014.

Putney, Clifford. *Muscular Christianity: Manhood and Sports in Protestant America, 1880–1920.* Harvard: Harvard University Press, 2009.

Reinharz, Shulamit. "Feminist Distrust: Problems of Content and Context in Sociological Work." In *The Self in Social Inquiry: Researching Methods*, edited by David N. Berg and Kenwyn K. Smith, 153–72. Beverly Hills: Sage, 1985.

———. *Feminist Methods in Social Research.* New York: Oxford University Press, 1992.

Reinharz, Shulamit, and Susan E. Chase. "Interviewing Women." In *Inside Interviewing: New Lenses, New Concerns*, edited by James A. Holstein and Jaber F. Gubrium, 73–90. Thousand Oaks, CA: Sage, 2003.

Richard Roberts Ministries. "Our History." http://oralroberts.com/about/our-history/.

———. "Our Mission." https://richardroberts.org/our-mission/.

Ricoeur, Paul. *From Text to Action: Essays in Hermeneutics, II.* Evanston, IL: Northwestern University Press, 2007.

Riemann, Gerhard, and Fritz Schütze. "Trajectory as Basic Theoretical Concept for Analyzing Suffering and Disorderly Social Processes." In *Social Organization and Social Process: Essays in Honor of Anselm Strauss*, edited by David Maines, 333–57. New York: Aldine de Gruyter, 1987.

Riessman, Catherine K. *Narrative Methods for the Human Sciences.* London: Sage, 2008.

Roach, Dale. *The Servant-Leadership Style of Jesus: A Biblical Strategy for Leadership Development.* Bloomington, IN: WestBow, 2016.

Robbins, Thomas. *Cults, Converts and Charisma: The Sociology of New Religious Movements.* London: Sage, 1988.

Robert, Dana L., and M. L. Daneel. "Worship among Apostles and Zionists in Southern Africa." In *Christian Worship Worldwide: Expanding Horizons, Deepening Practices*, edited by Charles E. Farhadian, 43–70. Grand Rapids: Eerdmans, 2007.

Roberts, Nancy C., and Raymond T. Bradley. "Limits of Charisma." In *Charismatic Leadership: The Elusive Factor in Organizational Effectiveness*, edited by Jay A. Conger and Rabindra N. Kanungo, 253–75. San Francisco: Jossey-Bass, 1988.

Robertson, Alexa. "Narrative Analysis." In *Analyzing Text and Discourse: Eight Approaches for the Social Sciences*, edited by Kristina Boréus and Göran Bergström, 122–45. London: Sage, 2017.

Robins, R. G. *Pentecostalism in America*. Santa Barbara: Greenwood, 2010.

Romano, Antonio. *The Charism of the Founders: The Person and Charism of Founders in Contemporary Theological Reflection*. Translated by Sr. Frances Teresa. Slough: St. Pauls, 1994.

Roof, Wade Clark. "Research Design." In *The Routledge Handbook of Research Methods in the Study of Religion*, edited by Michael Stausberg and Steven Engler, 68–80. London: Routledge, 2014.

Rosenthal, Gabriele. "Reconstruction of Life Stories: Principles of Selection in Generation Stories for Narrative Biographical Interviews." *The Narrative Study of Lives* 1 (1993) 59–91. http://www.ssoar.info/ssoar/bitstream/handle/document/5929/ssoar-tnsl-1993-91-rosenthal-reconstruction_of_life_stories.pdf?sequence=1.

Rosman, Doreen M. *Evangelicals and Culture*. Aldershot: Gregg Revivals, 1992.

Roulston, Kathryn. *Reflective Interviewing: A Guide to Theory and Practice*. London: Sage, 2010. https://books.google.com/books?id=IDUnAjUYRpQC&pg=PA51&source=gbs_toc_r&cad=3#v=onepage&q&f=false.

Rubenson, George C., and Anil K. Gupta. "The Initial Succession: A Contingency Model of Founder Tenure." *Entrepreneurship Theory and Practice* 21:2 (1996) 21–35.

Rüpke, Jörg. "Epideixis." In *Brill's New Pauly*, edited by Christine F. Salazar, 2006. http://dx.doi.org/10.1163/1574-9347_bnp_e331900.

———. "History." In *The Routledge Handbook of Research Methods in the Study of Religion*, edited by Michael Stausberg and Steven Engler, 285–309. London: Routledge, 2014.

Sakano, Tomoaki, and Arie Y. Lewin. "Impact of CEO Succession in Japanese Companies: A Coevolutionary Perspective." *Organization Science* 10:5 (1999) 654–71.

Salamone, Frank A., and Marjorie M. Snipes, eds. *The Intellectual Legacy of Victor and Edith Turner*. Lanham, MD: Lexington, 2018.

Sallnow, M. J. "Communitas Reconsidered: The Sociology of Andean Pilgrimage." *Man* 16 (1981) 163–82.

Sanders, J. Oswald. *Spiritual Leadership*. 3rd ed. Chicago: Moody, 1989.

Sashkin, Marshall. "The Structure of Charismatic Leadership." In *Leadership: The Cutting Edge*, edited by James G. Hunt and Lars L. Larson, 212–18. Carbondale, IL: Southern Illinois University Press, 1976.

Sasson, Diane. "The Shakers: The Adaptation of Prophecy." In *When Prophets Die: The Postcharismatic Fate of New Religious Movements*, edited by Timothy Miller, 13–28. Albany: State University of New York Press, 1991.

Satlow, Michael L. "'Try to Be a Man': The Rabbinic Construction of Masculinity." *The Harvard Theological Review* 89:1 (1996) 19–40.

Schattschneider, David A. "'Souls for the Lamb': A Theology for the Christian Mission According to Count Nicolaus Ludwig von Zinzendorf and Bishop Augustus Gottlieb Spangenberg." PhD diss., University of Chicago, 1975.

Schein, Edgar H. "The Role of the Founder in Creating Organizational Culture." *Organizational Dynamics* 12:1 (1983) 13–28.

Scheitle, Christopher P., and Kevin D. Dougherty. "The Sociology of Religious Organizations." *Sociology Compass* 2:3 (2008) 981–99.

Schenck, Rob. *Costly Grace: An Evangelical Minister's Rediscovery of Faith, Hope, and Love.* New York: HarperCollins, 2018.

Schreier, Margrit. "Qualitative Content Analysis." In *The Sage Handbook of Qualitative Data Analysis*, edited by Uwe Flick, 170–83. London: Sage, 2014.

———. *Qualitative Content Analysis in Practice.* London: Sage, 2012.

Schwalbe, Michael L., and Michelle Wolkomir. "Interviewing Men." In *Inside Interviewing: New Lenses, New Concerns*, edited by James A. Holstein and Jaber F. Gubrium, 55–72. Thousand Oaks, CA: Sage, 2003.

Scott, John. *A Matter of Record: Documentary Sources in Social Research.* Cambridge, UK: Polity, 1990.

Scott, W. Richard, and John W. Meyer. Preface to *Institutional Environments and Organizations: Structural Complexity and Individualism*, edited by W. Richard Scott and John W. Meyer, 1–8. Thousand Oaks, CA: Sage, 1994.

Shamir, Boas, et al. "The Motivational Effects of Charismatic Leadership: A Self-Concept Based Theory." *Organization Science* 4 (1993) 577–94.

Sheldon, Myrna P. "Wild at Heart: How Sociobiology and Evolutionary Psychology Helped Influence the Construction of Heterosexual Masculinity in American Evangelicalism." *Journal of Women in Culture and Society* 42:4 (2017) 977–98.

Shen, Wei, and Albert A. Cannella. "Revisiting the Performance Consequences of CEO Succession: The Impacts of Successor Type, Postsuccession Senior Executive Turnover, and Departing CEO Tenure." *Academy of Management Journal*, 45:4 (2002) 717–33.

Shields, Steven L. "The Latter Day Saint Movement: A Study in Survival." In *When Prophets Die: The Postcharismatic Fate of New Religious Movements*, edited by Timothy Miller, 59–77. Albany: State University of New York Press, 1991.

Simon, Hermann. *Hidden Champions: Lessons from 500 of the World's Best Unknown Companies.* Boston: Harvard Business School Press, 1996.

Simon, Rita J., and Pamela S. Nadell. "In the Same Voice or Is It Different? Gender and the Clergy." *Sociology of Religion* 56:1 (1995) 63–70.

Slater, Robert. *The New GE: How Jack Welch Revived an American Institution.* Homewood, IL: Business One Irwin, 1993.

Smith, David. "An Account of the Sustained Rise of New Frontiers International within the United Kingdom." *Journal of the European Theological Pentecostal Association* 23 (2003) 137–56.

Smith, Molly D., ed. *Transitional Ministry: A Time of Opportunity.* New York: Church, 2009.

Sonnenfeld, Jeffrey A., and Padraic L. Spence. "The Parting Patriarch of a Family Firm." *Family Business Review* 2:4 (1989) 355–75.

Sophocles. *Oedipus the King and Antigone.* Translated by Peter D. Arnott. Arlington Heights, IL: AHM, 1960.

South Sudan Customary Authorities Project. *Now We Are Zero: South Sudanese Chiefs and Elders Discuss Their Roles in Peace and Conflict*. London: Rift Valley Institute, 2017.

Spears, Larry C. "Tracing the Past, Present, and Future of Servant-Leadership." In *Focus on Leadership: Servant-Leadership for the Twenty-First Century*, edited by Larry C. Spears and Michele Lawrence, 1–16. New York: John Wiley & Sons, 2002.

Stevens, Susan K. "In Their Own Words: The Entrepreneurial Behavior of Nonprofit Founders." PhD diss., Union Institute and University, 2003.

Storkey, Elaine. *What's Right with Feminism?* London: SPCK, 1985.

Stott, John, ed. *Making Christ Known: Historic Mission Documents from the Lausanne Movement 1974–1989*. Carlisle, UK: Paternoster, 1996.

Svingen, Paul N. "The Interim Minister: A Special Calling." In *Temporary Shepherds: A Congregational Handbook for Interim Ministry*, edited by Roger S. Nicholson, 52–61. Bethesda, MD: Alban Institute, 1998.

Swartz, David. "Secularization, Religion, and Isomorphism: A Study of Large Nonprofit Hospital Trustees." In *Sacred Companies: Organizational Aspects of Religion and Religious Aspects of Organizations*, edited by N. J. Demerath et al., 323–39. New York/Oxford: Oxford University Press, 1998.

Swidler, Ann. *Organization without Authority: Dilemmas of Social Control in Free Schools*. Cambridge, MA: Harvard University Press, 1979.

Swift, Tracey A., and Michael A. West. *Reflexivity and Group Processes: Research and Practice*. Sheffield: ESRC Centre for Organization and Innovation, 1998.

Tashakori, Maryam. *Managerial Succession: From the Owner-Founder to the Professional Manager*. New York: Praeger, 1980.

Thatcher, Adrian, ed. *The Oxford Handbook of Theology, Sexuality, and Gender*. Oxford: Oxford University Press, 2014.

Thinkers50. "Fons Trompenars and Charles Hampden-Turner." https://thinkers50.com/biographies/fons-trompenaars-and-charles-hampden-turner/.

Thompson, James D. *Organizations in Action: Social Science Bases of Administrative Theory*. 6th ed. New Brunswick: Transaction, 2008.

Thomson, George. *Aeschylus and Athens: A Study in the Social Origins of Drama*. New York: Grosset and Dunlap, 1968.

THT Consulting. https://www.thtconsulting.com/partners/fons-trompenaars/.

Transparency International. "Corruption Perceptions Index 2017." February 21, 2018. https://www.transparency.org/en/news/corruption-perceptions-index-2017.

Trice, Harrison M., and Janice M. Beyer. "Charisma and Its Routinization in Two Social Movement Organizations." *Journal of Occupational Behavior* 7 (1986) 125–38.

Trompenaars, Fons, and Charles Hampden-Turner. *Riding the Waves of Culture: Understanding Diversity in Global Business*. 2nd ed. New York: McGraw-Hill, 1998.

Trompenaars, Fons, and Peter Wooliams. "Getting the Measure of Intercultural Leadership." In *Contemporary Leadership and Intercultural Competence: Exploring the Cross-Cultural Dynamics within Organizations*, edited by Michael A. Moodian, 161–74. Los Angeles: Sage, 2009.

Turner, Victor, ed. *Celebration: Studies in Festivity and Ritual*. Washington, DC: Smithsonian Institution Press, 1982.

———. *Dramas, Fields, and Metaphors: Symbolic Action in Human Society*. Ithaca and London: Cornell University Press, 1974.

———. *From Ritual to Theatre: The Human Seriousness of Play*. 2nd ed. New York: PAJ, 1992.

———. *The Ritual Process: Structure and Anti-Structure.* Hawthorne, NY: Aldine de Gruyter, 1995.

Turner, Victor, and Edith Turner. *Image and Pilgrimage in Christian Culture: Anthropological Perspectives.* Oxford: Blackwell, 1978.

———. "Religious Celebrations." In *Celebration: Studies in Festivity and Ritual,* edited by Victor Turner, 201–19. Washington, DC: Smithsonian Institution Press, 1982.

Tushima, Cephas. "Leadership Succession Patterns in the Apostolic Church as Template for Critique of Contemporary Charismatic Leadership Succession Patterns." *HTS Teologiese Studies/Theological Studies* 72:1 (2016). https://doi.org/10.4102/hts.v72i1.2968.

Ukaegbu, Chikwendu C. "Entrepreneurial Succession and Post-founder Durability: A Study of Indigenous Private Manufacturing Firms in Igbu States of Nigeria." *Journal of Contemporary African Studies* 21:1 (2003) 27–45.

Ukah, Asonzeh F. K. *A New Paradigm of Pentecostal Power: A Study of the Redeemed Christian Church of God in Nigeria.* Trenton, NJ: Africa World Press, 2008.

Ulrich, Marlene. *Celebrating 40 Years of God's Faithfulness: 1977–2017.* Ephrata, PA: Ephrata Community Church, 2017.

Vancil, Richard F. *Passing the Baton: Managing the Process of CEO Succession.* Boston, MA: Harvard Business School Press, 1987.

Virgo, Terry. *Does the Future Have a Church?* St. Louis: New Frontiers USA, 2011.

———. "The End of the Beginning." November 22, 2009. https://www.terryvirgo.org/articles/the-end-of-the-beginning/.

———. *Enjoying God's Grace.* St. Louis: New Frontiers USA, 2008.

———. "Firstline." In *Newfrontiers Magazine.* Special issue, *Forward Together: No Well-Worn Paths.* July–September 2011, 4–6.

———. *God Knows You're Human.* Weybridge: Roperpenberthy, 2009.

———. "Honouring the Future." November 19, 2009. https://www.terryvirgo.org/articles/honouring-the-future/.

———. *Men of Destiny.* Eastbourne: Kingsway, 1987.

———. "Newfrontiers Marches Forward into Multiplication." October 26, 2012. https://www.terryvirgo.org/blog/newfrontiers-marches-forward-into-multiplication/.

———. "Newfrontiers Redefined." November 16, 2010. https://www.terryvirgo.org/articles/transition-into-multiplication-newfrontiers-redefined/.

———. *No Well-Worn Paths.* 2nd ed. St. Louis: New Frontiers USA, 2008.

———. "The Presumption of Complementarianism." January 27, 2012. https://www.terryvirgo.org/articles/the-presumption-of-complementarianism/.

———. *Restoration in the Church.* Columbia, MO: Cityhill, 1989.

———. *The Spirit-Filled Church: Finding Your Place in God's Purpose.* Oxford: Monarch, 2011.

———. *The Tide Is Turning.* New Wine, 2006.

———. "Together on a Mission 2009: Newfrontiers—Past, Present and Future: Part 3. Our Future." July 5, 2009. https://www.terryvirgo.org/media/toam-2009-newfrontiers-past-present-and-future-part-3-our-future.

Virgo, Terry, and R. T. Kendall. *Soulfaring: Celtic Pilgrimage Then and Now.* London: SPCK, 1999.

Virgo, Terry, and Phil Rogers. *Receiving the Holy Spirit and His Gifts.* St. Louis: New Frontiers USA, 2013.

Vohra, Veena. "Using the Multiple Case Study Design to Decipher Contextual Leadership Behaviors in Indian Organizations." *The Electronic Journal of Business Research Methods* 12:1 (2014) 54–64.

Vonhof, John. *Pastoral Search Journey: A Guide to Finding Your Next Pastor.* Herndon, VA: Alban Institute, 2010.

Wagner, C. Peter, ed. *The New Apostolic Churches: Rediscovering the New Testament Model of Leadership and Why It Is God's Desire for the Church Today.* Ventura, CA: Regal, 1998.

Walker, Andrew. *Restoring the Kingdom: The Radical Christianity of the House Church Movement.* 4th ed. Guildford: Eagle, 1998.

Ward, John L. *Keeping the Family Business Healthy: How to Plan for Continued Growth, Profitability and Family Leadership.* San Francisco: Jossey-Bass, 1987.

Warnock, Adrian. "On the Future of Newfrontiers, Transition, But Not Retiring Just Yet. Interviews by Adrian Warnock: Part 6." July 13, 2011. https://www.terryvirgo.org/media/interviews-by-adrian-warnock-part-6-on-the-future-of-newfrontiers-transition-but-not-retiring-just-yet/.

Wasserman, Noam. "Founder-CEO Succession and the Paradox of Entrepreneurial Success." *Organization Science* 14 (2003) 149–72.

———. "Stewards, Agents, and the Founder Discount: Executive Compensation in New Ventures." *Academy of Management Journal* 29 (2006) 930–76.

Watkins, Clare. "Practising Ecclesiology: From Product to Process. Developing Ecclesiology as a Non-correlative Process and Practice through the Theological Action Research Framework of Theology in Four Voices." *Ecclesial Practices* 2 (2015) 23–39.

Watkins, Ralph C. *Leading Your African American Church Through Pastoral Transition.* Valley Forge, PA: Judson, 2010.

Weaver Swartz, Lisa. "Wesleyan (Anti)Feminism: A Religious Construction of Gender Equality." *Religions* 9:4 (2018) 1–11.

Weber, Max. *The Protestant Ethic and the Spirit of Capitalism.* Translated by Talcott Parsons. New York: Charles Scribner's, 1958.

———. *The Theory of Social and Economic Organization.* Translated by A. M. Henderson and Talcott Parsons. New York: Free Press, 1947.

———. *Wirtschaft und Gesellschaft: Grundriss der verstehenden Soziologie.* 5th ed. Tübingen: Mohr Siebeck, 2002.

Webster's New Twentieth Century Dictionary Unabridged. 2nd ed. Cleveland: The World, 1955.

Weese, Carolyn, and J. Russell Crabtree. *The Elephant in the Boardroom: Speaking the Unspoken about Pastoral Transitions.* San Francisco: Jossey-Bass, 2004.

Weil, Frederick D. "Cohorts, Regimes, and the Legitimation of Democracy: West Germany Since 1945." *American Sociological Review* 52 (1987) 308–24.

Welch, Catherine, et al. "Corporate Elites as Informants in Qualitative International Business Research." *International Business Research Review* 11:5 (2002) 611–28.

West, Michael A. "Reflexivity, Revolution and Innovation in Work Teams." In *Product Development Teams.* Advances in the Interdisciplinary Study of Work Teams 5, edited by Michael M. Beyerlein et al., 1–29. Stamford, CT: JAI, 2000.

West, Michael A., et al. "Group Decision-Making and Effectiveness: Unexplored Boundaries." In *Creating Tomorrow's Organizations: A Handbook for Future Research in Organizational Behavior,* edited by Cary L. Cooper and Susan E. Jackson, 293–316. Chichester: John Wiley & Sons, 1997.

Wheeler, Meredith E. "The Leadership Succession Process in Mega Churches." PhD diss., Temple University, 2008.

Whitehead, John W. *Servant Leadership: Leading Today for a Better Tomorrow.* Denver: Outskirts, 2019.

Widmer, Pascale S., et al. "Recent Developments in Reflexivity Research: A Review." *Journal Psychologie des Alltagshandelns/Psychology of Everyday Activity* 2:2 (2009) 2–11.

Wiersema, Margarethe F. "Strategic Consequences of Executive Succession within Diversified Firms." *Journal of Management Studies* 29 (1992) 73–94.

Wignall, Ross. "'A Man after God's Own Heart': Charisma, Masculinity and Leadership at a Charismatic Church in Brighton and Hove, UK." *Religion* 46:3 (2016) 389–411.

Williams, Craig. "A Time of Personal Growth." In *Saying Goodbye: A Time of Growth for Congregations and Pastors,* edited by Edward A. White, 18–22. Bethesda, MD: Alban Institute, 1990.

"Willowbank Report on Gospel and Culture." In *Making Christ Known: Historic Mission Documents from the Lausanne Movement 1974–1989,* edited by John Stott, 73–113. Carlisle, UK: Paternoster, 1996.

Wolff, Stephan. "Dokumenten- und Aktenanalyse." In *Qualitative Forschung: Ein Handbuch,* edited by Uwe Flick et al., 502–13. Hamburg: Rowohlts Enzyklopädie, 2005.

Woodley, Randy S., and Bo C. Sanders. *Decolonizing Evangelicalism: An 11:59 Conversation.* Eugene, OR: Cascade, 2020.

Yelle, Robert A. "Semiotics." In *The Routledge Handbook of Research Methods in the Study of Religion,* edited by Michael Stausberg and Steven Engler, 355–65. London: Routledge, 2014.

Yin, Robert K. *Case Study Research: Design and Methods.* 4th ed. Thousand Oaks, CA: Sage, 2009.

Zainiddinov, Hakim. "Institutional Isomorphism in Religious Entities of Post-Soviet Tajikistan." *Journal of Historical Sociology* 31:3 (2018) 346–62.

Zeelenberg, Marcel, and Eric van Dijk. "A Reverse Sunk Cost Effect in Risky Decision-Making: Sometimes We Have Too Much Invested to Gamble." *Journal of Economic Psychology* 18:6 (1997) 677–91.

Zhang, Yan, and Nandini Rajagopalan. "When the Known Devil Is Better Than an Unknown God: An Empirical Study of the Antecedents and Consequences of Relay Succession." *Academy of Management Journal* 47:4 (2004) 483–500.

Zott, Christopher, and Quy N. Huy. "How Entrepreneurs Use Symbolic Management to Acquire Resources." *Administrative Science Quarterly* 52 (2007) 70–105.

Zúñiga-Vicente, José Ángel, et al. "Facilitating and Inhibiting Factors behind Strategic Change: Evidence in the Spanish Private Banking Industry, 1983–1997." *Scandinavian Journal of Management* 21:3 (2005) 235–65.

www.ingramcontent.com/pod-product-compliance
Lightning Source LLC
Chambersburg PA
CBHW070910100426
42814CB00003B/118